TRIANGULATED
VISIONS

SUNY Series in Feminist Criticism and Theory
Michelle A. Masse, Editor

and

SUNY Series, Cultural Studies in Cinema/Video
Wheeler Winston Dixon, Editor

TRIANGULATED VISIONS

Women in Recent German Cinema

EDITED BY

Ingeborg Majer O'Sickey
and
Ingeborg von Zadow

State University of New York Press

Published by
State University of New York Press, Albany

For information, address State University of New York Press,
State University Plaza, Albany, N.Y. 12246

Production by Diane Ganeles
Marketing by Patrick Durocher

Library of Congress Cataloging-in-Publication Data
Triangulated visions : women in recent German cinema / edited by
    Ingeborg Majer O'Sickey and Ingeborg von Zadow.
        p.   cm. — (SUNY series in feminist criticism and theory)
    (SUNY series, cultural studies in cinema/video)
    Includes index.
    ISBN 0-7914-3717-5 (hc : alk. paper). — ISBN 0-7914-3718-3
    (pb : alk. paper)
    1. Women in motion pictures.   2. Women in the motion pic-
    ture industry—Germany.   I. Majer O'Sickey, Ingeborg.
    II. Zadow, Ingeborg von.   III. Series.   IV. Series: SUNY series,
    cultural studies in cinema/video.
    PN1995.9.W6T75   1998
    791.43'652042'0943—dc21   97-34327
                                                           CIP

10 9 8 7 6 5 4 3 2 1

Contents

Part V: Recovering (from) History: Memory and Film

Acknowledgments

We would like to thank the contributors for their generous gift of scholarship. We're also indebted to the following individuals for their supportive acts: Heinz Blumensath (Berliner Institut für Lehrerfortbildung—und weiterbildung); Mel Claasens (Hochschule für Künste, Filminstitut/HdK Kunst und Medien, Berlin); and Marie Shumin (Women's Studies Program, SUNY, Binghamton). Finally, we wish to express our gratitude to Mike Arnold and Elenore and Günter von Zadow for their steadfast support.

Introduction

Ingeborg Majer O'Sickey

About three years ago, in spring 1995, I coorganized a film series titled "Triangulated Vision(s): Women, Film, Identities" for the Women's Studies Program at SUNY, Binghamton. The weekly screenings of feminist films from all over the world were followed by intense discussions about the way in which feminist films represent race, sexuality, gender, and class in constructions of images of women.[1] When I first suggested the title for this series, I was thinking of "triangulated vision(s)" as a basic shorthand for the reality that a discussion of women's identities in film should include a discussion of women as images before the camera, as workers behind the camera, and as spectators in the theater. Of course, the film-theory-spectators structure of the film series itself reflected a more complex idea of "triangulated visions"; in the aftermath of Laura Mulvey's path-breaking 1975 essay, "Visual Pleasure and Narrative Cinema," and the rich discussions that followed, it is obvious that one cannot think of "triangulated" in cinematic terms without thinking of the underlying structures of visual identification and gender identity (the Imaginary and Symbolic orders) which collide with (or authenticate) the audience's horizons of expectations in all sorts of ways. The discussions after the film screenings put the intersections of the psycho-political terrain that cinema engages into sharp relief and reminded me anew that women's work in cinema is crucial to women's identities *tout court*, if for no other reason than to fill an absolute visual void of the range of possibilities of images of women.

Although the idea for the present collection of critical essays was induced by my excitement about this series on feminist/women-centered cinema, it follows a different agenda in that it is specifically concerned with women in recent German cinema. As such, we hope that it will go some way toward filling the gender gap in the scholarship on German film. As readers interested in feminist film theories and in German cinema know, *Triangulated Visions: Women in Recent German Cinema* is only the second volume that connects German film and

1

questions of gender.[2] When Ingeborg von Zadow came aboard as coeditor, we decided that the volume should fill that gap with essays that consider representations of and by women within recent German cinema.

The dangers of essentializing the term *women* in our title and in such an enterprise as a volume on "women in recent German cinema" became clear to us early on, and we recognize the fact that while we designate various sites and ways in which women are mapped and map themselves into the cinematic apparatus, the constituent parts of *woman* resist categorization: women may be actors, directors, spectators, and so on but inasmuch as *women* is not a stable category, the terms oscillate at the intersections of image and imaged, visions and revisions. At the very least class, race, gender, and sexuality inform the notion of the sign of women working in film, the sign of women as images, and of women watching film. So, rather than trying to contain filmworkers, images of women, and spectators under the common sign of women, the undertaking examines movements between image and imaged as well as movements from vision and revision as these resonate through the women's own fictitious works. In this regard, we intend our title "triangulated visions" to be not only a hieroglyph for a formula of women + cinema and cinema + women, but an invitation to retriangulate the construct at any point.

The essays collected in *Triangulated Visions* are representative of a wide range of theoretical approaches in current film theory. They are divided into five chapters for the sake of utility; the divisions are not intended to fence in meanings, but meant to loosely mark sociopolitical and psychosocial terrains. That one or another essay may seem out of place in "its" place is, given their wide range, inevitable. Some problematize political locations such as class, race, sexuality, and ethnicity and take up recent feminist film theory's challenge to examine the production of categories of femininity in terms of a politics of cinematic representation. Others trespass the boundaries of cinematic discourse by restaking the borders of psychoanalytic theory and genre studies. The dialogues with the German filmmakers Jutta Brückner, Seyhan Derin, Doris Dörrie, Helke Sander, and writer Helga Schubert reflect these concerns; their responses provide candid observations about the challenges female-centered filmmaking faces when attempting to produce images of women that deviate from traditional, Hollywoodian ones.

In part I, "Genre and Other Border Crossings," Nora M. Alter's essay confronts several questions of triangulation that pertain to the entire volume. Problematizing the notion of location(s), she maps the way in which fiction and truth, biography and autobiography weave designs that refuse to stay within critical frames. Using three moments and three "looks" in three films, Alter demonstrates that "these three moments have in common chiasmic performances that confirm, disrupt, and reconfirm the concept of triangulated vision: the look that circulates between director, actor, and viewer." Illustrating another kind of genre crossing, Douglas Kellner uses R. W. Fassbinder's 1972 film *The Bitter Tears of Petra von Kant* to give an example of Fassbinder's dual move of subverting and instrumentalizing genre conventions of the Hollywood melodrama. Fassbinder, argues Kellner, makes these moves in order to "screen" his critique of German bourgeois institutions and to examine the situation of women within these institutions. Margrit Frölich's "Behind the Curtains of a State-Owned Film Industry: Women-Filmmakers at the DEFA" examines the role of women in the DEFA, the only film studio in the former German Democratic Republic. The essay is among the first attempts to present a broad picture of how women took part in the East German film industry as directors, actors, and scriptwriters. Frölich pays particular attention to how women confronted and shaped notions of women's identity in light of the changing patterns of East Germany's cultural policy, and addresses how their work has been affected in the transition from a state-controlled studio system to the Federal Republic of Germany's free market system. In the final essay of this chapter Marcia Klotz resituates Monika Treut's work from a lesbian-filmmaker's space to a "*radical queer* political program." Klotz thus opens up a discussion of Treut's films to an expanded politics of representation. Asking whether "queer theory can be stretched in a way that might take on some . . . other fields of sexual marginalization," Klotz scrutinizes three films in particular: *The Virgin Machine* (1988), *My Father Is Coming* (1991), and *The Taboo Parlor* (1995).

Part II, "Triangulations of Ethnicity, Gender, and Class," leads off with Barbara Kosta's essay "'It Takes Three to Tango' or Romance Revised: Jutta Brückner's *One Glance and Love Breaks Out*." Kosta's highly original essay challenges ways of looking at cinematic triangulations of dance, desire, and gender by rereading and translating the figure of the tango. This dance, argues Kosta, is "anchored in a script of social arrangements that are culturally coded in terms of class, gender, and race" in which "the dancers adhere to prescribed patterns that, in their aesthetic formulations, conceal structures of power." While not originally solicited as a companion piece to Kosta's essay, but nevertheless valuable as such, Ingeborg von Zadow's exchange with Jutta Brückner about *Ein Blick und die Liebe bricht aus* (One Glance and Love Breaks Out, 1985); *Kollosale Liebe* (Colossal Love, 1983–91), and *Lieben Sie Brecht?* (Do You Love Brecht? 1993) illuminates Brückner's strategies of confronting artistic and functional challenges to feminist filmmaking. The dialogue also sheds light on the situation of this filmmaker's own generation and the new generation of women-filmmakers in German cinema.

Julia Knight's "Observing Rituals: Ulrike Ottinger's *Johanna d'Arc of Mongolia*," explores Ottinger's narrative of Mongolian women's culture by problematizing the filmmaker's notions of realism and representation, documentary and fiction as these are brought to bear on an "authentic community" (Mongolian) and a (West German) Other. Although cast in a different key from Knight's concerns, notions of transnational and interracial gender relations, alterity, and community also subtend David J. Levin's essay on Percy Adlon's *Bagdad Café* (1987); Levin focuses on the question of national harmony as grafted onto the problem of these gender relations and argues that Adlon's film triangulates these categories in problematic ways. Although he recognizes (indeed, illustrates) the enormous power of the rhetorical effects of alterity in *Bagdad Café*, Levin concludes that the film "mistakes the problem for the solution, and thus celebrates as a repudiation of racism what is, in fact, merely its restatement." The final piece in this chapter is Henriette Löwisch's interview with Seyhan Derin, a young Turkish-German filmmaker. Their dialogue reveals how Derin's first film, *ben annemin kiziyim* (I am my Mother's Daughter), which was praised highly at the 1996 Berlinale, came to be made. In many ways representative of the new generation of filmmakers in Germany, Derin provides a glimpse of the challenges that she and other Turkish-German women face in Germany's multicultural society, and how these challenges influence her work as a filmmaker.

Part III, "Images of Power and Pleasures," leads off with Kaja Silverman's highly suggestive reading of crucial sequences from Ulrike Ottinger's 1979 film *Bildnis einer Trinkerin* (Portrait of a Drinker) to make comprehensible her ideas on the "psycho-politics of representation," that is, on the film's presentation of the bodily ego, idealization, and identification. Significantly, "Narcissism: The Impossible Love" challenges "the larger assumption—that the female sometimes informs the equation of woman and spectacle—that the female subject stands outside lack, along with the particular reading of psychoanalysis from which it proceeds." Following Silverman's essay, Barbara Mennel focuses on the interplay of spectatorship, performance, and video film in her analysis of Monika Treut's *Verführung: Die grausame Frau* (Seduction: The Cruel Woman, 1985). Mennel argues that the triangulated structure of the film recasts the traditional masochistic scenario and offers alternative visual representations of women on one hand, and lesbians on the other, explaining that masochism is used as a vehicle to explore the role of the fetish in relationship to the multiple identities of the film's characters and diverse configurations of power, domination and submission, and love and desire. Ulrike Sieglohr's essay, too, relates to a number of issues surrounding performance and desire. "Why Drag the Diva Into It? Werner Schroeter's Gay Representation of Femininity" offers a comprehensive overview of Schroeter's oeuvre. Going beyond the general assessments of Schroeter's work as "camp artifice," Sieglohr offers bold readings of Schroeter's politics of representation and analyzes his films' strategic references to gay identity, to the cult of the diva, and to the inclusion of transvestite performers. Klaus Phillips's interview with Doris Dörrie concludes this chapter. Phillips situates Dörrie as a pathbreaking filmmaker in German cinema, remarking upon her ability to make "popular" yet difficult films. The dialogue reveals her views on a wide range of topics: her assessment of the challenges German women-filmmakers would face if they desired to work in Hollywood; filmmaking in Germany following the so-called Wende (unification of Germany); and the special challenges for films that wish to facilitate Germany's understanding of itself as a multicultural society.

Part IV, "Images of Women as Social Ciphers," begins with a much neglected filmmaker's work, Helga Reidemeister. Magda Mueller's essay "Commodified Body: Helga Reidemeister's *Mit starrem Blick aufs Geld* (Blank Stares and Hard Cash, 1983)" puts pressure on recent feminist theoretical works that privilege intellectual productions of femininity. Finding these constructions of femininity inadequate to her project, Mueller unfolds the significance of materiality as it manifests itself in the female body of the fashion model in Reidemeister's film, and shows that this materiality has a powerful effect on the production of the image of the woman on culture in general.

Addressing motifs and ways in which the GDR used women as celluloid alibis, Ute Lischke-McNab's interview with Helga Schubert focuses on women's roles in film production in the GDR. Schubert's straightforward answers about the policies that governed the official East German film studio, the DEFA, and her career as a scriptwriter and psychologist provide fascinating information and astute assessments of an era that is undergoing much examination. Further illumination of representations of women as social ciphers is offered in Andrea Rinke's essay that is intended as a companion piece to Margrit Frölich's essay in part I. Adding to Frölich's overview, Rinke's essay "Models or Misfits? The Role of Screen Heroines in GDR Cinema," analyzes L. Warneke's *Unser kurzes Leben* (Our Short Life, 1981) and E. Schmidt's *Das Fahrrad* (The Bicycle, 1982) as exemplary for two kinds of roles of screen heroines in the GDR, and examines how these films used the gender gap to critique institutionalized power. In the final essay of this section, "Wenders' Genders: From the End of the Wall to the End of the World," Scott Spector takes a fresh look at the way in which gendered vision is mapped onto the binary of image and history in *Until the End of the World* (1990). Wenders, explains Spector, may indeed have intended this film to be a feminist work, but failed because the film's confrontation of image and story (history) is determined by "figuring Woman in specific and predetermined relations to the male authorial subject and the (his) textual product."

The authors of essays in part V, "Recovering (from) History: Memory and Film," consider both documentary and feature films that represent events during and shortly after the twelve years of Nazi rule. Two essays, Rosmarie Thee Morewedge's on Helma Sander-Brahms's *Deutschland, bleiche Mutter* (Germany, Pale Mother, 1978), and Susan E. Linville's on Marianne Rosenbaum's *Peppermint Frieden* (Peppermint Peace, 1983), focus on these films' insertion of fairy tales or fairy-tale elements as a way toward some kind of Vergangenheitsbewältigung (coming to terms with the legacy of the Nazi regime's twelve years of terror). Morewedge argues that *Deutschland, bleiche Mutter* refracts fairy-tale elements (Sleeping Beauty, Little Red Riding Hood, and the Robber Bridegroom) through the historical background of Nazi Germany in order to make the Nazi's oppressive political and social policies more conspicuous. Linville's essay, "Fairy Tales and Reflexivity in Marianne Rosenbaum's *Peppermint Peace*," analyzes Rosenbaum's use of the fable "The Rabbit and the Hedgehog" within the context of a number of successful films by women that use the fairy tale as a vehicle for the social critique of Germany's political past.

Sabine Smith's dialogue with Helke Sander reveals the filmmaker's view of critical reactions to her film *BeFreier und Befreite: Krieg, Vergewaltigungen, Kinder* (Liberators Take Liberties), offering insights into alternate ways of thinking of the film as well as her perception of how the general public saw this film. Sander also talks about the specific challenges posed when making a documentary about rapes that happened over five decades ago, and reveals her views about feminist filmmaking, feminist documentary films, and the embattled term *feminist*. Unrelated to the Smith-Sander interview,[3] Marie-Luise Gättens analyzes *BeFreier und Befreite: Krieg, Vergewaltigungen, Kinder* from a perspective that has hitherto gotten short shrift: she refracts the film's interpretative framework (history/story) through its instrumentalization of the genre's strategies (insertion of voice-overs, use of experts, archival film footage, employment of photographic evidence, etc.). Arguing that the "historical enterprise" runs counter to the historian and documentarist's needs, Gättens identifies a resulting tension that is visible in the "disjuncture of narrative and images, and present and past."

For obvious reasons, many fine filmmakers' works could not be included in these pages, leaving much territory for further exploration. As is often pointed out, German women-filmmakers are usually marginalized in book-length studies on German cinema. The present collection is intended to ameliorate that situation. Furthermore, there is some reason for optimism for future scholarship on German women-directors. As the conversation between Ute Lischke-McNab and Jutta Brückner in the appendix announces, the "European Institute for Women and Film" provides an archive for films and materials relating to the production of Frauenfilm and films by women. The "last word" in this collection then, is on future possibilities and sites for research. As we hope the volume as a whole makes clear, film studies is at its best when it strives to enlarge our frames of intelligibility and when it puts pressure on the limits of current feminist film theories.

Notes

1. Films were the domain of SUNY Binghamton Cinema Department's Adele Brown; I helped facilitate the discussions with Prof. Marilynn Desmond, in the English and Women Studies Department.

2. *Triangulated Visions* follows the appearance in 1993 of *Gender and German Cinema: Feminist Interventions*, eds. Sandra Frieden, Richard McCormick, Vibeke Petersen, and Laurie Vogelsang.

3. It must be emphasized that Sabine Smith's interview with Helke Sander is not in response to Marie-Luise Gättens's essay, and the latter's essay does not incorporate Sander's remarks in the interview.

I

Genre and Other Border Crossings

1

Triangulating Performances:
Looking After Genre, After Feature

Nora M. Alter

J. L. Austin's examples of performativity [suggest] that the heterosexual-
ization of the social bond is the paradigmatic form for those speech acts
which bring about what they name. "I pronounce you. . . ." puts into effect the relation that it names. But from where and when does such a performance draw its force, and what happens to the performative when its
purpose is precisely to undo the presumptive force of the heterosexual
ceremonial?

—Judith Butler, *Bodies that Matter: On the Discursive Limits of "Sex"*

Jean-Luc Godard describes a scenario in which you enter a movie theater
late, without knowing what's playing. You see something on-screen ("All of a
sudden, pow, at 10:00 in the morning, just as you're coming in"), but exactly
what it is you see and how to describe it—that's the problem. At one percep-
tual level, a blond woman is walking up a hill in a city that you may or may not
recognize as San Francisco. For a few seconds, you don't know the epistemological and generic status of the image. Only as the woman comes into more detailed focus does it become apparent (at least to Godard's film-savvy viewer) that
she is the actor Kim Novak, and the film Hitchcock's *Vertigo*.[1] But the experience of radical generic undecidability lingers on, perhaps haunting all subsequent viewings.

Godard uses this anecdote to problematize the hoary binary division that
runs through film production, distribution, consumption, and categorization
between feature film and documentary. In his anecdote, fiction (or, more precisely, a spectator's eventual realization or interpretation of film footage *as* fiction) becomes for Godard a "moment of communication" that triangulates, so

to speak: everything on-screen displayed by camera and editing, including actors; how all this was constructed by the filmmaker's team; and the viewer. Part of the point of Godard's anecdote is to complicate this latter category ("the viewer"), so as to obscure the explanatory clarity of our triangle. For while it is obvious that viewers are key players in the game, "*the* viewer" is a notoriously unstable and untrainable beast, particularly because it is always haunted by more or less unconscious ghosts of class, race, gender, and sexuality.[2] So rambunctious is this category in empirical fact that it threatens to disrupt the stability of precisely that theoretical structure of triangulation of which it initially seems to be just one equally codetermining part. I take it that this constitutive tension (i.e., between the relatively stable, metanarrative structure of triangulated vision in theory and the comparatively instable, phenomenological way subjects and subject positions actually perceive and misperceive this same structure) is our concern here, particularly as it may relate to gender and genre.

What's more, the perspective of any viewer may shift imperceptibly even as s/he looks at what appears visible. As the art historian Donald Preziosi has noted (articulating Foucault's depiction of Bentham's prison with Lacan's analysis of Holbein's *Ambassadors*), the panoptical, centered aspect of our vision is often indelibly inscribed by an unsettling, labile countervisual moment of anamorphic projection.[3] Applied to Godard's anecdote, the (male?) viewer's initial, momentary indecision, indeed anxiety, about which genre is being viewed (Is that [female] person acting or not?) anamorphically disrupts "normal" categories of filmic expectation and response. On the one hand, Godard's anecdote happens to recuperate fiction for cinema, since the film in question turns out, objectively, to be *Vertigo*. On the other hand, by the same logic, the upshot could have been reversed. Another film might have turned out to be a documentary film or even, to complicate things somewhat, this very film might be documentary footage of the shooting of *Vertigo*. Godard himself alludes to this possibility elsewhere when he quips (à la Brecht) that his *Breathless* (1960) "is really a documentary on Jean Seberg and Jean-Paul Belmondo" playing their parts.[4] Furthermore, in addition to all the more or less *unconscious* pressures of distraction, free association, and daydreaming (as well as the baggage of cinema lore that has been brought into the theater), the viewer can *consciously* (if perversely) decide to look at what is seen *as* fiction or *as* documentary—irrespective of what is known to be the case.

The problem of specifying the precise epistemic locations of fact and fiction, and their oscillatory interrelationship, is also subtended by the notorious impossibility of distinguishing apodictically between autobiography and biography. And this brings us to the problem of performance. The ability of the viewer to "identify" (either positively or negatively by abjection) with what is seen and heard on-screen has to do with shifting transferential relationships between biography ("Ah, that's Kim Novak!") and more or less unconscious autobiography ("Maybe that's me?"). In a seminal argument, Paul de Man slyly suggested that "autobiography is not a genre or a mode, but a figure of reading or understanding that occurs to some degree in all texts."[5] Here another initially clear distinction between constating facts and performing alternative scenarios, collapses. By extension, all genres (in our case feature and/or documentary film) are not something (only) "in" a medium (including, say, its styles of camera, editing, and acting). For genres are (at least) codetermined by the multiple, performative gaze of spectators—part frontal, part anamorphic. The concept "triangulated vision" thus threatens to become an ultimately undecidable de Manian "figure of reading," indeed performative "de-facement." This unsettling possibility, if not undecidability, might undermine the confidence with which Brian Winston can assert that the film audience can "tell the difference between a fictional narrative and a documentary argument"—and hence that documentary might still "claim the real."[6] Similarly destabilized, if not reversed, is Dudley Andrew's dictum that "genres construct the proper spectator for their own consumption."[7] Now it is the spectators who construct genres, albeit in ways sooner or later recuperated by institutional conventions, including those of filmmaking, acting, and viewing. For his part, Godard concludes that "it's the look that creates the fiction" and that "fiction is the look, the text being the expression of this look."[8] But what, then, is this "look"? How, exactly, is it constructed, when, and by whom? And does gender have anything fundamental to do with the formal, epistemological, and technical problem of film production and reception?[9]

I am interested in moments in film when autobiography and biography become performances in which fact and fiction suddenly, momentarily exchange positions by chiasmic reversal: a single shot or short sequence assumed to be documentary shades into fiction or vice versa. I borrow the term *chiasmus* from Maurice Merleau-Ponty's unfinished last work, *The Visible and the Invisible*. Here the term refers to a "double and crossed situating of the visible in the tangible and of the tangible in the visible."[10] I want to extend this idea to the interaction between fact and fiction, biography and autobiography, in the audiovisual medium. According to Merleau-Ponty, what he calls these "two maps" (in his case, those of the visible and the tangible, in the sense of what can be felt but not seen, and hence maps of the visible and the invisible) "are complete, and yet they do not merge into one. The two parts are total parts and yet are not superposable" (134). Yet in film (and this might have something to do with Merleau-Ponty's notorious mistrust of the medium) the chiasmus in question would precisely entail superimposition: between and within images and sounds (what Godard calls *son + image*).[11]

In any case, not only moments "in" films but also critical concepts, such as "triangulated vision" are performative effects of "figures of reading" which, in our case here, both reconfirm and yet also "de-face" the stability of the triangulation between (woman)filmmaker-(woman)actor-(women)spectator. And we must again ask what gender has to do with this triangulation, and if it is something necessary or contingent. The Godardian "look" of documentary and/or feature is now configured slightly differently from what we noted earlier. We have three subject positions or constructions: the director (editor, camera crew, etc.); the actor (who may imitate certain signs conventionally understood to mark "fiction"); and spectatorial interaction with what is thus seen and heard.[12] Yet the phenomenal act of spectatorship—films as they are actually viewed— tends to play havoc with the metanarrative cogency of this tripartite theoretical model, as we glide more or less uncontrollably between the three "angles" of triangulated vision, always only to return eventually to ourselves, to our bodies. And, while it may matter very much whether the director, actor, and/or viewer is gendered (there is no escape from this in any case), I suggest that the deepest link between triangulated vision and gender may be a function less of gender than of this labile structure of triangulation and dis-triangulation. In other words, triangulated vision is a case of "immanent causation," in which a significant structure is not separate from, but continues to "indwell" its effects[13]—including those that take adapt explicitly gendered or sexualized forms. As another consequence of this undecidability, I also want to resist thinking of the notion of triangulated vision in only contemporary or national terms. Hence my use of Godard and my consideration presently of a film made by a male German director in 1942. At its deepest level, then, triangulated vision respects borders of neither time, nation, nor gender, even as it is manifested in and as these forms. Just as important, we typically "forget" this fact when watching films; and filmmakers and actors exploit this constitutive amnesia in various ways.

Let us cast our now complicated "look" at three films linked to one another vis-à-vis Godard's anecdote. Each involves an element of performance in potentially transgressive ways. In each case the transgression in question is simultaneously formal (technological) and thematic (i.e., key to the plot), whereby the normative generic distinction between feature and fiction enters particularly into risk. The first example especially problematizes heterosexual norms; the second overcodes this type of transgression with an ethnographic element in order to problematize Eurocentrism; the third asks us where formal and thematic transgressions are to be located in the history of cinema and what, if anything, they might have to do, necessarily, with contemporary women-directors, actors, and viewers. We begin in the city of Godard's anecdote.

> Susie Sexpert, contemporary California comedienne and performance artist, in direct address to the camera and then to passersby, hands out leaflets advertising sex shows. Location of the shot: the streets of San Francisco. Amongst the passersby, coming out of deep focus toward Sexpert and the camera, a woman approaches. She's suddenly recognized as the main actor in the movie. The voice of Sexpert changes, making it evident that she herself "becomes" a film

actress at this moment. This chiasmic, performative reversal occurs in Monika Treut's *The Virgin Machine* (1988).

We witness an elaborate ritual performance in which people dance in a circle with huge animal masks (which partly disguise their gender, though we may infer that they are male). The camera cuts to a group of western women, whose adventures we have been following, and one explains to her companions that this is a "tscham ceremony" intended to prepare all mortals for the journey our souls will take after death. Another western woman aims her camera at the film camera, our POV. Location of the sequence: steppes of Mongolia, in Ulrike Ottinger's *Johanna d'Arc of Mongolia* (1988).

A woman on stage sings a love song. The camera turns 180 degrees for a reaction shot: the audience applauding her performance. The singer onstage is Zarah Leander, the setting wartime Berlin in Nazi Germany. Or is it (also) here and now? This question is posed implicitly, if not also explicitly, in Rolf Hansen's 1942 feature film *Die grosse Liebe*.

These three sequences illustrate the constitutive tension between the three types of "look," but they also encourage a "look" that transcends and problematizes genre categorization—hence it is *after* genre in all senses, even *against* it. As I have argued, the "look" is both theoretically and phenomenologically located within the "triangle" but not firmly so, shifting as it does between its three "angles": director, actor, and spectator. For the sake of convenience (recognizing that these are analytic as much as empirical categories), I take each sequence to illustrate one of the angles of the triangulated "look," stressing at the same time that substantial overlappings occur that are both in and out of the ultimate control of director, actor, and spectator. (Also because of the overlappings, it's possible to spend more time with the first example and increasingly less with each succeeding one.) As opposed to films in which the documentary inserts are marked in contrast to the feature material, these three sequences are narratively and technologically sutured into the diegesis of each film, in a manner characteristic less of either feature or documentary films per se than to film essays. So it is that fact and fiction are tightly interwoven to produce an almost seamless— yet chiasmic—"postgenre" in which, among other things, commonly held categories of sexuality, geophysical region, and historical time become significantly problematized.

The Virgin Machine, or, The Look of the Actor

Treut's *Virgin Machine* can be viewed as a filmic rendering of a contemporary Bildungsroman (novel of education). Specifically, it both parodies and takes seriously the sentimental education of a young journalist, Dorothee, who is searching explicitly for "romantic love." Her picaresque leads from her native Hamburg, and from her lover Hans, to her arrival in an "exotic" San Francisco. Here she discovers "alternative" sexual practices (including S&M and dildos designed for and by women). The aforementioned sequence is pivotal because it introduces Dorothee to Sexpert and hence to initial liberation from heterosexual patriarchy. The film nears climax in Dorothee's lesbian encounter with a female call girl, Ramona (Dorothee has to pay for what she assumed was free), and ends with Dorothee's evidently most authentically liberating moment: performing on stage in a lesbian bar.

The Virgin Machine is shot in grainy black-and-white film stock, or so it is developed, the style associated with authenticity and/or documentary cinema. This reinforces the effect of both the scene just described and the coverage of the final performance in the bar. Here, as throughout the movie, the quality of the image suggests: "you are there."

This supposedly nonfiction style is overcoded by several binary sign systems or conventions: acting versus not acting; diegetic versus nondiegetic sound track; studio versus on-location shooting; and so forth. In what I've designated, for the sake of my argument, as the pivotal scene (i.e., when the camera focuses on Sexpert passing out advertisements for an upcoming sex show), there is no nondiegetic music, and after she addresses the camera frontally she subsequently appears completely unaware of its presence, at least until her telltale voice changes register to indicate (feigned or real?) "acting" or "stage fright." In this cinema verité mode, when a woman approaches from the crowd, the camera does not initially focus on her anymore than on any other pedestrian. Only when she comes into the visual and aural field of Sexpert do we interpellate her as Dorothee.[14] The documentary illusion (we now recognize our protagonist or "star," with whom we have already been asked to identify) is momentarily broken, before being reestablished later. We are further transported out of the documentary mode of looking when Sexpert first addresses Dorothee and the two enter into dialogue. Here Sexpert's voice changes to become that of an actor in this movie, aware of the camera, which, however, she had already been aware of at another level. The film camera interpellates Sexpert as a fictional construction only when she meets Dorothee, not when she is performing or preparing to perform. Her unexpected filmic artificiality shifts generic gears precisely at the moment when the two women join gender forces. Thus viewers and actors codetermine a genre after genre. In the one case it is our recognition of Dorothee as actor; in the second it is the self-consciousness of Sexpert, by means of which our own "look" is chiasmically transformed through a performance that combines elements that are at once "biographical" and "autobiographical." Remaining for a time within the fictional narrative reestablished by Sexpert's voice change, Dorothee accompanies her on a motorcycle to the next performance site where she'll discuss the pros and cons of various dildos. This time, the "look" is switched back from the fictional to the documentary, in a simple re-reversal. In direct address to the camera, Sexpert shows Dorothee and us her wares. To aid this transition, the camera cuts to several bystanders who have nothing to do with the plot. And Sexpert's voice changes back to how it was before she "first" encountered Dorothee, becoming again "herself."

In both shot sequences we are at one level "looking" at "real" performances that both suspend and then reestablish the distinction between "feature" and "documentary." Temporarily we are pointed in a different, third direction, only to be folded back into the familiar binarism and/or into one term or the other. This third possibility, which seems to exceed genre, is intimately linked to both the thematics and the form of *The Virgin Machine*. Indeed, it is not too much to say that the title suggests that this film is—quite literally as well as figuratively—a machine designed not merely to *record* (*constate*) at the level of "biography," the transformation of a heterosexually conflicted woman into a liberated lesbian but also actually to *produce* (*perform*) this transformation in the audience, as a form of "autobiography"—not merely Treut's but also "ours." Whether either transformation (of the actor playing Dorothee, of the filmmaker, or of us spectators) in fact occurs outside the film, is not quite the point. The point is rather that Treut's mode of production, *this* virgin machine, is *after* and *against* genre, if by genre one can only always mean "fact versus fiction," "documentary versus feature." Can we really distinguish who is acting from who is not?

Now, it may be true that, traditionally, strict adherence to categories and to the binary division of fiction versus nonfiction is symptomatic of, or at least undergirds, white, western, heterosexual, male cultural production. It might seem to follow, then, that effective transgressions can be expected to occur in films that problematize traditional gender and sexuality, including those that parody the Bildungsroman, which at least in German literature has been decidedly male-oriented and -dominated. Treut would thus attack this tradition cinematographically by showing that fantasy and reality are not polar opposites but part of a complex process of chiasmic performance. Her most explicit depictions of this performative strategy are in her discussions of sadomasochism.

Treut's earlier film *Seduction: The Cruel Woman* (1985) and her later *Female Misbehaviour* (1992) both focus on sadomasochism as a consensual, contractual practice that treads a fine line between fantasy, or the playing of a game or role, and the acting out of the real. *The Virgin Machine* also contains S&M scenes in Dorothee's hotel, but these are not explicitly remarked within or by *The Virgin Machine*: that is, neither diegetically from within by the actors nor nondiegetically by, say, a voice-over. Treut elsewhere has suggested that "the fantasy of masochistic submission draws its effectiveness not from the actual situation of an objectively existing and powerful dependency but rather from playing with the idea of such a dependency." [15] In other words, Treut's films are not purely real but also not purely fantasy, much as the aforementioned sequences with Doro-

thee and Sexpert on the street and in the bar are neither purely feature nor
purely documentary. And if, by the same logic, the actors' performances are not
pure biography or pure autobiography, either, then perhaps our response to the
film is expected to follow suit. (Not fortuitously, the plural in the German title,
Die Jungfrauen Maschine, indicates that the "machine" in question implicates
multiple "virgins.") Consequently, I argue that the specific (gendered and sexual) content of the sequences we've looked at eventually must give way to the
structural principle that determines them. Thus, the thematic shift away from
stable representations of sexuality are formally and technologically informed by
a move away from fixed categories of both genre and gender. It is significant that
in *The Virgin Machine* the final performance of the transformed Dorothee in the
bar takes place before an all-woman audience—but only *in the film*. In a preliminary shot sequence, we see that all men, one man in particular, have been
physically excluded from the performance at the club. But actual viewers watching the performance of the transformed actor Dorothee (on any format: in theaters or on VCRs) obviously can include males. At such points, the specificity
and geometrical rigor of triangulated vision is chiasmically breached, before it
reasserts itself. And so is problematized (for better or worse) its use-value in that
larger arena of sexual politics, films, and criticism in which the actors are, in a
sense, us.

Johanna d'Arc of Mongolia, or, The Look of the Director

Ulrike Ottinger's *Johanna d'Arc of Mongolia* shares with *The Virgin Machine*
a basic lesbian problematic, with a difference being that now this theme is implicitly homosocial as opposed to explicitly homosexual. Ottinger also considerably expands the ethnographic focus from the quite conventional sphere of
German-American relations depicted in Treut's film into the far more troubled
waters of Orientalism. Like Treut, Ottinger is intensely concerned with breaking down (easy) binaries between feature and documentary; indeed she is even
more explicitly articulate about intending to do so. It remains to be seen how
triangulated vision figures in this attempt, especially with regard to directing.

Ottinger's tripartite film in vibrant color begins on the trans-Siberian express through the former Soviet Union headed to China. Part 1 of the triptych
plays exclusively in the train and introduces the first main characters—white
Westerners (particularly, but not exclusively, women) of varying skin tones; natural and learned languages; and ethnic, national, and (apparently) sexual "identities"—not to mention (few critics do) social classes. These first scenes, filmed
within the train, as well as the shots through the train's windows of the spectacles
encountered at stops along the famous route, might be viewed as a homage (intentional or not) to the Soviet feature and documentary filmmaker Alexandre

Medvedkin. For he created "the cinema train" that traveled (with fully equipped editing and developing rooms) to all regions of the nascent Soviet Socialist Republic, chronicling the lives of its radically diverse peoples and attempting to unite them, at least filmically.[16] Be influence as it may, and under Ottinger's postmodern conditions, the first part of her film focuses on various types of musical and narrative performances. These both differentiate the various actors (male and female) and yet also bind them together from a more or less Western point of view. Part 2 centers on the passengers' "abduction" by a group of renegade Mongolians led by a "fierce" female leader, to whom one of the female abductees, Johanna, is increasingly, and reciprocally, attracted. This portion of the film concerns less the Western travelers than the visual detailing of customs, costumes, and mores of the "natives."

It is at this point that we seem to be entering into the realm of documentary ethnography. But just as Treut parodies the Bildungsroman, so Ottinger—arguably—ironizes ethnographic and anthropological filmmaking.[17] Part 3 (where my exemplary sequence occurs) continues where part 2 left off: namely, with the dominant focus on the elaborate tscham festival with its ritual slaughters of animals, dances, and set performances. The film ends with the Westerners boarding the train to continue their journey. The significant difference now is that there is a new voyager. Either she is another Mongolian princess or, as other critics think, the first princess again but this time in Western garb. This somewhat ambiguous figure explains that she lives part of the year in Paris and summers in Mongolia. So it is, then, that "the enlightenment West" meets "the exotic East" once again, upholding and/or problematizing a long tradition of overdetermined "attraction," albeit this time with a feminist twist—specifically homosocial.[18]

My question here involves the paradoxical anthropological status of one sequence, indeed the one image: the tscham. Clearly, Ottinger has restaged the "documentary" event. Nonetheless, it remains a performance based on an actual ritual—a re-creation of an actuality—thus paying a certain, imaginary or symbolic, homage to the real. In a sense, by staging and directing this real, Ottinger avoids giving the misleading impression that her camera is a neutral, objective, invisible witness to the event "as it really is." (To paraphrase Lacan, if the real resists symbolization absolutely, this is not to say that symbolization can be avoided.) So when Lady Windemere speaks of the ceremony of death to her audience, it makes sense that it remains unclear if she is speaking to us, to all her compatriots, to Johanna intimately leaning over her shoulder, and/or to the assembled Mongolians also watching (and coproducing) the performance. The camera crosscuts to all of these parties. The cut to us is suggested by Frau Vohwinkel, the one who, as surrogate viewer, raises her camera and aims it at Ottinger's camera, thereby folding us in/visibly, chiasmically into the performance. Also suitably ambiguous is the referent or recipient of what is meant by "death."

In a sense, the tscham death at stake is the obliteration of the question of what is real, what is fictional. But this, too, is an old story, and one here involving less closure than the opening up of new possibilities.

Ethnographic filmmaking at its origins, as well as many early feature films, had "exotic settings" with "real natives." These films thus functioned at once as entertainment but also as a form of surrogate, visual tourism for spectators.[19] In Ottinger's version of this "cinema of attractions," the "chronicling" of Mongolia, largely staged by Ottinger, and by the seductively beautiful images that she permits us to watch, in this nearly one-hour segment, are neither reenforced nor disrupted by much narrative. This "sublime" sequence may be intended primarily as unadulterated viewing pleasure, a certain suspension not only of disbelief but of cognitive distance itself.

Questions of the ethics of "ethnographic" filmmaking aside, Ottinger has been commonly viewed as a problematic exception in the canon of West German women-filmmakers. Despite the fact that her films "bring together elements of autobiography, documentary, and fiction, they depart from the manner in which these tendencies have been represented in West Berlin's women's films."[20] This includes the tendency to adhere to a relatively clear separation of genres, fiction or documentary, but not both at once, and not in the same image. Thus, "fantasy and visual opulence predominate over the kind of realism associated with everyday life and vision."[21]

In the very first scene of the film, Lady Windemere asks us to consider this question: "Was it a confrontation with reality or with the imagination . . . must imagination shun the encounter with reality? Or are they enamoured of each other? Can they form an alliance?" And henceforth, as Brenda Longfellow notes, the film "is structured around a spectacular alliance of reality and the imagination."[22] Or, in terms of my argument, it becomes an essay film "after" nonfiction and/or fiction, feature film and/or documentary, and biographical and/or autobiographical performance. Ottinger seeks to transcend at least generic limits. In her words, "The continuing endeavours of the film industry to limit filmmakers and directors to the most narrow, stereotyped genre cinema possible cannot be overlooked."[23] Roswitha Mueller duly points to Ottinger's interrogation of the "fixity of oppositions."[24] Longfellow, basing her arguments on Ottinger's claim that she is trying to create "a new kind of realism," concludes that *Johanna d'Arc of Mongolia* represents a "hybridization of categories in which the distinctions between fiction and documentary begin to break down."[25] Clearly, this "hybridization" is also linked to the importance of the figure of the nomad for Ottinger. As she explains in an interview with Therese Grisham, "I became quite interested in nomadism . . . nomad thought is very important."[26] And, importantly, nomadism, as the constant moving between cultures, genres, and concepts, is reflected in the film's cinematographic style. This is why Ottinger in effect directs the viewer into a spectatorial position of nomadic oscillation, not only between documentary and feature, not only between varieties of homosocial experience, but also across wide expanses of space and, in terms of ritual performance, time. Not for nothing do Deleuze and Guattari view what they call nomadology as the figure par excellence of the "war machine" disruptive of all power, not least the "spatiogeographic."[27]

Cinema has been called the Last Machine.[28] *The Virgin Machine* can be read—particularly in its "look" of the actors—as a virtual machine for the reproduction of a simultaneously triangulated and distriangulated vision. So also Ottinger's film can be read as another type of "machine," as the attempt to fuse—particularly at the level of her directing, camera work, and editing (over all of which she keeps notoriously firm control) the aforementioned crosscuts uniting all the audiences of the performance: namely, the "Western self" with the "Oriental other." Although critics rarely attempt to explain the title of Ottinger's film, perhaps an answer may be found in the heroic—albeit unclarified—allusion to the original Jeanne d'Arc de France, the unique woman-warrior-maiden who led her people to at least momentary victory over the foreign invader, before finding death at the stake. And this may be the ultimate reason why Ottinger literally "directs" attention to the tscham ceremony, as preparation for death at what may be the axial point of her film in terms of the triangulated look. The re/performance of this ceremony arguably *is* the film—if not exactly "war machine"—*Johanna d'Arc of Mongolia*.

Die große Liebe, or, The Look of the (Historical) Viewer

My final scene opens up the argument beyond the spatial into the temporal and historical in order to problematize the "newness" of what might otherwise appear to be a specifically postmodern and (lesbian) feminist problematic of cinematic triangulation circa 1988 and its critical aftermath. Today, with increasing frequency and intensity, lines between documentary truth and feature fiction are being blurred. This corresponds to the more general social and cultural meltdown of traditional genre and media categories of representation and to the coterminous tendency toward hybridity that seem to be a condition of postmodernity. One result, I have been suggesting, are moments of chiasmus in a cinema that radically problematizes the distinction between "documentary" and "feature," and "biography" and "autobiography," and these moments are particularly im/perceptible around performances with, and of, these films. In such moments the validity of the notion of triangulated vision is at once confirmed, disrupted, and confirmed again. This almost imperceptible mixing of the two basic genres may seem to contrast sharply with the earlier film practice of directly intersplicing documentary footage into features but in such a way as to keep them relatively distinct and recognizable. Furthermore, this postmodern problematic may also be part of the overall drift of cinema to shift away from a more or less unquestioned concern to depict human movement through time and space and toward a desire to interrogate space and time themselves, in tandem with various types of their audiovisual compression.[29] However, it should also be noted that in the earliest silent cinema, the conflation of nonfiction footage with narrative was sometimes equally and systematically blurred; indeed films did not become formally divided into the two basic categories until the twenties.[30] Thus we are cautioned against viewing current problematics of cinema as being wholly new—after all categories that we may imagine to be empirical and historical often turn out to be our own analytic projections.

Now, *Die große Liebe* (The Great or True Love) is a love story set in wartime Nazi Germany involving a heartthrob singer and performer, played by Zarah Leander, and an ostensibly not untypical Luftwaffe pilot, played by Paul Wendlandt. The inevitable conflict arises when duty for the fatherland overrides his duty as her lover. Needless to say, in the end she has to accept that service to the führer must come first, family and personal life second. Set against the backdrop of the actual war, the film includes several insertions of newsreel war footage— the kind that was shown before feature films and performance, including this one. Thus we can imagine an audience in 1942 as being sutured into a real that was increasingly, publicly horrific (particularly, for many, after the defeats in North Africa and Stalingrad and the bombing of German cities) in this very film, by its use of newsreels. But I'm interested here in another, rather less obvious, "documentary" moment within the film: Leander's performance as a singer. Based on her most popular songs, these performances are smoothly integrated into the plot yet they may seem to exceed the fictional frame for audiences not merely in the forties but today as well. So it is that a "feature" moment becomes for viewers in, say, 1996 a documentary moment that is just as "real" as it was for viewers back in 1942. This is not any singer performing or any actor reenacting the role of a historical person (such as Hannah Schygulla's performance of Lili Marleen in Fassbinder's eponymous film) but—for a certain viewer or viewing formation—this is actually Zarah Leander momentarily transcending space and time. The two documentary "looks"—that of the 1942 and the 1996 spectator—suddenly coalesce audiovisually, the distinction momentarily moot. The body and voice of Leander exceed their mortal boundaries to become an excess—an excess beyond interpretation precisely because it blurs reality and fiction. In its overabundance this moment becomes Bill Nichols's "one Body too many."[31] Such bodies can barely contain multiple subject positions within triangulated vision. In the case of Leander, she was among other things a gay male and lesbian fetish object as well as heterosexual. In the performance scene in question, Rolf Hansen's camera turns from the view of the theater (both in the film and in our own) toward the reverse angle from Leander's point of view on the audience. In this chiasmic moment we suddenly see (ourselves as) the two Luftwaffe officers. And it is here that their reaction to Leander's singing is to exchange deep glances between themselves, before the one, our hero, bolts out of his chair, headed for his unannounced first meeting with Leander, or her character, backstage—and from now on the plot, of course, thickens.

But to what exactly does the title *Die große Liebe* refer? Exactly whose "love of a lifetime" is here in play and at risk? According to the plot, it is obviously the love of fatherland, specifically Hitler, which overrides all other love, even the most profoundly personal. This includes the tacit (homoerotic) male bonding between two Luftwaffe officers, and the explicit (heterosexual) bond between one of them and Zarah Leander and/or her character in the film. But the film cannot determine the sexuality or gender of each member of its real audience. In other words, this performative moment is after genre, in which the distinctions between documentary and feature, biography and autobiography, are momentarily reversed or obviated. It is also, in a sense, a moment after gender and after sexuality. But which historical audience are we now imagining? During this scene, if the film is working properly, there is likely a momentary forgetting, during Leander's performance of her love song, that the war is—or was—going on. For a German audience in 1942 or in the next few years (the film was screened only in Germany and in its occupied territories), this chiasmic performance can be expected to have one kind of historical effect, as otherwise heterogeneous as it must have been on individual members of the audience. But what Leander's performance ought not to make us forget—today—is another thing that audiences may well be led to "forget" by this film and particularly this one moment in it: namely, that many other people besides Nazis and other Germans were at physical risk at the time. This is the problem with all the so-called entertainment films of the Third Reich, so actively supported by Goebbels, in his peculiar "great love" of Germany and German cinema. But it remains our problem as film critics.

One lesson we may take from *Die große Liebe* is that chiasmic performances can have enormous power within the supple structure of triangulated vision. While they can be adopted to serve what some of us at least imagine to be progressive and liberatory ends—as arguably in the virgin machines and war machines of Treut and Ottinger—their basic mechanism can serve virtually any purpose imaginable. Indeed chiasmic performances open up our audiovisual synapses momentarily, suspending our cognitive powers, and in such moments theoretically any type of ideology can penetrate. This is perhaps not the least reason why the topic of triangulated vision is important. Even as we perform, we are performed; even as we are performed, we have at least some capacity to change our performance.

My main focus has been the interplay between fiction and truth, and biography and autobiography, as it appears in three moments in three films and/or viewing experiences more or less controlled or prefigured by audiovisual technologies. I have argued that these three moments have in common chiasmic performances that confirm, disrupt, and reconfirm the concept of triangulated vision: the look that circulates between director, actor, and viewer. One way of viewing these performances would be in terms of what Tom Gunning, referring to early silent films, has called the "cinema of attractions." According to Gunning, "Rather than being an involvement with narrative action or empathy with character psychology, the cinema of attractions solicits a highly conscious awareness of the film image engaging the viewer's curiosity. The spectator does not get lost in a fictional world and its drama, but remains aware of the act of looking, the excitement of curiosity and its fulfilment." [32] But we have seen that, at least as film history has developed, this "solicitation" does not result—necessarily—in high levels of consciousness. Rather, audiences have to help produce it. Part of the fascination with cinema at its inception a century ago, according to Gunning, was a simple marveling at the sheer technology and what it could reveal, before the days of television. He also suggests that elements of this same attraction continue to persist "in later cinema, even if it rarely dominates the form of a feature film as a whole"; for instance, "It provides an undercurrent flowing beneath narrative logic and diegetic realism, producing those moments of cinematic dépaysement beloved by the surrealists" (123). In contrast, Godard finds prefigured already in the earliest cinema a split: "Cinema," Truffaut said, "is spectacle—Méliès—and research—Lumière. If I analyze myself today, I see that I have always wanted, basically to do research in the form of spectacle." [33] Which may lead us to think that the split in question, which includes the cinema of attractions, is at least as much something that we viewers produce as it is something that historians and critics find readymade in films.

Notes

1. Jean-Luc Godard, "Introduction à une véritable histoire de cinéma," *camera obscura* 8–10 (1980): 75–88; especially 78. I am indebted to Robert Ray for this reference.

2. For representative current scholarship on spectatorship, see *Viewing Positions: Ways of Seeing Film*, ed. Linda Williams (New Brunswick, N. J.: Rutgers University Press, 1995).

3. Donald Preziosi, *Rethinking Art History: Meditations on a Coy Science* (New Haven: Yale University Press, 1989), chap. 3, "The Panoptic Gaze and the Anamorphic Archive."

4. Godard, "Interview with Yvonne Baby" (1960), trans. Dudley Andrew, in *Breathless*, ed. Dudley Andrew (New Brunswick, N. J.: Rutgers University Press, 1987), 165–66; especially 166. Godard generally works from the principle that documentary fact and narrative fiction are mutually imbricated, remarking that "I started from the imaginary and discovered reality; but behind reality, there is again imagination" ("Interview with Jean-Luc Godard" [*Cahiers du Cinéma*, 1962], *Godard on Godard*, trans. and ed. Tom Milne, foreword by Annette Michelsen, 2d ed. [New York: Da Capo Press, 1986], 171–96; especially 181).

5. Paul de Man, "Autobiography as De-Facement," in *The Rhetoric of Romanticism* (New York: Columbia University Press, 1984), 67–81; especially 70.

6. Brian Winston, *Claiming the Real: The Documentary Film Revisited* (London: British Film Institute, 1995), 253. Also thus complicated is Winston's hope that "Grounding the documentary idea in reception rather than representation is exactly the way to preserve its validity. It allows for the audience to make the truth claim for the documentary rather than the documentary implicitly making the claim for itself" (253).

7. Dudley Andrew, *Concepts in Film Theory* (New York: Oxford University Press, 1984), 110.

8. Godard, "Introduction à une véritable histoire," 78.

9. I hope it goes without saying that my intent is not to diminish the importance of gender and sexuality in film or film analysis; but I do want to caution against reducing complex filmic issues to these terms and, more generally, against confusing the filmic transgression of any norm with other, perhaps more significant types of social change.

10. Maurice Merleau-Ponty, *The Visible and the Invisible*, ed. Claude Lefort, trans. Alphonso Lingis (1959–61; reprint, Evanston, Ill.: Northwestern University Press, 1968), 134.

11. Although she does not deal with film, for a substantial critique of Merleau-Ponty for having neglected sound in his phenomenology, alongside neglect of the sexualized aspect of his own discourse generally, see Luce Irigaray, *An Ethics of Sexual Difference*, trans. Carolyn Burke and Gillian C. Gill (1984; reprint, Ithaca, N.Y.: Cornell University Press, 1993), 151–84. See Godard, *Son + Image*, ed. Raymond Bellour, trans. Mary Lea Bandy (1974–91; reprint, New York: Museum of Modern Art, 1992).

12. This structure bears similarities, of course, to Laura Mulvey's foundational essay, "Visual Pleasure and Narrative Cinema" (1975), on the tripartite construction of the "male gaze" in cinema—splitting it between the gaze of the director, the characters, and the audience. However, whereas Mulvey locates her theory firmly within one film genre, the feature, I want to expand her theory to problematize gender essentialism and to include not only nonfiction but the very distinction between feature and documentary. Elsewhere I have argued that this results in a third "genre" (or, more precisely, antigenre) called essay film (see my article "The Political Im/perceptible in the Essay Film: Harun Farocki's *Images of the World and the Inscription of War*," *New German Critique* 68 (spring 1996): 165–92.

13. On the use and abuse of structural causality in its application to the human sciences, see Fredric Jameson, *The Political Unconscious: Narrative as Socially Symbolic Act* (Ithaca, N.Y.: Cornell University Press, 1981), especially chap. 1.

14. A similar moment, famously, occurs in Godard's *A Woman Is a Woman* (1961) when Anna Karina emerges from a building into the street full of passersby before she begins recognizably to act.

15. Monika Treut, "Female Misbehaviour," in *Feminisms in the Cinema*, eds. Laura Pietropaolo and Ada Testaferri (Bloomington: Indiana University Press, 1995), 106–21; especially 109.

16. On Medvedkin's project, see Chris Marker's *Train en marche* (1971) and *The Last Bolshevik* (1993). In the former, the voice-over comments that, in Medvedkin's project, "imagination is no longer the enemy of reality."

17. Immediately before *Johanna d'Arc of Mongolia*, Ottinger made *China: The Arts, Everyday Life* (1985), a four-and-a-half-hour "documentary" film based on her travels in China. According to her, it functioned as a preliminary version of *Johanna d'Arc of Mongolia*, adding that "What's also important about this particular documentary is the way it functions for me as a sketchbook: reality connected together" (cited by Janet Bergstrom, "The Theater of Everyday Life: Ulrike Ottinger's *China: The Arts, Everyday Life*," *camera obscura* 18 (1988): 42–51; especially 50). For a detailed analysis of the latter film through the lens of contemporary theories of ethnography and postcoloniality, see Katie Trumpener, "*Johanna d'Arc of Mongolia* in the Mirror of *Dorian Gray*: Ethnographic Recordings and the Aesthetics of the Market in the Recent Films of Ulrike Ottinger," *New German Critique* 60 (fall 1993): 77–99. Trumpener interprets the film as a serious ethnographic foray informed, however, by unintentional German neoimperialism. In contrast, Therese Grisham and Brenda Longfellow read the film as being considerably more complex and nuanced in its treatment of the "exotic." Grisham supports her argument by analyzing Ottinger's camera movement, concluding that "This underscores, tongue in cheek, the sweeping, objective view of the western cultural anthropologist" (Grisham, "Twentieth Century *Theatrum Mundi*: Ulrike Ottinger's *Johanna d'Arc of Mongolia*," *Wide Angle* 14, no. 2 [April 1992]: 22–36; especially 24). Also see Brenda Longfellow, "Lesbian Phantasy and the Other Woman in Ottinger's *Johanna d'Arc of Mongolia*," *Screen* 34, no. 2 (summer 1993): 124–36.

18. One of the final lines in the film is that "The mutual exotic attraction has a long history"—leaving the antecedent somewhat ambiguous. On the early cinema of attractions, see Tom Gunning, "An Aesthetic of Astonishment: Early Film and the (In)Credulous Spectator," in *Viewing Positions*, 114–33.

19. One obvious example of this was Flaherty and Murnau's joint production *Tabu* (1931), which, according to the credits, was "filmed entirely on the island of Bora Bora using only natives"; yet, predictably, the resulting narrative was decidedly Eurocentric in its imposition of its particular version of romantic love, and so forth.

20. Bergstrom, "Theater of Everyday Life," 43.

21. Ibid., 43.

22. Longfellow, "Lesbian Phantasy," 126.

23. Ulrike Ottinger, "The Pressure to Make Genre Films: About the Endangered Autorenkino," in *West German Filmmakers on Film: Visions and Voices*, ed. Eric Rentschler (1983; reprint, New York: Holmes and Meier, 1988), 90–93; especially 90.

24. Roswitha Mueller, "The Mirror and the Vamp," *New German Critique* 34 (1985): 176–93; especially 188.

25. Longfellow, "Lesbian Phantasy," 129.

26. Therese Grisham, "An Interview with Ulrike Ottinger," *Wide Angle* 14, no. 2 (April 1992): 28–36; especially 31 and 33.

27. See Gilles Deleuze and Félix Guattari, *A Thousand Plateaus: Capitalism and Schizophrenia*, trans. Brian Massumi (1980; reprint, Minneapolis: University of Minnesota Press, 1987), chap. 12, "1227: Treatise on Nomadology—The War Machine," especially 380–87.

28. The phrase is attributed to the avant-garde filmmaker Hollis Frampton, a protégé of Ezra Pound. See Ian Christie, *The Last Machine: Early Cinema and the Birth of the Modern World* (London: BFI, 1994), 7. Frampton appears wrong to have added that it "is probably the last art that will reach the mind through the senses," unless of course one takes "cinema" in an extended sense.

29. See Gilles Deleuze, *Camera 1: The Movement-Image*, trans. Hugh Tomlinson and Barbara Habberjam (1983; reprint, Minneapolis: University of Minnesota Press, 1986); and *Camera 2: The Time-Image*, trans. Tomlinson and Robert Galeta (1985; reprint, Minneapolis: University of Minnesota Press, 1989). One of the interesting problems with this work is that—partly by design—Deleuze blurs the distinction between claims made about a shift in the history of cinema from one kind of image to the other with claims the status of which is purely analytic and might be used to view all films.

30. Though the first recorded application of the term *documentary* to film occurred as early as 1898, by the critic Boreslaw Matuszweski, and in 1914, by the filmmaker Edward S. Curtis to describe his work, these are isolated incidents. Documentary film practice and theory was not formally institutionalized and formalized until the late twenties and early thirties by John Grierson. For a detailed history of the documentary, see Winston, *Claiming the Real*.

31. See Bill Nichols,"Questions of Magnitude," in *Documentary and the Mass Media*, ed. John Corner (London: Edward Arnold, 1986), 107–22; idem, *Representing Reality: Issues and Concepts in Documentary* (Bloomington and Indianapolis: Indiana University Press, 1991), 229–66; and idem, *Blurred Boundaries* (Bloomington and Indianapolis: Indiana University Press, 1994).

32. Gunning, "Aesthetic of Astonishment," 121.

33. "Interview with Jean-Luc Godard," 181.

2

Fassbinder, Women, and Melodrama: Critical Interrogations

Douglas Kellner

Rainer Werner Fassbinder's representations of women have continued to provoke controversy long after his untimely death. In this study, I wish to probe Fassbinder's use of melodrama to interrogate the situation of women and to criticize German bourgeois institutions and ideology. I argue that Fassbinder effectively deploys the often-despised genre of melodrama to position the audience to view critically exploitative and oppressive personal relationships (a constant in Fassbinder's universe). Fassbinder's deployment of melodrama forces the audience into an uncomfortable realization of the ways in which money, power, and social conventions structure sexual relations and especially oppress women. I discuss how Fassbinder uses melodrama and contrast his use of the genre with Douglas Sirk and with the classical Hollywood cinema. Through a reading of *The Bitter Tears of Petra von Kant* (1972), I discuss melodrama and how it enables Fassbinder to critically dissect the social constructions of gender and sexuality, gender and class oppression, and the structures of domination. My argument is that popular genres like melodrama can be turned against their conventional uses and be used as vehicles of cinematic expression and social critique.

Fassbinder and Melodrama

Fassbinder's films are varied in style and genre but he has consistently used the genre of melodrama to probe the oppression of women in bourgeois society and the intersection of gender, sexuality, race, and class in the dynamics of domination. Melodrama has classically focused on the domestic sphere and particularly on family situations, sexual relationships and politics, and the domain of everyday life, though this need not always be so. The conflicts portrayed in melodrama are extremely dramatic and often given to excess; sex and violence are thus constants in the genre. The world of melodrama is generally bifurcated into conflicts between good and evil, marked either by the triumph of good or its defeat. In either case, a moral lesson is transmitted, and in classical melodrama at least a moral order of the universe is affirmed or presupposed.[1]

Melodrama is frequently held in contempt because of its simplistic dichotomy between good and evil, its simplified moral lessons, and its use of stock characters who generally represent stereotypes of virtue or vice. The narrative strategy of melodrama is to produce familiar characters and situations and to use techniques to induce the audience to identify with them. The "good" characters are generally sympathetic representatives of domestic normality who are usually threatened by "bad" characters whom the audience is positioned to abhor. The protagonists find themselves in readily recognizable conflicts and problems, and the audience is led to feel pity or empathy with their suffering, and either to be relieved when the "good" characters triumph over adversity or to feel sorrow or pain when they suffer or are defeated.

Although early forms of melodrama aided bourgeois social revolution, by showing members of the aristocracy to be decadent and corrupt, with the institutionalization of bourgeois society, melodrama assumed increasingly conservative social functions by legitimating dominant institutions, gender roles, social practices, and the values of bourgeois societies by punishing characters who broke with dominant social norms and behavior and by rewarding those who conformed. Whereas there is a tradition in which melodrama has been used as an instrument of social protest and critique (Smith 1973), for the most part, melodrama tended to produce morality plays that served as instruments of dominant ideologies—especially those of the family, traditional masculine and feminine gender roles and well-defined sexual differences, romantic love, the naturalness and rightness of conservative values, and so on.

Melodrama, in this form, became a major genre of Hollywood film and world cinema. In particular, Hollywood melodrama focused on domestic suffering and conflict, while producing genre cycles of the so-called women's film, or women's weepies. Eventually, formal and thematic conventions, stock themes and characters, and formal features solidified into a recognizable cinematic generic form (Elsaesser 1972, Haskell 1973, Schatz 1981, Kellner-Ryan 1987). But in contrast to the genre-dominated Hollywood cinema, the so-called New German Cinema has been an "auteur-cinema" (Autoren-kino) which has developed in opposition to the classical Hollywood film and genres developed in the United States. Consequently, most major German directors have tended to avoid Hollywood genres like the melodrama. Rainer Werner Fassbinder, however, is an important exception to the avoidance of Hollywood melodrama in German cinema, though I shall argue that he turns Hollywood melodrama upside-down, using a genre that upholds dominant societal norms to subvert them.

Fassbinder's early cycle of experimental films in the late 1960s and early 1970s feature extremely melodramatic situations and have some thematic resemblance to classical melodrama; they usually focus on domestic situations, present intense conflicts between the characters, or between the characters and external social forces like the police, and contain excessive amounts of sex and violence. Stylistically, however, Fassbinder's early films are extremely diverse and contain few of the formal features and strategies of Hollywood melodrama. In these films, Fassbinder generally employs aggressively Brechtian and Godardian distancing devices: *Katzelmacher* (1969), for instance, uses long takes that scrutinize the environment, the interaction of the characters, and, in good Brechtian fashion, their varying forms of social and asocial behavior. It also employs repetition, stylized and artificial acting, and has generally unpleasant characters with whom it is difficult to identify. In this way, the film positions the audience to view critically the social environment and dominant forms of exploitation and oppression.

Thematically, Fassbinder's early films subvert the ideology of the classical melodrama by refusing to delineate clear lines and conflicts between good and evil, and by projecting an extremely pessimistic view of the universe where oppressive forces usually triumph and the more sympathetic characters are defeated and often killed. Many of these films feature betrayal, and one gets the impression that intense romantic love and sexual passion generally brings suffering and death (i.e., *Love Is Colder than Death* 1969, *Katzelmacher* 1969, and *Gods of the Plague* 1969)—a theme that is also at the center of many of Godard's early films (i.e., *Breathless* 1959, *Le Petit Soldat* 1960, and *Pierrot Le Fou* 1965) where romantic love of a man for a woman brings about Godard's protagonist's downfall. In Fassbinder's *American Soldier* (1970), for example, every sexual relation in the film is marked by violence and betrayal, and at the end the concern of his mother and brother for the protagonist results in his death. In these films, it is as if sexual love and the family were sources of suffering and disaster for the individual—a position that reverses the ideology of the classical melodrama that presents the family and romantic love as a positive force in an often cruel world.

Fassbinder's first cycle of films thus present critical visions of relationships, practices, and values in the domestic sphere. At this time (the early seventies) Fassbinder began to be fascinated by classical Hollywood melodrama and especially by the films of Douglas Sirk. In a famous and oft-cited article, Fassbinder wrote: "Sirk has made the tenderest films I know, the films of someone who loves people and doesn't despise them. . . . I have seen six films by Douglas Sirk. Among them were the most beautiful in the world" (Fassbinder 1975, p. 88). In this article, he praises Sirk's efforts at using Hollywood cinema as an instrument of social critique, and lauds Sirk's style, his character construction, his ability to render psychological states in cinematic terms, and his representations of women. Fassbinder's own films would exhibit many of the very traits that he attributed to Sirkian cinema.

It is no accident that Fassbinder would be attracted by the genre of Hollywood melodrama and particularly by the films of Sirk. Melodrama has traditionally been a genre that deals with conflicts and problems in the domestic sphere, and especially interpersonal and sexual relations, while sexual politics, relations, and identity have been a recurrent concern of Fassbinder's cinema (and theater). Melodrama has also been a form of excess—emotional, stylistic, and existential—and certainly both Fassbinder's texts and life have been marked by outrageous excess. Sometimes, in his films, the excess is controlled and distanced (as in depictions of violence in his early films) and sometimes it is allowed to explode (as when Herr R runs amok in the film of that title, or the excessively flamboyant behavior of his film team is put on display in *Beware the Holy Whore*, 1970).

Melodramatic cinema, especially in masters of the genre like Sirk, is highly stylized and lends itself to formal play and display—extravagant colors, expressive symbols, elaborate design, and so forth—and certainly Fassbinder is interested in form and style. Furthermore, the thematics of the Hollywood melodrama would appeal to Fassbinder with its intense interpersonal conflicts and highly charged sex and violence, as would Hollywood's dramatic presentations of stories that contain a moral of some sort, especially those that contain a moral critique of an immoral society. To an extent not fully appreciated—but that we can now begin to discern—Fassbinder was a highly theatrical storyteller who, more than most of his modernist contemporaries and fellow stars of the New German Cinema, loved narrative story telling and dramatic, entertaining stories. Consequently, it is not surprising that he would be attracted to a form of melodrama that traditionally dramatized highly emotional stories of domestic and sexual conflict. For of all the major New German filmmakers, Fassbinder was probably the most attracted to the entertainment value and functions of the Hollywood cinema.[2] Fassbinder's most important films of the early to midseventies partake of many conventions of the Hollywood melodrama and display the stylistic influence of Sirk. Such films as *The Merchant of the Four Seasons, The Bitter Tears of Petra von Kant, Ali: Fear Eats the Soul, Fox and His Friends*, and most of his succeeding films of that period are much more conventional than his earlier films in their use of formal and thematic conventions of the melodrama and Sirkian aesthetics.

Many Fassbinder critics have noticed this and have stressed the impact of Sirk and the Hollywood melodrama on Fassbinder (Elsaesser 1976, Mayne 1977). Here, however, I am going to pursue a somewhat different critical strategy: while the influence of Sirk is clear and undeniable, I want to stress instead the *differences* between Fassbinder and Sirk, attempting to analyze the specificity of the Fassbinderian melodrama, the ways in which he refunctioned the genre, and his more radical sexual politics. In particular, I want to show how Fassbinder takes melodrama to its limits and goes beyond both the thematics and form of the classical melodrama while using its conventions.

During this period, Fassbinder stated in an interview: "Any life-story that deals with a relationship or whatever is a melodrama and for this reason, I think melodramatic films are correct films. The American method of making them, however, left the audience with emotions and nothing else. I want to give the spectator the emotions along with the possibility of reflecting on and analyzing what (she or) he is doing" (Fassbinder 1977).[3] Fassbinder's 1970 melodramas explore and question sexual identity and gender construction; relationships of domination and subordination; and connections between sexuality, work, and the social world. They scrutinize and criticize dominant forms of bourgeois morality and social (really asocial) behavior and thus carry the Brechtian project into the realm of contemporary morals and behavior. Stylistically, despite the Sirkian influence in their artifice, framing, and careful formal strategies of image construction, they are much more "realistic" in both aesthetic and psychological senses than Sirk's rather contrived and often farfetched melodramas with their idealized unitary characters (played by Rock Hudson in three major Sirkian films), their chance encounters, their rigorously dichotomized moral world, and so on. But, most crucially, as I shall now argue, Fassbinder's melodramas generate more powerful and subversive social criticism than the more liberal and affirmative films of Sirk.

Petra von Kant and the Politics of Representation

Although Fassbinder's films from the early to midseventies contain somewhat different aesthetic strategies and uses of melodrama, most of them refunction conventions of the Hollywood melodrama to criticize dominant forms of bourgeois morality and behavior, while radically interrogating bourgeois sexual politics. In a distinctive manner, Fassbinder uses conventional Hollywood modes of subject positioning and moral address to produce a socially critical "progressive" melodrama in a form that traditionally deployed very little distancing or cinematic reflexivity. In *The Bitter Tears of Petra von Kant* (1972), Fassbinder's use of the emotional pyrotechnics of melodrama and highly stylized image construction is highly exaggerated and mixes strategies of identification and distantiation—a unique combination that would henceforth characterize the Fassbinderian melodrama.

In the film, a manipulative and egotistical dress designer, Petra von Kant, falls madly in love with a model, Karin, who eventually leaves Petra and who drives her to extreme emotional distress. Fassbinder explores here the difficulties of maintaining nonexploitative sexual relations, and criticizes various forms of domination and manipulation, thus using formal and thematic conventions of the melodrama to engage in moral critique. But unlike Hollywood melodrama, *Petra* is highly aestheticized; none of the characters is particularly sympathetic, nor does Fassbinder employ conventional strategies of identification or positioning. Indeed, his image and character construction frequently serves to distance the spectator to view the characters and their behavior critically.

The film deploys a profusion and excess of formal and stylistic devices to engage in moral critique. The artificiality of Petra's *haute-bourgeois* behavior, for example, is signaled by the elaborately designed exteriors (gigantic paintings, lace and curtains, mirrors, etc.). Her hypocrisy is exposed in an early scene where she lies to her mother on the telephone, and her manipulativeness is signaled throughout by her treatment of her employee Marlene who seems to do all the work for Petra's business. The mise-en-scène is marked by cinematic excess that itself calls attention to the artificiality of the cinematic apparatus and in several scenes explicit parallels are drawn between the dreams that fashion and cinema produce and the fantasies of the characters.[4]

Departing from realism, Fassbinder limits the action to the claustrophobic and intense enclosure of a single apartment where all the action takes place. This enables him to construct a visual iconography that is used to intensify his themes. Lesbian sexual desire, for example, is connoted by the large paintings of nudes in her room, though a painting by Poussin containing male nudes signals the presence (and threat) of male sexuality though no males actually appear onscreen. Rather, in several scenes, Fassbinder frames the portrait with an exposed male penis between Petra and Karin, signaling the eventual triumph of the phallus (i.e., heterosexuality and the male sexual order) over Petra's desire to possess and control Karin, while in another scene the penis hangs directly over Karin in a menacing fashion when she is talking of her troubles with men (thus coding the phallus as a symbol of oppressive patriarchy rather than, say, of male power or sexual desire; for analysis of the polysomic excess of connotation in the dialectic between and within painting and film, see Kirby 1985).

The many themes of the film include the destructiveness of bourgeois desires to possess and totally control a lover, and the instability of sexual relationships, desire, and identity. When Karin eventually leaves Petra to reunite with her husband, who has returned from Australia, Petra, previously the manipulator, is herself devastated. Philosophers might be amused here by Fassbinder's joke of using the name "Kant" in a story that illustrates Hegel's master-slave dialectic whereby the dominated becomes the dominator in an inversion of power relationships. The general theme seems to be the ways in which desires to possess and control inevitably bring manipulation and domination into sexual relationships, and the instability in which the dominated can become the dominator in a vicious circle of sexual predation.

An accompanying theme is the instability of sexual identity and difference. Lesbian identity and practice is threatened by the perpetual presence of the male and the possibility of heterosexuality, which in turn is threatened by the possibility of homosexuality. Petra herself slides indeterminately from conventional female to conventional male behavior (i.e., domination, business, and seduction), and from positions of regal power to abject powerlessness. The frequent shifts of costumes and roles, and the fact that Petra is a designer who produces images for display and identification, points to the conventionality of gender roles and to the possibility of continually constructing and reconstructing one's image and identity. Although the film is structured into five segments where the characters wear different clothes and play different roles, the order is subverted by the excess of emotional display and by the disorder of the shifting roles, positions, and power relations. In this way, the very style or form of the film signifies a radical disorder, excess, and indeterminateness beneath social and sexual roles, relations, and gender identity.

The film poses the challenge of breaking from the chain of sexual domination and role-playing, but the story is ambivalent on this point. At the end, a distraught Petra turns to her employee, Marlene, and proposes that they work and live more closely together. Marlene has been a silent observer of the (melo)-drama and is obviously in love herself with Petra. The device of the silent observer, Marlene, has enabled Fassbinder to construct a surrogate for the audience since much of the action is depicted from her point of view in frequent long takes with deep focus that show her silently observing the goings-on. Other scenes position the audience as voyeurs who watch Marlene observing the action, and mirrors with reflections of the cinematic reflections of the actors further point to the constructedness of both the cinema and subjectivity. And Marlene is frequently coupled imagistically with the mannequins for whom she creates fashions (identity) which might be read as a figure of indeterminateness that at once signifies that possibility of being molded into an object of display or openness to mold and produce one's own self-(bodily) identity.

From a formal point of view, all of these techniques can be read as Brechtian devices to distance the spectator and to frustrate identification in order to promote critical reflection. Identification is also frustrated by Fassbinder's character constructions: most of his main characters are flawed, most are outsiders, and few are the sort of people that one would want to identify with in any profound way. At the film's conclusion, when Petra turns to Marlene, the latter silently packs up her bag and leaves as "The Great Pretender" plays on the sound track. The film is dedicated to "one who here has become Marlene" and one possible reading of the conclusion is that one must break out of exploitative relationships in order to become oneself, to be a person. In this reading, Fassbinder ends his film with a gesture and figure of liberation that points to the need for revolt against oppression and domination. In another possible reading, suggested by Fassbinder himself, Marlene leaves because

> The servant accepts her own repression and exploitation, and is therefore afraid of the freedom she is offered. What goes with freedom is the responsibility of having to think about your own existence, and that is something she has never

had to do. . . . When she leaves Petra she is not . . . heading for freedom but going in search of another slave-existence. . . . It would be wildly optimistic, even utopian, to imagine that someone who has done and thought nothing for thirty years except for what others have thought for her would all of a sudden choose freedom. (Fassbinder 1977, p. 83)

Yet the very theme of sexual indeterminacy that is at the heart of the Fassbinderian universe makes possible such a reading as does the film's open-endedness and possibilities for multivalent reading. And it is precisely the in determinacy and possibility of multivalent readings of *Petra* that distinguishes Fassbinder's use of melodrama from conventional Hollywood practices of providing conventional and often comforting messages, reassurance, and closure. Throughout Fassbinder's films, there are unusually empathetic portrayals of homosexuals and women, which helps explain why feminists in West Germany have generally not been critical of the more problematic aspects of Fassbinder's representations of women and gays. They believe that as a homosexual Fassbinder was better able to sympathize with women, gays, and other oppressed groups than most male filmmakers and that therefore he is viewed, with reservations, as an ally in the struggle against patriarchal capitalism.[5]

Fassbinder's Melodramas

Fassbinder's unique mixture of identifactory and distancing strategies in the service of radical social critique is probably the distinguishing trait of his use of melodrama. Fassbinder typically uses deep focus middle shots with one of the characters in the background looking on at the action to get the viewer to view the characters and events from the position of onlooker, and perhaps to signal that film itself positions audiences to be voyeurs of artificially constructed dramas. In these ritualistic displays of asocial behavior, characters look at other characters being exploited, humiliated, and oppressed and the audience is forced to observe these rituals of exploitation. If one sees them as the product of bourgeois society and as typical asocial manifestations of bourgeois values and behavior then Fassbinder has realized the Brechtian ambition of producing a socially critical spectacle that will politicize the viewer.

Fassbinder also uses well-constructed and sometimes dazzling aesthetic images and effects to both provide aesthetic pleasure and to get the spectator to scrutinize the images and scenes and to reflect upon what they are portraying. Odd camera settings and angles and aesthetic excess in image construction both distance the spectator from the action and provide formally pleasing aesthetic images. Likewise, Fassbinder uses a moving camera both to provide pleasing aesthetic effects and to allow the spectator to scrutinize the environment portrayed.

Mirrors, staircases, deep focus, eccentric camera angles, a profusion of objects in front of the characters, chiaroscuro lighting, excessive color, expressive music, and other aesthetic devices involve the spectator in the scrutiny of images and image construction and distance her from getting lost in the story. Yet unlike more formalistic exercises in image (de)construction, Fassbinder tells stories, produces sympathetic characters, and uses mise-en-scène, style, and aesthetic strategies to engage in radical social critique. In this way, his formal-aesthetic strategies and moral-narrative ends blend together and complement each other in a cinema that combines moral purpose with aesthetic inventiveness and expressiveness.

As mentioned, most of the literature on Fassbinder and Sirk emphasizes the impact of Sirk on Fassbinder, his admiration for Sirk, and the ways both use melodrama as a vehicle for social critique; in this discussion, however, I wish to argue that the differences between both filmmakers are significant and should not be overlooked. Indeed, a comparison of Fassbinder's melodramas with Sirk's should help elucidate how the former undercuts the predominant conservative and liberal uses of these conventions in the Hollywood and Sirkian melodrama. Conservative Hollywood melodrama uses its conventions to dramatize the pain and suffering produced by transgressions of bourgeois morality, or idealizes the sacrifices of women for their children or husbands. They frequently reward virtuous behavior with "happy endings" that either rectify injustices perpetrated on the protagonists (this is a central trope of Victorian melodrama that Hollywood appropriated) or that affirm certain modes of traditional behavior, sexual roles, and institutions as correct. In Sirk's more liberal variety, melodrama often is used to criticize oppressive forms of conformist, provincial, mean-spirited small-town conservative behavior or excessive forms of egotism and untamed sexuality (i.e., Kyle and Marylee Hadley in *Written on the Wind*).

Sirk practices what the Frankfurt School called immanent critique, that is, using more liberal bourgeois values to criticize conservative and repressive values from the standpoint of a more liberal cosmopolitanism or earthy humanism. For example, in *Written on the Wind*, venial small-town Texan values are criticized from the standpoint of New York cosmopolitanism (represented by the Lauren Bacall character) or rural values (i.e., the Rock Hudson figure and his father). In *All that Heaven Allows*, Hudson plays a gardener who becomes romantically involved with an older widow (Jane Wyman) to the evident disapproval of her offensive, upwardly mobile children (fifties Yuppies) and set of snobbish, upper-class friends. In the story, the Rock Hudson character represents nature, goodness, and Thoreauvian integrity while those who oppose the relation represent spitefulness, pettiness, social conformity, and the like.

Fassbinder and others have praised Sirk's critiques of small-town America (Fassbinder 1975, p. 89), but I do not consider the critique as sharp or penetrating as Fassbinder's radical critique of bourgeois sexual relations and interro-

gations of the social construction of gender and sexuality. Sirk was under contract to conservative studios during the last hurrah of the Hollywood studio system and was under constraints not suffered by the independent Fassbinder. But
like Sirk, Fassbinder forces his audiences of *Petra von Kant* and his other melodramas of the period to observe oppression, greed, manipulation, venality, and
domination that characterize, in his view, contemporary bourgeois-capitalist societies. But Fassbinder never idealizes the family, romance, or any type of normative behavior, while Sirk tends to idealize various ideological institutions like
the family or the redemptive power of romantic love.

Fassbinder, on the other hand, depicts sexual and social relations as inher-
ently problematical and unstable, and is sensitive to the complex ways in which
manipulation, oppression, and domination enter into all relationships. Most important, Fassbinder refuses on principle the happy endings and melodramatic
closure of most Sirkian and Hollywood melodrama, and affirms, if he affirms
anything at all, emancipation from bourgeois values, relations of domination,
and institutions.[6] For his working-class or petty bourgeois protagonists there is
indeed little hope of self-emancipation or happiness in a world where the rules
of the game, or organization of society, are against them from the start. Thus, I
would argue that in opposition to Sirk's liberal humanism, Fassbinder's use of
melodrama is much more radical, and his humanism is more anarchic, displaying sympathy for human beings and their sufferings but without affirming liberal or conservative ideology to provide solace or to patch over or resolve conflicts and problems.

Some glimmers of hope appear in Fassbinder's melodramas, but they are
fragile and precarious at best. Although Marlene rejects the sadomasochism in
Petra von Kant's circle and finally revolts against her exploitation and mistreat-
ment, the liberation is a gesture of refusal rather than an ideological affirmation
of something like true love, a reconstructed family, or the like with which Sirk's
films usually conclude. Consequently, Fassbinder uses the melodrama differently
than Sirk in that he uses the genre to sustain more radical social critique. In addition, Fassbinder produces more open-ended and less affirmative films than
Sirk, and therefore departs more radically from the conventional thematics and
ideology of the Hollywood melodrama. Furthermore, Fassbinder differs from
Sirk in character construction and identification strategies. Sirk generally constructs traditional Hollywood characters who are both extremely attractive and
virtuous (i.e., the roles played by Rock Hudson and Jane Wyman); the audience
is invited to identify with these characters through the use of close-ups, shot-
reverse shots (the suture), romantic music, expressive color, and symbols associated with the characters. Fassbinder, on the other hand, attempts to position the
audience to sympathize with his characters' situation (as oppressed individuals)
rather than to identify with the characters in a psychological and personalized
way. In other words, Fassbinder distances us more from his characters by mak-

ing them unattractive in conventional terms; marginal or atypical; and flawed, fragmented or contradictory (unlike the unitary and generally virtuous middle- or upper-class characters in Sirk or Hollywood's melodramas). Yet his victims are often sympathetic and the audience is positioned to empathize with their suffering and to view the oppressors critically.

Perhaps a distinction between spectator-identification and spectator-positioning might both illuminate Fassbinder's cinematic practice and put into question a highly questionable notion of "identification" that has found some currency in contemporary film theory (I am thinking of Stephen Heath's use of Metz and Lacan; for a critique of this model see Elsaesser 1980, Carroll 1982, and Kellner-Ryan 1987). The theory of identification presupposes not only that the spectator literally identifies with the characters on the screen but that in addition a process of subject-positioning is going on that would create a sense of a unitary, coherent, self-satisfied subject. A school of film theory associated at one point with *Screen* magazine in the English-speaking world claimed that Hollywood cinema essentially consisted of strategies to engage spectator identification and to produce what it called the subject effect (i.e., the sense of being a unified subject).

Now I would imagine that Fassbinder himself would snort with disbelief at this theory and several critics have attacked its inconsistencies and reliance on questionable psychological and cinematic assumptions. Indeed, it is not even clear that audiences *identify* with characters in the strong sense presupposed in the Metzian-Lacanian structuralist theory, let alone that films produce coherent, ideological subjects simply through narrative strategies. It is more plausible, I believe, to see films *positioning* spectators to view certain roles, behaviors, attitudes, and so forth, as positive and others as negative, and to invite spectators to identify with and emulate these representations and forms of behavior. From this perspective, Fassbinder utilizes certain Hollywood strategies for positioning audiences to see some characters in a sympathetic light and to view other characters and forms of behavior critically. Although this process of audience reception of his films might involve some sort of identification, Fassbinder also attempts, as I've argued, to distance his audiences at this same time.

Sirk, too, employed strategies that combined techniques of identification and distanciation but I believe that Fassbinder more radically distances his audience from dominant conventions and institutions. For Fassbinder continually attacks dominant forms of oppression, including marriage, the family, and romantic love that are strongly valorized in Sirk's films. In his article on Sirk, Fassbinder writes: "After seeing Douglas Sirk's films I am more convinced than ever that love is the best, most insidious, most effective instrument of social repression" (Fassbinder 1975, p. 92). Now I submit that this is Fassbinder's own position and not Sirk's, who generally celebrates romantic love as life's most desirable experience. Furthermore, Fassbinder's couples and families seem imprisoned in claustrophobic, closed interiors that produce feelings of entrapment within the institution of marriage or family. Fassbinder uses deep-focus, long shots, characters looking at other characters, and various point of view shots to force the audience to observe, to reflect upon, and to criticize (rather than simply to emotionally participate in) the behavior being presented.

From this perspective, Fassbinder uses melodrama to display how the dominant sex, class, and race exploit, manipulate, and destroy less privileged and powerful members of the opposite sex, class, and race. These films question social hierarchy and privilege, and critically scrutinize dominant forms of class relations, sex and gender construction, and more generally relations of domination and subordination. Thus, Fassbinder's films exhibit deep sympathy for the working class, foreign workers, homosexuals, the aged, and even oppressed members of the lower middle class and petty bourgeoisie, as well as women. Consequently, while Fassbinder is often criticized for his misanthropic or nihilistic projections, I consider his films to be informed by a radical humanism and sympathy for the oppressed. Thus, Fassbinder uses melodrama to dramatize different forms of oppression and domination and either depicts their destructive results or potential (though precarious) routes of escape.

Notes

1. Melodrama has often been one of the most scorned and despised members of the family of genres. Held in contempt by cultural conservatives who see it as a clichéd, stereotyped, and crude form of popular art, it is also the subject of attack by cultural radicals who see it primarily as a conservative form that generally upholds the rightness and goodness of established institutions, social practices, gender roles, and ideologies. From the 1970s to the present, however, there have been attempts to rehabilitate the genre. On the history of melodrama, see Rahill 1967, Smith 1973, and Brooks 1976. For attempts to show how melodrama can be used for social critique, see Elsaesser 1972, Kleinhans 1978, Williams 1984, and Byers 1980; these texts describe how melodrama has both been used as a form of social critique and to engage sexual politics critically, strategies I find exemplified in some of Fassbinder's work.

2. Fassbinder has often expressed his positive evaluation of Hollywood films. When asked, "Do you want to make German Hollywood films?" Fassbinder answered: "Yes. I'm all for it. Yes, that's what I want." Cited in Elsaesser 1976, p. 24. See also the interview where Fassbinder stated: "American cinema is the only one I can take really seriously, because it's the only one that really reached an audience. . . . Our films have been based on our *understanding* of the American cinema" (Fassbinder, cited in Corrigan, 44–45).

3. Fassbinder 1977, p. 20. This interview specifies Fassbinder's perceived differences from Brecht: "With Brecht you see the emotions and you reflect upon them as you witness them but you never feel them. That's my interpretation and I think I go farther than he did in that I let the audience *feel and think*" (20). One might also add that Brecht's

plays, at least in his Marxist period, were constructed to promote an explicit sort of so-cial critique and change—a goal absent in Fassbinder. On Brechtian elements of Fass-binder's cinematic practice, see Moeller 1980 and 1984.

4. Other readings that stress the complex use of images, symbols, cinematography, and strategies of distanciation in *Petra* include Johnson 1980, Corrigan 1983, and Kirby 1985. These studies provide abundant examples of how image construction, the use of space and time, empathic camera movement, a profusion of symbols, and so forth serve to distance the spectator and to signal the presence of the cinematic apparatus. Kirby pro-vides a brilliant reading of *Petra* from the role of Poussin's painting in the film.

5. This point was made to me by Renate Moehrmann in a discussion in Austin, Texas. Yet Fassbinder has also been sharply criticized by gays for his representations of lesbians and homosexuals. See, for example, Dyer 1980, and the exchange in *Jump Cut 16* between Bob Cant 1977 and Andrew Britton 1977.

6. Both Sirk and Fassbinder claim that Sirk's hyperbolically and unrealistically vir-tuous characters and contrived happy endings subverted the conservative ideological clo-sure of traditional Hollywood melodramas by showing how artificial such closures really are, but such accounts fail to consider how audiences responded to and experienced the films, particularly in the 1950s when they appeared. Consequently, I believe that a so-cially progressive use of melodrama today must resist and subvert the ideological closure traditional to the melodrama form—as Fassbinder often does.

3

Behind the Curtains of a State-Owned Film Industry: Women-Filmmakers at the DEFA

Margrit Frölich

Many of the DEFA documentary and fiction films, especially since the 1970s, focus on women characters, but not many were conceived through the lens of a female director. Despite women's legal equality inaugurated through legislative action in the early days of the German Democratic Republic (GDR),[1] only very few women worked as directors in East Germany's state-owned film enterprise DEFA. Although provisions in all fields of society promoted women through a quota system (Frauenförderungspläne) and granted special benefits for working mothers, the number of women in the directing chair did not rise over the years. Moreover, in the GDR, in contrast to other Eastern bloc countries, young aspiring directors, regardless of their gender, received fewer opportunities to make their own films. At best, for many years they had to content themselves with assistant-directorships, and, due to the absence of an independent cinema, they could not find alternative venues.[2] In the 1960s, only a few women entered professional film training. Among the student films produced at the film academy in Potsdam-Babelsberg, between 1961 and 1968 no films were directed by women, and until the midseventies, the percentage of films directed by women was still very slim.[3] In the 1980s, the number of male and female students graduating from the East German film academy was almost equal. But women graduates frequently occupied middle-range positions (dramaturgy), often in traditional female careers (design or editing), or found employment either in television or in children's film.[4]

Among the large staff of permanent employees at the DEFA, dramaturges had a special significance.[5] In charge of the development of film themes, they mediated between film directors and scriptwriters. The DEFA's emphasis on a film's preproduction phase, and the large number of people involved in this multistage process, ideally engendered a fruitful and thorough exchange of ideas in collective discussions. However, this structure also provided the means to influence the film production in that it prevented violations of taboos or norms already in the preproduction stage. Sibylle Schönemann (until her imprisonment and subsequent expulsion to West Germany in 1985) and Tamara Trampe were among the twenty-seven dramaturges. Both became well-known to international audiences in the aftermath of the political upheaval in the East due to their investigative documentaries *Verriegelte Zeit* (Locked Up Time, 1990) and *Der schwarze Kasten* [with Johann Feindt] (The Black Box, 1992), respectively, in which they probe into the sinister methods of East Germany's state security (Stasi).[6]

The first women-directors at the DEFA feature film studio were Bärbl Bergmann, who directed several children's films, and Karin Reschke, the first female student in the directing program at the East German film academy at Potsdam-Babelsberg. Among her films are *Kennen Sie Urban* (Do You Know Urban? 1971), which is about the difficulties of a young man with a criminal record to reintegrate himself in society. This was Reschke's last film before she died in a car accident in 1971. Iris Gusner was the third woman to direct fiction films at the DEFA in the early 1970s. She left the GDR in the summer of 1989 and moved to West Germany. Until the demise of the GDR, only two other women-directors were employed by the studio: Hannelore Unterberg, who worked in the children's film division, and Evelyn Schmidt. In the documentary film studio, which comprised a variety of different branches, chances for women were slightly greater in that they could find directing opportunities in fields such as industrial or popular science films and commercials, as well as informational films produced for schools and research institutions. During the early construction period, when the DEFA film was mainly concerned with topical political issues, the immediate Nazi past, and the building of a socialist society, Eva Fritzsche joined the DEFA documentary film division. Trained in film editing during the Weimar Republic through her work with Erwin Piscator, she became the first woman ever to direct a film at the DEFA. Among her films is the docudrama about the reconstruction of a bridge, *Die Brücke von Caputh* (1949). She also made *MAS "Fritz Reuter"* (1950) and *Haus der Kinder* (1950) before she moved on to work in the theater. Annelie Thorndike, a first-hour pioneer of socialist documentary film associated with East Germany's antifascist legacy, and repeatedly a national prize holder, made herself a legend through the propagandistic historical chronicles she produced with her husband. The Thorndikes substantially contributed to the shaping of the GDR's official image of history with their numerous films such as the antiwar documentary *Du und mancher Kamerad* (1956); *Das russische Wunder* (1963), a two-part documentary mythologizing the Soviet Union as a modern industrial and scientific power; their portrait *Waldimir Iljitsch Uljanov-Lenin* (1970); and *Die Alte Neue Welt* (1977), an extensive compilation film about world history. In the 1960s, when documentary film had developed more artistic ambitions, the renowned director of numerous films, Gitta Nickel began her career as a filmmaker. Since her directing debut in 1965, she completed more than forty films for movie theaters and television about a wide spectrum of topics.[7] Although Nickel is open to controversial issues, she regards her role of filmmaker as firmly rooted in the struggle to build a socialist society that is worth living in. Thus, her films never completely abandon the bottom line of the dominant party politics. In the 1980s, two noteworthy documentary filmmakers, Petra Tschörtner and Helke Misselwitz began to direct films, bringing an unprecedented critical dimension to the DEFA documentary film.

To make a film in the GDR, whether fiction or documentary, was always a highly political issue. It inevitably meant that the filmmaker had to have the ability to navigate the fine line between addressing controversial issues and tempering the view to a level acceptable to the regime's cultural functionaries. Otherwise the film would not make it through the state-controlled centralized review procedure that existed until 1990. With the relative liberalization that had begun with the Honecker era[8] in the early seventies, more DEFA films examined contemporary reality and addressed controversial topical issues.[9] Erich Honecker's statement made at the *Sozialistische Einheitspartei Deutschland* (SED) Central Committee's Fourth Session in 1971, according to which there no longer should be any taboos in literature and art as long as the works have a solid grounding in the principles of socialism, introduced this new climate in cultural life.[10] The changes in leadership at the feature film studio in the late seventies, when Hans Dieter Mäde became general director of the studio (1977), was a hopeful sign that filmmakers would have more freedom in the choice of topics and in approaches to controversial subject matter, even though Wolf Biermann's expulsion had ended the period of détente of the previous years. It quickly became clear, however, that the space within which a critical view of society could be articulated was still rather narrow. Nevertheless, the films produced in the late seventies and at the turn of the eighties indicated an increased awareness of modern alienation in socialist society.

As a result of the turn away from historical subjects to topical themes, and those about everyday life, both fiction and documentary film began to focus on women. In documentary film, this trend had been clearly noticeable since the 1960s. During this period, the emergence of television took over from documentary film the primary function of transferring the propaganda of the official ideology, subsequently loosening some of the restrictions that previously had been imposed on documentary films. With a new generation of documentary filmmakers, such as Volker Koepp, Winfried Junge, and Gitta Nickel, a small group of slightly more critical films appeared gradually and developed throughout the 1970s, after an increased tolerance in cultural politics made moderate criticism acceptable.

Famous examples of the women's documentary film are Jürgen Böttcher's *Stars* (1963) and *Wäscherinnen* (Washerwomen, 1972), Winfried Junge's *Studentinnen* (Female Students, 1965), and Volker Koepp's *Die Mädchen von Wittstock* (The Girl from Wittstock, 1975). In of all these films, women talk willingly and frankly about their living and working conditions, point out problems, and openly voice their criticism of social structures. In these documentary films, women thus became the real-life agents for the filmmakers to lay bare antagonisms in East German society. In fiction film, the so-called women's film became a genre of its own in the late seventies and at the beginning of the 1980s. The earliest forerunner of this genre was Slatan Dudow's *Frauenschicksale* (Women's Lives, 1952), a film about various women in pursuit of happiness and their disillusionment with romance. The women's films that emerged in the early 1980s include, among others, Erwin Stranka's *Sabine Wulff* (1978), Konrad Wolf's famous *Solo Sunny* (1979), Lothar Warneke's *Unser kurzes Leben I* (Our Short Life, 1981) and *Die Beunruhigung* (1982), as well as Hermann Zschoche's *Bürgschaft für ein Jahr* (1981).[11] They all feature nonconformist female protagonists and their struggles with a problem-ridden or unsatisfactory life. These women's films, in addressing antagonisms in socialist society through narratives about rebellious women, were the last attempts to create a space for resistance against the dominant order and were aimed at making the viewer aware of its defects, before the stagnation of the GDR's final years made such liberty impossible. Given the opposition to handed-down norms and patterns of thinking prominent in these narratives, it is perhaps not surprising that the women-directors at the feature film studio, through many if not most of their films, contributed to the genre of the women's film.[12] Both their fiction and documentary films focusing on women depict the contemporary state of East German society. Through a female protagonist and perspective, they examine the social structures of East German society as they were experienced in everyday life. To varying degrees, these films take advantage of the limited space available for criticism of society. Their constructions of East German reality allow us to explore their images of women in relation to the official image of women in socialist society and to reflect upon the continuity of historically derived gender roles within socialism as they are seen through the lens of female directorship.

One of the women's films emerging in the early eighties is Iris Gusner's *Alle meine Mädchen* (All My Girls). It opened in 1980 at the GDR's first national fiction film festival in Karl-Marx-Stadt. The film received overall positive notices and succeeded in a way that Gusner's later films did not. Gusner used the documentary portraits of women in East Germany's industrial production as a model for her fiction film. The emphasis of her film is not on the labor process as such. Rather, the atmospheric images of workaday reality serve as a backdrop for a delineation of relationships and conflicts between individuals as they develop in the industrial working environment.

The plot, unfolding in impressionistic sequences, motivates the film's documentary realism: a film student receives a commission to make a documentary film about a women's brigade. Present with his camera at any moment, he documents the interactions between the effervescent young women performing their jobs at the conveyer belt. His camera captures the women's cheerfulness behind which the monotony of their demanding work seems to disappear. Furthermore, he films aspects that subtly debunk the pathos of the official image of the socialist production sphere. For example, the election of the union's representative among the brigade members turns out to be only a routine procedure. Furthermore, when a delegation of political leaders—consisting of only men and one older woman—visits the plant, one of the brigade women fails to hand a bouquet of flowers to the right person. Rather than concentrating on the celebrities and on the representative side of the official visit, the film student focuses on marginal events, which we see as the black-and-white images of his film. He films how the young woman, still with the flowers in her hand and amused about her own clumsiness, laughingly embraces one of her colleagues; and as the other women join in a dance to the tunes of a popular Russian folk song, the image suddenly shifts back to color.

A stranger and at first an intruder to the industrial environment, the film student induces a crisis between the *kollektiv* (workers' league) and their brigade leader, Marie Boltzin. A middle-aged, energetic woman, she has created a sense of community in the brigade and keeps its spirits high, despite all the diversity among the personalities of her five young protégés. While the women-workers are watching, the film student is interviewing the brigade leader in front of the camera. Through outright questioning, he discloses the management's decision to introduce new technology that will jeopardize the existence of their *kollektiv*. The argument between the brigade and their leader intensifies when they learn that Marie is keeping a notebook in which she enters the failures of each to comply with the required discipline (coming late, missing shifts, etc.). In an earlier scene with the manager, she herself disapproves of the management's decision made without her prior knowledge. Now, however, when the women reproach her for withholding from them information about a decision that vitally affects them, she evades the issue at stake. Cornered by her workers, she begins to enumerate the observations she listed in her book. The film treats the brigade leader's bookkeeping as one of her idiosyncratic obsessions that she practices without the intention of denouncing anybody (later, she keeps records of her companion's alcohol consumption). Gusner's portrayal of the brigade leader does not show a politically questionable individual. Rather, she emphasizes Marie's overall positive human traits, whom her protégés respect for her dedication, and she focuses on the ability of the brigade to handle this crisis.

The film within the film structure adds to the exposition of the conflict. The images that show the confrontation between Marie and the workers that we saw a moment before as "real," appear once more in black and white. This time, we recognize them as a sequence of the student film that is screened at the editing table as a work in progress. Remarkably, the underlying sound comes from another episode. It is taken from a scene, when the film student Ralph visits Marie at home and talks with her about her personal life. She tells him about her disappointment with her husband, who abandoned her after returning from the war where he had been injured. While he went to North America, she got stuck at her new job at the factory. Now she lives with an alcoholic live-in boyfriend, who is fond of her, but who nevertheless lacks the strength to give her enough emotional support. The nonsynchronous relationship of sound and image, which Ralph edited from two previous unrelated scenes, underscores the gap between Marie's strong performance at work and the tragic dimension of her private life, which she never mentions at work.

As a result of the conflict between Marie and the five women, Marie suffers a nervous breakdown and is hospitalized. Much of the ensuing plot focuses on the joint effort of the brigade and Ralph to win their leader back and to help her recover. Here, the portrayal of these young industrial workers moves beyond the rapport possible within workday reality at the conveyer belt. By tracking the attachments that develop between the women of the brigade and with Ralph, Gusner delineates an optimistic view of rewarding human relationships that admit the possibility of individual self-realization within the *kollektiv*. A paradigmatic example is a sequence when the young women and Ralph stay overnight at an inn in the little village where Marie is hospitalized. In underscoring the intimacy and gaiety that unfolds among the women (and toward Ralph) as they party and spend the night together, Gusner insists on uninhibited sensuality as the prerequisite for more sincere and tolerant human relationships.

Alle meine Mädchen proposes female collectivism as an effective means to solve conflicts. Eventually, the brigade's efforts in helping their leader recover are successful, and Marie returns to the workplace. Their rebellion against the management's decision is equally successful. Whereas by herself, Marie, in spite of her quick temper and her general ability to accomplish things, had only been able to voice her discontent about the management's decision that was made without consulting the workers, it is the group's assertiveness that results in actual change now. By directly confronting the male superior about his leadership methods, the five women manage to push through their demand for an older model of machine, thus preventing their brigade from being broken up. Other tensions within the brigade, however, remain unresolved.

In delineating the dynamics within the brigade, Gusner also opens a critical perspective on East German society's difficulties in reintegrating outsiders who have come into conflict with social norms and legal authority. Kerstin is an outsider to the *kollektiv*; similar to the protagonist of Erwin Stranka's memorable film, *Sabine Wulff*, Kerstin meets with her environment's distrust and rejection because she has a criminal record. Convicted for theft, she works with the brigade on probation. Because of her high school background, she also has a higher level of education than her colleagues. This social difference is the source of a quarrel between Kerstin and Anita, the most responsible member of the brigade; they argue about a missing comma on a poster that Anita is preparing for the anniversary of the German Democratic Republic. Through the social difference between Kerstin and the other women, Gusner unmasks the official notion that GDR society is classless. When, later in the film, money is missing, the brigade immediately suspects Kerstin. Even Ralph, who has gotten involved in a romantic relationship with Kerstin, assumes responsibility for her theft. Although the money turns up again (even though it turns out that Kerstin indeed tried to take it), and the brigade finally begins to realize the damaging effects of their scapegoating, it is already too late: Kerstin has left.

The fictionalized women's brigade portrayed in *Alle meine Mädchen* surely does not fit the notion of a socialist *kollektiv*'s prototype. With its emphasis on conflicts within an industrial environment and on problematic aspects of social reality, the film raises issues that official public discourse in the GDR did not address (presenting elections of worker representatives as routines without significance; the existence of alcoholism and loneliness in a socialist society that prided itself on assembling each individual within its community; prejudices against individuals from different social backgrounds such as those with a criminal record, etc.). The film also does not conceal the fact that in spite of the state's legal measures to guarantee equal opportunities for both sexes in the labor force, which allowed about 90 percent of women to be employed or trained for a profession, comparatively few women occupied leading positions (e.g., in the plant's management and among the delegation of politicians).

In summary, Gusner's *Alle meine Mädchen* presents a critical view, however moderate it may be, of the contemporary state of socialist society. In emphasizing the collective spirit of a women's brigade, Gusner conforms to a core socialist ideal. By showing the effectiveness of the fictional women's brigade as it resolves a deplorable situation at work and settles the conflict with the brigade leader through compassion toward her and among each other, Gusner expresses an optimistic view of the possibilities for improving social conditions at work and in the personal sphere within the existing framework of social structures. Even though the film encourages viewers not to conform and to struggle for solutions to social problems, it is this optimism that ultimately keeps the film within acceptable boundaries within which filmmakers were allowed to criticize the GDR's social problems.

Similar to *Alle meine Mädchen*, Evelyn Schmidt's film, *Das Fahrrad* (The Bicycle, 1981) focuses on a protagonist who is working in East Germany's industrial production. As was typical of many DEFA films in the eighties, *Das Fahrrad* focuses on contemporary reality and portrays an average character who usually remains invisible in society. The film tells the story of Susanne Becker, a single mother around thirty who works as an unskilled laborer at a punching machine in a factory. Examining the role of women within East German society and of the actual status of women's emancipation, Schmidt delineates the process her protagonist has to go through to gain self-confidence and self-determination. Furthermore, by way of the plot line of a romantic relationship between Susanne and Thomas, a young, promising engineer, the film treats the subject of social differences in East Germany's socialist society. In doing so, it calls into question the official notion of East Germany as a society with equal opportunities for everyone.

Das Fahrrad, like many DEFA films in the 1980s, gives priority to milieu and situation over dramatic conflict.[13] More than the characters' laconic interactions, the precise images of a minuscule section of everyday life locate the characters within their social environment. The film's expository sequence gives us a concise image of Susanne's everyday life and her role in society.[14]

In *Das Fahrrad*, as in two of her other films examining the role of women in socialist society, *Seitensprung* (The Affair)[15] and *Der Hut* (The Hat),[16] Schmidt bestows her female protagonist, however weak she may appear in the beginning, with the courage and ability to give her life another direction. She does so, without, however, discrediting her male character as the one to be blamed for her protagonist's previous inability to take charge of her life. Through the confrontation with the authorities and in separating from Thomas, Susanne has gained a new strength. Although the film does not offer a solution to the problems determined by Susanne's social position, Susanne in the end emerges as someone capable of letting go of the anxieties that hampered her before. In the last scene, we see her relaxed and laughing as she coaches her daughter to ride her mother's bike. Thomas, obviously willing to come around, approaches them, but when he sees Susanne absorbed with her daughter, he stops and does not interrupt them, thus leaving it open to the viewers' imagination whether Susanne and Thomas will get back together or not. In this last scene, the bicycle becomes the symbol for self-determination in taking one's life into one's own hands to give it motion and direction. In the same way that it was a long struggle for Jenny to learn how to ride the bike autonomously, it was a strenuous process for Susanne to reach this state of self-determination.

What triggered the negative criticism of the film was the characterization of the protagonist and the social critique implied in it.[17] With her protagonist's lack of high spirits and zest for action, her inability to articulate herself, which predominates until the last scene, Schmidt developed a character who is far away from the cliché ideal of the well-rounded socialist personality. With this social portrait of a young woman helplessly trapped in social misery, Schmidt raises her audience's awareness about the numerous cases of women who inconspicuously live their daily lives, are inactive, and accept the limitations imposed upon them.[18] Yet unlike films with a similar conflict, such as *Bürgschaft für ein Jahr* and *Solo Sunny*, which both focus on an unbalanced female character's search for a place in society, Schmidt's film did not earn favorable recognition.[19] The nonconforming protagonist bewildered many critics. This reaction is not surprising. After all, she challenges social expectations: she insists on a better life even though she has not done anything noteworthy to achieve it. She is, more often than not, helpless, dejected, and inhibited; she has no skills, but wants a better job; and she rejects a man striving for success. These traits evidently carried more weight than the nurturing relation Susanne has to her daughter, and her anxieties, insecurities, and the pressure to cope with everyday life. The fact that Susanne is someone who does not always bounce back, who is not able to combine effortlessly the double burden as a mother and a full-time worker, created a contradiction in the image of the strong and competitive working mother, which predominated in the official discourse of a society that for reasons of economic necessity relied on the availability of women for the labor force.[20] Another reason for the critics' dismissal must be attributed to the fact that Schmidt does not provide a corrective for her protagonist's life-style (the gloomy bar, her one-night stands, the insurance fraud, etc.) that corresponds to the socialist ideal of a young mother and proper citizen. Nor does she correct Susanne's attitude toward labor, her discontent with her job at the factory, and her claim to a better life to which she holds on despite her apparent lack of zeal and effort. The unwillingness of Schmidt's protagonist to accept her situation touched on sensitive nerves because it brought to the foreground an unresolved problem in socialist society: in theory, it granted all its citizens equal opportunities to develop and broaden their personalities, but, in practice, tiring and monotonous jobs, such as Susanne's, existed even in the GDR and somebody had to do them. Schmidt thus undermines the East German state's political self-understanding according to which the laws protecting women's legal and economic equality had brought women's emancipation already to completion and had supposedly made superfluous any further discussion of the actual situation of women under socialism.

Similar to *Das Fahrrad*, Gitta Nickel's documentary film *Gundula—Jahrgang 58* (Gundula—Class of 58, 1982) focuses on a young woman and her self-realization within the pressures of everyday life. Unlike Schmidt, however, Nickel presents a more favorable view of the possibilities for self-realization within socialism. *Gundula* is one among several other films by the renowned DEFA documentary filmmaker that examines the social experiences of women under socialism. Nickel's films about women include:

- *Sie* (She, 1970) (about the introduction of the contraceptive pill);
- *Im Märzen die Bäuerin* (The Farmer, 1971) (about a group of female peasants in a farmer's cooperative);

- *Gret Palucca* (1971) (a portrait of the famous modern dancer from the 1920s);
- *Heuwetter* (Weather for Harvest, 1972) (about a female calf breeder);
- *Und morgen kommen die Polinnen* (Arrival of the Polish Women, 1974) (one of Nickel's most noteworthy films, about Polish women working in an East German chicken-broiling combine);
- *Das ist einfach mein Leben* (The Simple Life, 1975) (about the chairwoman of a Ukrainian collective farm);
- *Wir von Esda* (Us, 1976) (about a women brigade in a stocking combine);
- *Die May* (1976) (a portrait of the actress Gisela May);
- *. . . und das Weib sei nicht mehr untertan* (Free at Last, 1978) (about the social role of women in socialism;
- *Wenn man eine Liebe hat* (1986);
- *China—mein Traum, mein Leben* (China—My Dream, My Life, 1990) (a portrait of the German-Jewish photographer and documentary filmmaker Eva Siao); and
- *Un de Mäuse sin mir* (1992) (about Fidel Hönisch, "Saxony's cheekiest grand-mother").

While Gitta Nickel insists—as most East German women-directors probably would—that her films do not reflect a particular feminine point of view, she ac-knowledges that the role of women in society is a crucial topical subject matter because women's emancipation is of key significance in the larger process of changing social structures.[21]

Gundula, the film's protagonist is a boisterous, self-confident nurse in her early twenties, who works at a nursing home in an East German district town. Unlike Susanne in Evelyn Schmidt's fiction film *Das Fahrrad*, Gundula is deter-mined, does not mince matters, and is constantly bubbling over with excess en-ergy. "You always have to do something for your claim to life," is her maxim. Similar to Sunny, the heroine from Konrad Wolf's famous fiction film *Solo Sunny*, Gundula has ambitions as a pop music star and sings in a pop band. On weekends, her band travels through East Germany's provinces and performs in clubs and at other festivities. Unlike Wolf's character, however, who gives up her monotonous job in a factory in favor of her singing career, Gundula is thor-oughly devoted to her career as a nurse and regards singing as a hobby. Yet she is unwilling to subordinate her hobby to the job and insists on combining them. The workaday routine alone does not satisfy her; she tries to give her life more meaning by doing something that she enjoys.

After an expository sequence that blends images of Gundula in a dressing room preparing herself for a stage performance with her narration about her ex-perience as a singer, we accompany Gundula throughout her working day at the nursing home and observe her as she performs her routine tasks. Images of her demanding job, of which she never seems to tire, predominate throughout most of the film. Evidently, Gundula knows how to work hard and never spares herself from doing so. Another one of her maxims is to be generous, so that your surroundings respond to you in a friendlier way. Her effervescent uplifting attitude inspires the old people she takes care of. It has earned her much popularity among them. In various scenes, we see her cheerfully interact with her patients, chatting, playing a game of dice, and always making them laugh. Other scenes reveal a more vulnerable side of Gundula. This is shown when she silently and mournfully parts from a patient who has died.

It is only much later in the film, after we have witnessed Gundula taking care of the old people, that we also see her at home with her baby daughter. A single working mother and a singer, she does not have much time for her daughter. Her daughter stays at a crèche, except when Gundula has a few days off. Even though she is aware that people think that she is neglecting her daughter, she herself is convinced that it is more sensible to take her daughter home when she can really spend a longer stretch of time with her, instead of taking her home every evening, when there are only a few hours and she is tired from work. Asked about any plans of getting married, she rules it out for the moment. She could not expect a man to live with her, she claims, while she is trying to combine her job and singing, since she has no time. However, later in life, she envisions marriage as a possibility. In this respect, Gundula is a typical example of an East German woman. Although a single mother, she is able to rely on the state's provisions, such as the crèche and special benefits allowing women to combine work and motherhood, which in the GDR coexisted with free access to contraceptives and legal abortion (since 1972).

The benefits for working mothers in the former GDR, which allowed the state to integrate women in the labor force in order to substitute manpower for the lack of technological advancement, and that was also a response to the large numbers of divorces, included generously paid maternity leaves, reduced workload, priority assignment day care and kindergarten places, as well as monthly supplements for dependent children. Gitta Nickel's 1970 film *Sie* examines the extent to which the introduction of the contraceptive pill made it easier for women to combine education, job, and family, praising its advantages for the realization of women's emancipation. In an insightful essay, Elke Schieber has argued that the legalization of abortion in the GDR was never discussed in public and that media projects about the subject were rejected.[22] Given this lack of a public discourse, Sibylle Schönemann's student film *Kinderkriegen* (Having Babies, 1975) is an intervention that attempts to cast light on the social practice surrounding abortion.[23] Due to the veto of one of the women portrayed, the film never received any public screening in the GDR. In this documentary film, Schönemann examines the negative side of legalized abortion and how women handle this new freedom. From today's conservative climate and campaigns by prochoice opponents, the film's perspective might appear as an antiliberal statement. It is in effect not a criticism of the women's legal access to abortion, but rather a criticism of a social practice in which women were frequently pressured by their environment to interrupt their pregnancies.

With the support of the state's programs for working mothers, Gundula in Nickel's film can stay competitive in the labor force and remain economically independent from a man. It is remarkable that her responsibilities as a nurse, as a mother, and as a singer do not seem too much for her, and that she aims at taking on further ones: through continuing job training, Gundula would like to gain the qualification required for an advanced position. However, the advancement of her career depends on the approval of her colleagues and superiors. As was common practice in the GDR, she needs their delegation. In one sequence, we observe Gundula discussing the issue with her superiors and the collective leader, the latter being the only man in a profession dominated by women. Fragments of their conversation alternate with scenes in which we see Gundula amicably interacting with her old patients. In assessing Gundula's performance, the superiors and the *kollektiv* leader argue that, regardless of her popularity with the patients, her hobby as a singer interferes with her work and with their expectations of a devoted socialist. In order to receive their approval for advanced job training, she would have to improve her job performance so that the *kollektiv* could be proud of her. During this polite, though uncomfortable conversation, Gundula, whose mouth usually never stands still, is oddly quiet, abashed, and trying to hide her emotions as she listens to the criticism by her superiors. She only occasionally explains her viewpoint. The conversation ends with a compromise that seems to satisfy both parties. Upon the suggestion of her supervisor, Gundula performs with her band in the nursing home, allowing her patients and colleagues to relate to her also on the level of her hobby. In the last sequence, we see Gundula with her band on stage in the home, while the old patients and her colleagues listen to her and later dance.

With her portrait of a young professional woman who energetically insists on her somewhat unusual hobby of singing in a pop band while being sincerely dedicated to her work as a nurse, Nickel gives voice to the demand of the young generation to have the freedom to develop their own values, to give meaning to their lives, and to find their place in society. The film pleads for social responsibility and tolerance vis-à-vis contemporary youth. With *Gundula*, as with her other films, Nickel follows her self-definition as a filmmaker who contributes to the shaping of society,[24] attempting to set models that positively influence others.[25] The film's harmonic ending signals the filmmaker's belief in the ability of socialist society to integrate the young generation's controversial views and to be open to alternatives, as long as they confirm with the socialist basis of society. Gundula, though she has an unusual personality, becomes the prototype of contemporary youth: regardless of her rough edges, she is a reliable individual who seeks to take on responsibilities, who wants society to need her, and who engages with the same dedication and joy in her "serving" profession as she does in her singing. In portraying how young women cope with the complex challenges of everyday life, Nickel sets a positive model for a future generation of young women. It implies the expectation that these young women would step into the footprints of the strong socialist heroines—be they antifascists, working mothers, or brigade leaders—deserving honor for their proven commitment. As did numerous DEFA films, Nickel romanticizes these empowering images in . . . *und das Weib sei nicht mehr untertan* (1978). These images had little to do with real life under socialism. They corresponded, however, to the East German state's propagandistic viewpoint of women's emancipation. This viewpoint reflects the socialist ideal of women who are able to cope with multiple burdens or hardships. The paradigm of the strong woman provided the socialist state with the ideological tool to use women for reproductive work as well as for service in society and family. It further allowed the state, as Elke Schieber has convincingly argued, to withdraw from any responsibility for the actual realization of women's emancipation and to allocate it exclusively to the women themselves, since the state, by inaugurating legal equality between the sexes, had already done its duty.[26]

It was then through Petra Tschörtner and Helke Misselwitz that a new dimension was brought to the documentary genre. With their unvarnished look into women's everyday experiences and into the relationships between men and women, their films articulate, more than any other film before, the gap between the official claim to a fully accomplished women's emancipation in socialist society and actual reality. Thus these filmmakers also contributed substantially to the critical turn of DEFA documentary films in the late eighties.

Petra Tschörtner's thesis film, *Hinter den Fenstern* (Behind Closed Doors, 1983), one of the most significant film projects directed by a graduate of the East German film academy, examines the continuity of gender-specific inequalities under socialism with regard to family and marriage.[27] Afterward, several other of her films examined the role of women in East German society. These include her women portraits *Meine Mutter ist Lehrerin* (My Mother, the Teacher, 1986) and *Schnelles Glück* (Fleeting Happiness, 1989) as well as a film about single mothers, entitled *Und die Sehnsucht bleibt* (1987). Tolerated by GDR officials for the benefit of gaining Western currency, she completed the latter documentary for the West German television channel *Zweites deutsches Fernsehen* (ZDF). It was, however, never broadcast on East German television. In later films, Tschörtner approached a variety of other topics. Some examples are her documentary of a East Berlin neighborhood at time of the currency reform, entitled *Berlin—Prenzlauer Berg* (1990) and *Marmor, Stein und Eisen* (Marble, Stone and Iron, 1994), where she traces the development of her fellow students at the film academy.

In 1984, the board of the East German film school sent *Hinter den Fenstern*, without the prior knowledge of the filmmaker, to the Oberhausen film festival.

At the festival, it earned strong applause and won several awards. What contributed to this success in the West was that for the first time, a documentary film allowed viewers to gain insight into the internal dynamics of private lives and into the relationships between men and women in the East as they reflected upon the state of East German society. Whereas the image of the strong working mothers, which provided the socialist state with the ideological tool to use women for reproductive work as well as for service in society and family, attributes no significance to the notion of partnership, Tschörtner's film is based on the assumption that the actual state of women's emancipation can be grasped through an investigation into personal relationships between the sexes.

In *Hinter den Fenstern*, Tschörtner interviews three married couples about their ideas of life and partnership, their problems and crises, and their attempts to solve them. All three couples live in the same housing block. All are in their late twenties or early thirties, have one or two children, and live in a modern apartment. Though they are of different social backgrounds, all are professionals (except one husband, who has returned to graduate school). In spite of these characteristics signaling social advancement, the reality of their relationships indicates a rather retrogressive state. In all three cases, the husbands' tolerance does not extend very far; and it is the wives who compromise the most. (1) Christel (a clerk) and Rüdiger (a plumber) divorced once before because Christel could no longer tolerate Rüdiger's drinking and unwillingness to work, but later they reconciled. Both agree that what is keeping them together, more than love and their children, is habit as well as their joint investments in furniture, a car, and so forth. (2) Glazek (a graduate student of pedagogy) casually philosophizes about his views on marriage while enjoying himself being interviewed in the bathtub. For him, marriage is primarily a way of getting an apartment. He claims that he likes everything about his wife Birgit (a teacher). As we later learn from her, he makes her feel, however, as though she should be glad that he married her. He maintains that he would not prevent her from leaving him for another man if he was no longer satisfying her expectations. Birgit reveals, however, that he tried to persuade her to content herself with him. As she continues talking, she admits that she is missing a lot in the relationship with her husband, that she adapts much more to his needs while hers come to grief, and that it is only through another man who she recently met that she feels appreciated. (3) Karin (an assistant professor of aesthetics) and Lutz (a locksmith) overcome the gap between their diverse educational backgrounds and interests by talking about everything together. They have to tell each other a lot, as their lively conversation about what makes their marriage work out indicates. However, when Karin poses the hypothetical situation that she would continue her studies, perhaps abroad, to gain further qualifications and improve her career opportunities, Lutz adamantly vetoes such a possibility. Blocking any negotiation for a compromise, he insists that his wife's additional studies would be too much sacrifice for him and their son. In a final sequence, months later, the filmmaker talks to Karin again. In the meantime, Karin decided to give up her job in the university and to relocate with her family to the countryside where her husband grew up. While Karin justifies the decision to relocate with health concerns about her son, she reveals that it has been a difficult decision for her. Her statement, "I have to work on wanting it," betrays the extent to which she has to force herself to subordinate her own self-realization to that of her husband and son.

These sobering insights into three average marriages paradigmatically reveal the discrepancy between the self-understanding of the GDR as a society that had taken up the cause of improving the relationships between all individuals as well as between the sexes, and reality. This critical view of the GDR's private sphere, of the relations between the sexes in the so-called really existing socialism, and of the discrepancy between the legal equality of the sexes and the actual continuity of their historically derived inequality, was never before publicly addressed. In doing so, Tschörtner breaks with the dominant view of women in many films, which admires women's strength and capabilities, but that neglects to probe deeper into their real problems.

Six years later, Helke Misselwitz made *Winter adé* (1988), her first first full-length documentary film. A film about women's experiences in the GDR, *Winter adé* challenged the officially praised achievements of women's emancipation in the GDR to an extent unparalleled by any other film and laid bare the brittleness of human relationships underneath the public facade of East German society.[28] From her earliest film projects, such as her thesis fiction film *Die fidele Bäckerin* (1982), Misselwitz's work has centered on women. With its unembellished introspection into women's everyday experiences, its ironic view of East Germany's male-dominated society, and its compelling poetic images, *Winter adé* was an overwhelming success, both in the GDR and internationally. Recalling Maxie Wander's well-known collection of interviews with women in East Germany from the seventies, *Guten Morgen, Du Schöne*, as well as Sarah Kirsch's *Pantherfrau*, *Winter adé* portrays women of different generations and social backgrounds. Unlike Gitta Nickel's film . . . *und das Weib sei nicht mehr untertan*,[29] which juxtaposes the perspectives of women from three different generations to illustrate the increased possibilities for women in socialist society compared to the past, Misselwitz presents a far more critical view of the social position of women in East Germany. In *Winter adé*, women openly talk about their experiences, hopes, and disappointments in front of the camera to an extent that was never achieved in any film before. Misselwitz's empathetic representation allows viewers to understand the biography of average individuals as unique, and to reflect upon their own lives in these terms.[30] The film's visual and narrative frame is a train journey across the GDR. Suggestive of the filmmaker's being on the road in search for stories about women's lives, and of her attempt to move against the stagnation within East German society are the repeated images of

moving trains and tracks, shot from within a moving train. These images alternate with sequences of conversations between the filmmaker and several women
whom she meets on her journey as well as impressionistic images of random visual sensations. Through diverse individual life stories, Misselwitz examines what
changed in nearly forty years of legal and economic equality of the sexes. There
are two sixteen-year-old punk girls; there is a woman in her thirties, who works
in a coal factory; a successful advertising manager in her forties, who frankly
comments upon the almost complete absence of women in leadership positions;
furthermore, a self-confident, dedicated middle-aged director of a home for
children of dysfunctional families, who rejected the man who loved her in order
to live alone with her two children; an elderly owner of a private dance school;
an older woman operating a store in which she repairs dolls; finally, an eighty-
four-year-old woman whose seemingly intact marriage is clouded by her husband's infidelities.

    With the portrayal of two punk girls, who dropped out of school, Missel-
witz focused on a group of social outsiders who, according to official doctrine,
were subjects unsuited for public representation. In close-ups of the playful
young girls, as they put on makeup and style their hair in a public restroom in
a no-man's-land somewhere along the train route, the camera delineates their
fragility as well as their stubborn insistence on their unconventional life-style.
However, their dream of freedom and their unwillingness to conform to the
norms of society soon afterward end in a juvenile reformatory. In portraying
these two punk girls, Misselwitz touched on a taboo. The juvenile reformatory
was a subject that at best was tolerated in fictions only (e.g., in Erwin Stranka's
film *Sabine Wulff*). By pointing to the merciless rigor with which the East German state criminalized individuals who were unwilling to adapt to social norms
and whose families failed to give them sufficient emotional security, Misselwitz
challenged the GDR's public self-image of a harmonious human society.

    Particularly memorable is also the encounter with Christine, a woman in
her thirties, on whose fragile-looking and soft face the camera rests for a long
time. She has a tough job and a demanding private life, but she exhibits an inner strength to handle her life without complaint; and despite her hardships, she
has preserved an open-mindedness that allows her to dream of traveling in order to learn about people in other cultures. We first see her in the coal factory
where she works, cleaning soot out of the ovens. At home, she lives with her two
teenage children. Since her daughter is mentally ill, she needs special care and a
great deal of patience. Yet, despite the daughter's aggressive outbursts, Christine
prefers to provide her with a home instead of delegating the responsibility and
committing her to an institution. Christine calmly looks into the camera as she
talks about the people in the village who shun and blame her for the mental illness of her daughter, which they regard as the result of a lack of education.
While Christine talks, we cut from her kitchen to a long shot of an old couple

working in their garden. Christine's account shatters the atmospheric image of the elderly people peacefully gardening by revealing the heartlessness and prejudiced mind underneath the seemingly friendly surface.

Misselwitz's portrait of an eighty-five-year-old grandmother may have been influenced by Gabriele Denecke's noteworthy thesis film, *Wolters Trude* (1977), a documentary film about an old woman who spent her life working hard to bring up her eight children.[31] Like the protagonist in Denecke's film, the women in Misselwitz's film do not distinguish themselves through any official commitment to the socialist cause. It is the ups and downs of their individual lives in which the filmmaker is interested, not a biography suited to fit the ideological framework of dominant discourse. In the episode with the old woman, the center of focus is the celebration of the sixtieth anniversary of her wedding. A large crowd of family members have gathered to celebrate the event. We see husband and wife enjoying themselves as they dance together, an image conveying a sense of intact family ties. This impression of the happy family is further confirmed through the relatives who assure the filmmaker that none of the family members is divorced, except for one or two extended relatives who live in the West. The impression of the happy family and the harmonious couple, however, instantaneously breaks apart when the old woman talks to Misselwitz alone. While she is holding a large frame with a photograph of her as a young woman, she confesses to Misselwitz that she would not marry her husband again. Threatened to be thrown out of her parents' home by her father when she became pregant, she did not see any other choice but to wed, only to find herself married to a repeatedly unfaithful husband.

What provoked the cultural politicians the most about Misselwitz's film, resulting in the film not being broadcast on East German TV until after the political changes, was the report of Hillu, a successful advertising manager in her forties. Talking about a prize being awarded to her *kollektiv* at the Ministry of the Interior, she expresses her bewilderment about the small number of women among the party functionaries present at the award ceremony. Hillu wonders whether the male-dominated structure of the GDR's seemingly classless society should be compared to a "kingdom." *Winter adé* further adds an ironic commentary to the discrepancy between the official appraisal of the successes of women's emancipation and the actual inequality of the sexes that Hillu observed when the film inserts TV coverage of the celebration of the official women's day in East Berlin.

In dismantling the official image of women and replacing it by more realistic portrayals of individual lives, *Winter adé* alerted viewers to the urgent necessity of social change that could already be sensed at the time when the film opened at the Leipzig film festival in 1988. The fact that it only won the second prize, a silver dove, indicates the disturbance that the film created among the cultural politicians for its uncompromising view of East Germany's defective social structure and of its male-dominated society, at the same time trying to diminish the film's significance, despite ovations from the festival audience. Through its title *Winter adé* bid farewell to the silence about grievances and social pressures governing the relationships between individuals. In doing so, it was a call for a more democratic socialism in which problems could be openly addressed. Its release, however, only shortly preceded the demise of the GDR. In retrospect, the film thus became a document of a near-extinct system.

Helke Misselwitz—after completing two more documentaries, *Wer fürchtet sich vorm schwarzen Mann* (1989), which is about a private coal business in East Berlin, and *Sperrmüll* (1990), a film about a young man and his unconventional music group during the political upheaval in the fall of 1989—shot her first fiction film, *Herzsprung*, in 1992. This film, named after a village in Germany's northeast, with its atmospheric images and its romantic plot line of a young East German woman falling in love with an Afro-German bohemian nomad, pays tribute to a forgotten run-down area. It represents a poetic reflection about postunification reality and some current social problems, such as unemployment in the East, right-wing youth, and xenophobia in Germany. Misselwitz's *Herzsprung* is a first attempt to reestablish the DEFA's tradition of women's films. Various factors, however, have diminished the chances for a critically engaged German cinema: increased market pressures, pronounced attempts by functionaries in the film industry for a more viable and internationally competitive German cinema through focus on subjects attracting mainstream audiences, and tight budgets limiting funding possibilities. Given these constraints, it remains yet to be seen, to what extent filmmakers, especially women-directors, in the future will be able to make critical films that draw upon female perspectives in order to address topical issues concerning postunification German society.[32]

Notes

1. See *Außerhalb von Mitten Drin: Literatur/Film*, Berlin: Neue Gesellschaft für bildende (Künste, 1991), 181–83.

2. See Jörg Foth, "Forever Young" *Filmland DDR: Ein Reader zur Geschichte, Funktion und Wirkung der DEFA*, eds. Harry Blunk and Dirk Jungnickel (Cologne, Germany: Verlag Wissenschaft und Politik, 1990), 95–105; Elke Schieber, "In alter und neuer Gangart—Eine Generation im Mittelzustand," *Aus Theorie und Praxis des Films* 1 (1989); idem, "Ein kleines Boot in großer Flut: Zur Situation des Dokumentarfilms in der ehemaligen DDR," *Film und Fernsehen* 10 (1990): 30–32; Evelyn Schmidt, "Zur Helden- und Themenwahl—vorerst Fragen," *Beiträge zur Film—und Fernsehwissenschaft* 3 (1982): 32–41; idem, "Eigene Arbeit zu haben, ist kein schlechtes Gefühl," *Film und Fernsehen* 5 (1977): 7–8; Erika Richter, "Porträt einer Generation," *Film und Fernsehen* 4, no. 5 (1994): 110–12; and Wolfgang Gersch, "Film in der DDR: Die verlorene Alternative,"

Geschichte des deutschen Films, eds. Wolfgang Jacobsen, Anton Kaes, and Hans Helmut Prinzler (Stuttgart and Weimar, Germany: Metzler, 1993), 358.

3. Tamara Trampe, "Die Schere im Kopf: Notizen zur Sichtung der Filme, die Frauen (Regie) an der Hochschule für Film und Fernsehen in Potsdam-Babelsberg in 40 Jahren realisiert haben," manuscript, cited in Claus Löser, "Im Dornröschenschloß: Dokumentarfilme an der Babelsberger Filmhochschule," *Schwarzweiß und Farbe: DEFA-Dokumentarfilme 1946–1992*, ed. Filmmuseum Potsdam (Berlin: Jovis, 1996), 349.

4. See *Außerhalb von Mitten Drin*, 113–80. A research project on the professional histories of female graduates of the East German film academy in Potsdam-Babelsberg has been conducted at the *Hochschule für Film und Fernsehen "Konrad Wolf."* Uta Becher's contribution to this project, "Balance-Akte—Anspruch und Wirklichkeit von Absolventinnen der HFF," will be published in a forthcoming issue of *Beiträge zur Film—und Fernsehwissenschaft*.

5. Sibylle Schönemann, "Stoffentwicklung im DEFA-Studio für Spielfilme," *Filmland DDR* 71–81.

6. See Christel Gräf, "Nachwuchs-Nachlese: Regie Nachwuchs der 80er Jahre im DEFA-Film," *Film und Fernsehen* 6 (1994): 100–115; Margrit Frölich, "Locked Up Time: An interview with Sibylle Schönemann," *GDR Bulletin* 1 (1994): 21–24; Eggo Müller, "Dokumente der Distanz: Identitätsbestimmungen in Dokumentarfilmen über die DDR, November 1989 bis zur Vereinigung," *Mauer-Show*, eds. Rainer Bohn and Knut Hickethier (Eggo Müller, Berlin: Edition Sigma, 1992), 139–55; Marc Silberman, "Post-Wall Documentaries: New Images from a New Germany?" *Cinema Journal* 33, no. 2 (1994): 22–41; Karen Rosenberg, "Up Against the Wall: German Cinema Confronts a Divided Past," *The Independent* (November 1991): 22–25; Frank Schnelle, "Der schwarze Kasten," *Epd Film* 7 (1992): 42; and Dorothee Wenner, "Der schwarze Kasten," *Film und Fernsehen* 3 (1992): 76–77.

7. See Evelin Matschke, "Gitta Nickel," *Filmdokumentaristen der DDR*, ed. Institut für Filmwissenschaft (Berlin: Henschel, 1969): 364–75; Regine Sylvester, "Den Vorhang beiseite schieben: Die Dokumentaristin Gitta Nickel," *Kino- und Fernseh-Alamanach* 17 (1987): 32 63; and Heinz Baumert, "Gitta Nickel: Mutige Filme fordern mich heraus," *Film und Fernsehen* 4 (1977): 26–31.

8. Dietrich Staritz, *Geschichte der DDR 1949–1985* (Frankfurt/Main, Germany: Suhrkamp, 1985), 198–203.

9. See Erika Richter, "Alltag und Geschichte in DEFA-Gegenwartsfilmen der siebziger Jahre" (diss.) *Filmwissenschaftliche Beiträge* 1 (1976).

10. An example of films that addressed more controversial topics, enjoying tremendous popularity among audiences, is Heiner Carow's box office hit *Die Legende von Paul und Paula* (1973), among others.

11. See Elke Schieber, "Anfang vom Ende oder Kontinuität des Argwohns: 1980 bis 1989," *Das zweite Leben der Filmstadt Babelsberg: DEFA-Spielfilme 1946–1992*, ed. Filmmuseum (Potsdam, Berlin: Henschel, 1994), 264–327; Sigrun D. Leonhard, "Test-

ing the Borders: East German Film between Individualism and Social Commitment," *Post New Wave Cinema in the Soviet Union and Eastern Europe*, ed. Daniel J. Goulding (Bloomington: Indiana University Press, 1989), 60–71; Heinz Kersten, "The Role of Women in GDR Films since the Early 1970s," *Studies in GDR Culture and Society*, ed. Margy Gerber (Lanham, Maryland: University Press of America, 1988), 8:47–64.

12. Examples are Iris Gusner's *Alle meine Mädchen* (1980), *Wäre die Erde nicht rund* (1981), and *Kaskade rückwärts* (1984), and Evelyn Schmidt's *Seitensprung* (1979) and *Das Fahrrad* (1982).

13. Schieber, "Anfang vom Ende," 305.

14. See Andrea Rinke's discussion of *Das Fahrrad* (The Bicycle) in this volume.

15. *Seitensprung* focuses on the relationships between men and women within the family and the responsibility of adults toward children.

16. One of the last films produced by the DEFA, *Der Hut* (1991) is a comedy about women's emancipation. The film signals its concern with average women through its dedication to "the GDR's last female citizen." See Schieber, "Der Hut 1991," *Film und Fernsehen* 5 (1991): 46.

17. By contrast, see the positive review of the West German film critic Heinz Kersten, "Eigene Sicht vom Fahrrad: Ein DEFA-Film und Babelsberger Nachwuchsprobleme," *Frankfurter Rundschau*, 16 November 1982. Although Evelyn Schmidt was able to realize a few other films in subsequent years, the bad press concerning *Das Fahrrad* had significantly hampered her career as a film director, and more often than not, she was in jeopardy of losing her contract with the studio. See "Evelyn Schmidt" *DEFA NOVA— nach wie vor?* (Berlin: Freunde der Deutschen Kinemathek, 1993), 129–34.

18. Interview with Evelyn Schmidt by Detlev Friedrich, "Das Fahrrad als Stein des Anstoßes: Der Alltag, das Alltägliche, der große und der kleine Konflikt—Auskünfte einer DEFA—Regisseurin," *Berliner Zeitung* 17, no. 18 (July 1982).

19. It was not until the Fifth Convention of the Members of the Film and Television Industry in 1988 that the film was recognized as one of the most significant works of the younger generation of East German directors. See Schieber, "Anfang vom Ende," 269.

20. See *Frauen in Deutschland 1945–1992*, eds. Gisela Helwig and Hildegard Maria Nickel (Bonn: Bundeszentrale für politische Bildung, 1993); Helwig, *Frau und Familie: Bundesrepublik—DDR*, 2d ed. (Cologne, Germany: Verlag Wissenschaft und Politik, 1987); Herta Kurig and Wulfram Speigner, *Zur gesellschaftlichen Stellung der Frau in der DDR* (Leipzig, Germany: Verlag für die Frau, 1978); and Harry G. Shaffer, *Women in the Two Germanies* (New York: Pergamon, 1981).

21. Baumert, "Gitta Nickel," 29.

22. Elke Schieber, ". . . und das Weib sei nicht mehr untertan: Frauen der siebziger und achtziger Jahre im Dokumentarfilm der DDR," *Außerhalb von Mitten Drin*, 82–90.

23. See Christel Gräf, "Nachwuchs-Nachlese," 103, 107. Schönemann completed her studies at the East German film academy with her thesis film, *Ramona* (1979), a sensitive fiction film about a young girl from an orphanage in search of her father.

24. Sylvester, "Den Vorhang beiseite schieben," 40–41.

25. See Peter Neumann and Raymund Stolze's interview with Gitta Nickel, "An der Seite jener, die den Schritt ins Neuland wagen," *Junge Welt*, 30 March 1984.

26. Schieber, ". . . und das Weib sei nicht mehr untertan," 82–84.

27. Two other examples of films focusing on the role of women in East German society, which were directed by female students of the film academy, include Juliane Richter's *Nur eine Frau* (1974) and Gabriele Denecke's thesis film *Wolter's Trude* (1977).

28. See Beate Schönfeldt, "Frauen, Alltagserfahrungen und gesellschaftliche Realität: 'Winter ade,'" *Beiträge zur Film- und Fernsehwissenschaft* 37 (1990): 100–110.

29. See Schieber, ". . . und das Weib sei nicht mehr untertan," 85.

30. See Beate Schönfeldt's interview with Helke Misselwitz, "Wenn einer eine Reise tut: Begegnungen—Meinungen: 'Winter adé'—Ein abendfüllender DEFA-Dokumentarfilm über Menschen in unserer Gesellschaft," *Berliner Zeitung* 28, no. 29 (January 1989).

31. Another example of a filmic portrait of older women in society is Leonja Wuss-Mundeciema's portrait *Die älteste Greisin* (1987). Other works by Denecke, who was employed by East German television, which focus on women, are *In Zwickau* (1980) and *Tell Me Tales* (1991), a video about women of different generations and social backgrounds and their experiences in relationships with men.

32. In the meantime, Misselwitz completed her second fiction film entitled *Engelchen* (1996).

4

The Queer and Unqueer Spaces of Monika Treut's Films

Marcia Klotz

As Julia Knight points out in *The Meaning of Treut?* Monika Treut's works have generally been received first and most positively by people who identify as "gay," "lesbian," or "queer," often opening at gay and lesbian film festivals in North America and Germany.[1] While Treut, an out lesbian who makes films primarily about lesbian thematics, is often received as a "lesbian filmmaker," Knight argues that her films move beyond this kind of labeling. Treut supports the freedom to choose among any number of different sexual options, according to Knight, and promotes "tolerance of different sexualities—*whatever* those sexualities may be" (48). Knight's characterization of Treut's goals, however, strikes me as much too liberal, since Treut does not generally try to move her audience to merely *tolerate* nonmainstream sexual practices, but rather actively affirms those practices as nondeviant, emancipatory, and fun. In this essay, I will examine Treut's works within the context of a *radical queer* political program, and critique them on that basis.[2]

While *queer* is often employed as synonymous with "gay and lesbian," or as an umbrella term for "gays, lesbians, and bisexuals," queer theory tends to focus on readings of cultural texts which, according to Alexander Doty's definition, "can be marked as contra-, non- or anti-straight."[3] However, queer theory, particularly as practiced by Judith Butler, has sometimes distinguished itself from the identity politics of the gay and lesbian movement by calling attention to the instability inherent in any fixed identity categories, such as "male," "female," "heterosexual," and "homosexual." For Butler, "straight" can no more be understood as representing a coherent sexual identity or set of sexual practices than anything else:

> Heterosexuality is always in the process of imitating and approximating its own phantasmatic idealization of itself—*and failing*. Precisely because it is bound to

fail, and yet endeavors to succeed, the project of heterosexuality is propelled into an endless repetition of itself. Indeed, in its efforts to naturalize itself as the original, heterosexuality must be understood as a compulsive and compulsory repetition that can only produce the *effect* of its own originality.[4]

Butler's vision is somewhat at odds with Doty's notion of queer as "contra-, non- or anti-straight," because "queer," as she uses it, is not the simple antonym to "straight," but points rather to a set of theoretical practices that challenge the logic that would set these terms up as binary opposites in the first place.

This understanding of queer theory, namely as a radical critique of gender and sexuality that serves to challenge both dominant and marginal understandings of identity,[5] can be pushed one step further with help from a second article by Butler.[6] In "Against Proper Objects," she critiques a definition of lesbian and gay studies that had appeared in the introduction to *The Lesbian and Gay Studies Reader* and reads as follows: "Lesbian/gay studies does for *sex* and *sexuality* approximately what women's studies does for gender."[7] Butler is dissatisfied with this formulation not only because it neglects the rich feminist tradition that has focused on sex and sexuality (particularly by such theorists as Gayle Rubin),[8] but also because lesbian and gay studies is not an adequate field for addressing many realms of sexual oppression:

> Not only do central notions like the racialization of sexuality get dropped or domesticated as "instances" of either feminism or lesbian and gay studies, but the notion of sexual minorities, which include sex workers, transsexuals, and cross-generational partners, cannot be adequately approached through a framework of lesbian and gay studies. (10–11)

The categories of marginalization mentioned here as beyond the scope of gay and lesbian studies represent only a few of the kinds of sexual outlawry treated by Monika Treut's films. The question I would like to ask here is whether queer theory can be stretched in a way that might take on some of these other fields of sexual marginalization—rather than being restricted to a critique of gay and lesbian marginalization based on same-sex desire.

Indeed, it is only if one accepts this more expansive understanding of "queer" that Treut can be viewed as a "queer filmmaker" at all. Clearly, she does not intend to simply portray positive images of lesbian relationships, of the sort seen in *Go Fish* (Guinevere Turner, 1994) or *The Incredibly True Adventures of Two Girls in Love* (Maria Maggenti, 1995). Treut has been critiqued, in fact, for not sticking more closely to lesbian thematics; Julia Knight reports that when *My Father Is Coming* opened in New York in 1991, *The Village Voice* criticized Treut for the "excessively heterosexual" thematics of the promotional poster, which showed Alfred Edel lying supine on a table, dwarfed beneath the breasts of Annie Sprinkle, who smiles into the camera. With the poster Treut had "betrayed the label of lesbian filmmaker," according to *The Voice*.[9] In a sense, *The Voice* is correct; this is less a lesbian than a queer film, portraying many different kinds of nonstraight sexualities. But even the supposedly "straight" encounter between Annie and Hans that the poster depicts is carefully framed, within the film itself, as anything other than a heterosexual love story—or even a straight seduction. Annie refuses the cake Hans brings her on the evening of their date ("I don't eat any sugar"), then refuses his kisses as he tries to seduce her, insisting instead that he join her in watching a film about transsexuals. The final sex scene between them shows him lying flat on his back with a very unflattering camera tilting from his flabby stomach up to Annie, who stands over him, cooing while she massages his shoulders. Her words to Hans, "And now I want you to squeeze the muscles in your genitals and just pump up that sexual energy. Let that sexual energy heal and nourish every cell in your body," are not addressed to him, but spoken directly into a camera that is focusing in close-up on her face; the shot does not include the recipient of her attention. This scene could not be further removed from filmic tropes of passionate lovemaking, but represents instead a performance of sexual healing, staged melodramatically and professionally by a well-practiced sex goddess. Moreover, when Hans finally leaves to return home, Annie sees him off, reminding him of his promise to line her up some performance opportunities in Germany. This suggests that the sexual pleasure she has given him was actually exchanged for future favors Hans would do for her, and that their encounter was closer to prostitution than to seduction. If we understand sex work as a kind of eroticism that both threatens and is policed by hegemonic sexual culture, this development might be understood as "queering" the Hans-Annie relationship.

A second "heterosexual" relationship in *My Father Is Coming* is similarly queered, though along different lines. The videotape that Annie shows to Hans as he tries to kiss her focuses on a female-to-male transsexual whose face is familiar to the viewer: we recognize Joe (Michael Massee), the same man who, at that same moment in the film's time, is making love to Hans's daughter, Vicky (Shelley Kastner), with a passion that underscores what is lacking between Annie and Hans. The viewer is thus let in on Joe's secret before Vicky is—he only lets her know *after* their sexual encounter that he was born female. While Vicky's attraction to Joe is certainly that of a woman to a man, it can hardly be considered simply "straight." As Judith Halberstam notes:

> While Judith Butler's dictum . . . that some girls like "their boys to be girls" has been understood widely in terms of a butch-femme aesthetic, it can also apply quite literally to those girls who like their boys to have been genetic girls. As in the . . . example of the man who had been looking all his life for a guy with a pussy, there are some women who have always been searching for a woman with a dick or a dyke with a dick. (220)

Vicky's ignorance of Joe's transsexual status at the time she has sex with him does nothing to detract from the queerness of the encounter, but simply strengthens the fantasy value of the female-to-male's ability to pull off the masquerade successfully.

The queering of these two straight relationships is typical of Monika Treut's entire oeuvre. All of her narrative films are structured around the creation of what I would call queer havens, meaning spaces in which all kinds of sexual free play are allowed and encouraged, and where women tend to be in control. Thus *Seduction: The Cruel Woman* (1985) revolves around the opening of a house/ gallery in which erotic fantasies can be staged for pay by Wanda (Mechthild Grossmann), while *Virgin Machine* (1988) slowly leads Dorothee (Ina Blum) out of a heterosexual life in Hamburg and into the separated space of the women-only erotic dance club in San Francisco, where she loses her inhibitions and joins the performers on stage. *My Father Is Coming* (1991) similarly locates Vicky's journey of sexual self-discovery in two locales of erotic emancipation: Annie Sprinkle's theater and the gay nightclub where Vicky finally performs. *The Taboo Parlor* (1995)[10] also moves between erotic free zones: the luxury apartment of the two women, chock-full of sex toys, and an S&M club located in a boat that is anchored in the Hamburg harbor.

The world outside of these queer havens lives under the sign of straightness. Treut's characters who live there, like Dorothee before her journey of sexual self-discovery in *Virgin Machine*, find themselves surrounded by selfish, repulsive men. Sex between Dorothee and Heinz (Gad Klein) is represented in a flashback sequence that emphasizes the disgusting. The camera portrays the round, balding head of Heinz with a leering grin on his face, rising above the camera and falling into close-ups in twisted angles. This cuts to an outdoor shot of Heinz blowing his nose, then a microscopic close-up of the head of a penis ejaculating into liquid. His orgasm is thereby reduced to the biologic function of discharging mucus. The frequent intercuts between scenes of their relationship and the clogged and belching drain in Dorothee's apartment are hardly needed to underscore that Dorothee will never get what she wants from this man.

Virgin Machine is not a simple story of a woman who escapes a repulsive life of heterosexuality to find love and happiness among lesbians, however, but a polemic against the ideology of love itself. Dorothee's romance with Ramona (Shelly Mars) in San Francisco sets up the viewer to expect that, while she had been enslaved to a world of compulsory heterosexuality as enforced through the boring, endless repetition of vanilla sex, Ramona might provide something different. Instead, Ramona presents her with a bill for her services after they sleep together, and we realize that Ramona has made good on the promise of her television advertisement; what she has to offer is in fact a "cure for love." The "straightness" of the outside world is not defined simply by the law of compulsory heterosexuality, but also by the imperative to couple. Dorothee will not find a simple solution to her problems by substituting a woman for a man as her romantic partner. She finally gives up her search for bourgeois love and joins the dancers on the stage at the erotic dance club, embracing a kind of pleasure that revolves around voyeurism and exhibitionism. Sex is not an expression of the bonds that join the romantic couple here, but rather a diffused source of pleasure, shared between a number of onlookers and dancers, less about orgasm and more about performance. In refusing a utopian view of relationships between women in this film, Monika Treut queers lesbianism itself.[11]

Dorothee's escape from the heterosexual world of romantic love in Hamburg to the queer haven of the strip show in San Francisco is contingent, of course, on the existence of a safe space where women control what happens and who is watching. However, as in many of Treut's films, the boundaries that separate the queer haven from the surrounding straight world are not secure in *Virgin Machine*, but must be defended against threats from the outside. When Marvin Moss, owner of the club and self-proclaimed "king of porn here in San Francisco," tries to shove his way in to view the women performing on ladies' night, the border of the queer haven is defended by a group of very tough butches who meet him at the door. Intimidated by their obvious physical superiority, he can only flip them off while beating a quick retreat.

The repulsion of Marvin Moss from the queer space of the erotic dance club represents only the most obvious means of defending the sexual free zone. A much more complex strategy is pursued in the earlier film, *Seduction: The Cruel Woman*, when a journalist (Peter Weibel) appears in Wanda's fantasy house to interview her for what promises, judging from the harsh questions he puts to her, to be a very unflattering article. His threat, however, is quickly neutralized as Wanda seduces him. First he proposes that he see her "as a client," but she coolly responds that that kind of sexuality holds no interest for her anymore. His second proposal, however, meets with a warmer reception: he offers to serve as her "toilet."

The sequence in which Wanda satisfies this desire is perhaps the most controversial in all of Monika Treut's films (it was the reason she lost government funding for *Seduction* in 1985).[12] While much of *Seduction* is loosely based on Sacher-Masoch's *Venus in Furs*,[13] the film refocuses the fantasy structure, making it less about the pleasure of the masochistic man (as in Sacher-Masoch's novel) and more about the pleasure of the dominant woman. This recentering of the fantasy around the woman's position is crucial to the framing of the "toilet" sequence as well, which depicts Wanda watching a video of herself. As the journalist crawls around a restroom on all fours, slavishly begging her to allow him to serve as her toilet, Wanda kicks him, orders him around, and shouts abuses at him. Then her tone changes, and she addresses the camera warmly, offering advice to other dominatrixes on how to deal with this kind of slave:

> The slave worships the substances that are considered the absolute worst in our social circles. His submissive soul clings to you and to everything around you,

even that which you value the least, paradoxical though that may be. Overcome your disgust and revulsion. Say to yourself: my excrement is the most
normal thing on earth, neither especially beautiful nor especially terrible.
Stand by your shit! A last word: don't spoil your slave. The best thing for both
of you is to keep him in a constant state of longing.[14]

This how-to message for the would-be dominatrix is intercut with shots of the
viewer, Wanda, attentively watching herself on the screen, laughing at her own
jokes, and looking generally mesmerized by what the Wanda who speaks before
the camera is saying, as if seeing it all for the first time. This framing device recasts one of the most potentially offensive kinds of pleasure (that taken in con-
suming excrement) into a very woman-centered framework: we are not asked
to identify with the journalist's pleasure, but rather with Wanda's enjoyment
in viewing the tape. This framing device serves to recuperate the scene for the
sex-positive feminist viewer. The video shown here is a film made by a woman
(Wanda) about a woman (Wanda) and for women (dominatrixes, instantiated
here yet again in Wanda). The journalist who had initially threatened to write
an article condemning her for transgressions against the mores of a straight
world is neutralized as she discovers his perverse desire and exploits it, transpos-
ing him into a prop in a video that allows her to voyeuristically enjoy the spectacle of herself as the cruel and dominant mistress she enjoys playing. She incorporates him into the queer haven, but in a way that changes him into a mere
accessory in a woman-centered fantasy world.

A second controversial sequence in *Seduction* touches on the sticky issue of
transgenerational sex. In this sequence, Wanda's lover, Caren (Carola Regnier),
an avid shoe-fetishist, is shown in her shoe store waiting on a very unhappy customer, a girl who looks to be somewhere between thirteen and sixteen years old,
shopping at the behest of her domineering mother. The girl's long hair hangs in
her face, while her surly expression betrays obvious irritation with her neatly
groomed mother, who arrogantly makes decisions on her daughter's behalf. A
shot of Caren making eye contact with the unruly girl then cuts to a fantasy sequence that first shows the daughter stretching across Caren's lap wearing a tight,
short skirt and fishnet stockings. Both she and Caren cast a mocking smile at the
camera, which cuts to a countershot of the mother, bound to a chair and gagged.
Shots of the girl alone stretching across the sofa follow, with Caren now situated
obligingly behind the restrained mother, peering with kind interest at the girl.
Caren delivers the voice-over to this fantasy: "You see my dear? When your
heart breaks, it's like theater without the audience." (Siehst du, Liebes? Wenn
dein Herz bricht, ist es wie Theater ohne Publikum.)

Just as many sequences set in Wanda's house of pleasure rewrite various
scenes from Sacher-Masoch's *Venus in Furs*, this fantasy sequence in the shoe
store suggests a rewriting of the Marquis de Sade's *Philosophy in the Bedroom*.
That novel depicts the education of a pubescent girl, Eugenie, at the hands of a

group of libertines (two men and a woman), in which Eugenie is deflowered (both vaginally and anally), then taught to reject the moral code she has learned from her mother, which teaches girls to value chastity above all else. Her education concludes with a newly orgasmic Eugenie turning against her repressive mother and joining the libertines in torturing her. Despite the brutal misogyny of this ending, the novel contains a number of lines that can be read as very supportive of women—or at least of women's pleasure, as when Madame de Saint-Ange instructs Eugenie:

> Is there anything more ridiculous than to see a maiden of fifteen or sixteen, consumed by desires she is compelled to suppress, wait . . . until it pleases her parents, having first rendered her youth miserable, further to sacrifice her riper years . . . when they associate her, despite her wishes, with a husband who either has nothing wherewith to make himself loved, or who possesses everything to make himself hated? . . . Fuck, Eugenie, fuck, my angel; your body is yours alone; in all the world there is but yourself who has the right to enjoy it as you see fit.[15]

In rewriting the *Philosophy in the Bedroom* (Monika Treut made *Seduction: The Cruel Woman* in collaboration with Elfie Mikesch as a kind of filmed version of her dissertation on Sacher-Masoch and Sade),[16] the shoe store sequence offers another response to an intrusion of straightness into the queer haven of the fetishized shoe store, as represented in the mother's control over her daughter. In Sade's novel, that control centers around the mother's insistence on maintaining the girl's virginity until control over her sexuality can be placed in the hands of her husband. Rebellion against the mother is thus central in affirming the girl's own pleasure, both in *Philosophy in the Bedroom* and in this sequence. The film changes a key element, however: whereas Sade's narrative depicts *real* events, at least in the fictional world of the novel, this sequence only represents a *fantasy* within the fictional world of the film. Moreover, there is no way to tell whose fantasy the sequence depicts: the voice-over is cast in the second-person ("When *your* heart breaks. . . .") indicating that this is not Caren's fantasy at all, but rather that of the girl herself—though shared with Caren in some unclear manner. Or it may be the fantasy Caren *would imagine* the girl having if she could only visualize it. In any case, the triumphant smile on the girl's face as she glares at her distraught, squirming mother while stretching her long legs across Caren's lap indicate that the girl's pleasure is much more at stake in this fantasy than Caren's, and in the following tableaux, Caren is altogether absent. This is not surprising, for it is the girl who stands the most to gain here, as this performance of herself as a sexual being before her mother's unwilling stare enacts not only her own desire, but also her emancipation from the repressive regime of parental authority.

The touchy topic of intergenerational sex is framed in a way that focuses the fantasy—not on the adult's pleasure in having a minor sit on her lap—but rather on the active affirmation of a pubescent girl's erotic pleasure and how it might be used to liberate her from her mother's control. As in the toilet sequence just discussed, this fantasy scene functions to recuperate a potentially offensive sexual act by reframing it within a system that affirms women's pleasure and freedom, remaking it into part of the utopian world that lies within the boundaries of the queer haven. This is a very distinct project from a kind of feminist utopianism that would locate women's emancipation solely in relations between women. The very fact that it is the daughter's *mother* who here invokes the prohibitional voice of patriarchy, rather than some sort of father figure, is quite significant in signaling Treut's rebellion against an essentialist form of feminism that tends to portray woman-to-woman relationships in utopian terms.

I would like to turn now to the question of what lies on the outside of those queer havens in Treut's films. This is a space, for example, where sex workers are not always as fully in control of their business as the self-possessed Annie Sprinkle of *My Father Is Coming*. In a scene from *Virgin Machine*, Dorothee watches an emaciated white prostitute, carrying a bottle in a paper bag, look for business on a corner of the poverty-stricken Tenderloin District of San Francisco, as a number of thin, African-American men mill about round her. As she watches, Dorothee muses to herself, "Die Sex-Industrie ist deswegen so trostlos, weil Frauen darin so wenig zu sagen haben." [17] There is obviously something wrong with the kind of sex work she is witness to here—something the erotic dancers in the women's club have managed to escape. Dorothee does not think about this question for long, but sets off on her own path of personal emancipation, landing eventually in the queer haven of the women's club. Although this seemingly random comment occupies a minutely small space within the film, it points to a kind of prostitution that has nothing to do with erotic emancipation, but that is coerced—whether financially, by dependence on alcohol or drugs, or by other means. The fact that most of the people on that street corner are black leads one to wonder just what the relation might be between race and class here—or why the sad, coerced kind of sex is at home in a black neighborhood while the world of the erotic dance club is all white.

If there is a suggested relationship between race and a class position that limits one's erotic possibilities in the straight space of *Virgin Machine*, ethnic conflict resides there in some of Treut's other films. In *My Father Is Coming*, Vicky and her father go into a deli in Coney Island, for example, but discover that the Jewish owners are unwilling to wait on them because they are German. Later, a Jewish man strikes up a conversation with Vicky's father and asks him point-blank what he had been doing during the Nazi years. Hans is so uncomfortable that he flees into the women's rest room, where he has the fateful encounter with Annie Sprinkle that marks the beginning of his erotic education. Like the Tenderloin prostitute in *Virgin Machine*, the memory of the Holocaust, marked by Jewish anger and German guilt, is left at the periphery of the film's frame of reference, never fully thematized and certainly never resolved. It is invoked as a vague source of discomfort for the main characters, who are nevertheless able to escape it by losing themselves in the eroticism of the queer havens where the main action is situated.

The contrast between the utopianism that lies within the emancipatory space of Treut's queer havens and the social ills that lie outside is drawn most starkly in her most recent short film, *The Taboo Parlor*, which depicts a lesbian couple, two wealthy and glamorous women in traditional Hollywood style, who decide to supplement their sex life by picking up a man to join them one evening. They find what they are looking for at a party on a boat in the Hamburg harbor—a man of unsavory reputation, as the bartender informs them, with sexual politics that are, at least from a Treutian perspective, reprehensible (which is to say, utterly straight): he is openly disdainful of a dance being directed by a dominatrix in the next room, and he even tries to convince one of the women to leave her lover and go home with him alone. When he is given to understand that both the women want to sleep with him, however, he happily leaves with them. But before this paragon of straightness is able to get what he wants from the two women, the tables are turned on him. Just as he is about to climax in the missionary position with one of the women, her partner rapes him anally with a strap-on dildo. Angered, he storms out of their apartment, but a bomb that has been planted at the behest of one of the femmes fatales in his sports car bursts into flames when he gets in, while the two women look on dispassionately through a window.

The ending of *The Taboo Parlor* sets up a new dynamic in Treut's filmed world; this is the first time that queerness ever becomes predatory. And while there is an oblique hint in the bartender's reference to the victim's criminality that he may in fact deserve his fate, the film itself provides no justification for his death. With this film, Treut's queer haven goes to war with the outside world, but it is a war that can hardly be taken seriously. *The Taboo Parlor*, as I read it, sends up a genre of horror/slasher film, in which it is often sexually promiscuous *women* who are raped, brutalized, killed, and sometimes dismembered.[18] These deaths are generally not justified; the women often barely appear onscreen before they are killed. The victim in *The Taboo Parlor* is dealt with in a similar kind of absentminded way; his death does not need to be justified because he is simply inconsequential to the logic of the film; what matters here is the lesbian couple. Yet this absentminded treatment of his plot development is quite intentional and somewhat tongue-in-cheek; Treut is deliberately provoking the audience by dealing with the man—who would otherwise be the central character in a more traditional pornographic fantasy about a man with two women—as peripheral to the main action.

The Taboo Parlor would thus seem to be Treut's boldest affirmation of the queer haven, a clear statement that what lies inside its borders is important and interesting; what lies outside is not. Yet this is also the film where she comes closest to critiquing how these spaces are constructed—in a very quick sequence that might seem, at first glance anyway, itself inconsequential. As the lesbian couple and their male escort dreamily make their way home from the party, they encounter another trio, two German men who are taunting and physically threatening a man they derogatorily refer to as "Ausländer" at a bus stop. As the eroticized group passes by, decked out in elegant, expensive clothing, the violence is interrupted for a moment while all three men are enraptured by the sexy vision of the two women and the man, already lost in kissing, caressing, and fondling one another. The contrast between the two trios is marked not only as physical extremes: violence in one group, eroticism in the other, but also in terms of class: the poor men at the bus stop might be just as fascinated by the elegant riches conspicuously displayed by the group as by their exhibitionistic sexuality. The two women and their escort enjoy the good fortune that seems to accompany the rich; they no sooner arrive at the stop than the bus comes to whisk them away, while the camera returns to the two men who have resumed their harassment of the foreigner, but only for an instant, and we never see them again.

The viewer is left to wonder what the parallels between these two groups might indicate. Both trios consist of a couple that stands in a predatory relationship to the third member based, in the first instance, on his gender and straightness, in the second, on his ethnicity. Does the foreigner wind up dead at the end of the film, like the man the two women bring home? Or is Treut deliberately contrasting her wealthy protagonists here with the Hamburg underclass, showing, perhaps, that their sex games are somehow connected to class privilege? How might those games be related to what is happening between this other trio—a kind of violence that is anything but playful, absolutely involuntary, and utterly inescapable?

These three men, like the prostitute on the streetcorner in *Virgin Machine* or the Jewish resentment toward Germans in *My Father Is Coming*, threaten to rupture the entire structure of the film in which they appear. They are located, like the others, on the periphery of the film's visual field, in that uninteresting, straight space through which the main characters wander somnambulistically, lost in dreams of the adventures they will return to in the erotic free zones. Yet the appearance of these conflicts on the perimeter begs the question of what exactly the class and racial status of the players at the center—that is, *within* the queer haven itself—might be. Would the fantasy presented in *The Taboo Parlor* operate differently if one of the women were Kurdish? Or if the man they picked up were a Turk? Would Hans's sexual education flow as smoothly if Annie Sprinkle were Jewish in *My Father Is Coming*? And what would happen if the dancers at the women's club in *Virgin Machine* were in desperate need of cash for the dances they perform? Or if they had pimps waiting outside to see how much they had taken in, and expecting a cut?

Although we see a number of instances in Treut's films of how straightness threatens to violate the boundaries of the queer haven and how those threats are repelled, neutralized, or destroyed, inequalities based on class or race never seem to threaten the queer space at all. Do they "naturally" reside only on the outside, intrinsically connected to the straight world? If so, it would seem that the fantasy of the queer haven is itself predicated on escaping from a social reality where class and race continue to play a role. Thus, while Monika Treut repeatedly challenges the utopian assumptions that have been connected to the radical lesbian movement in her films, *she re-creates a new kind of utopianism that is here based on a radical queer political agenda.* Although the kinds of sexual practices that lie within this program are certainly much more diverse than those of radical lesbianism, there is still an essentializing element in the line that separates the polymorphous perversity of Treut's queer world, with its multiplicitous possibilities of erotic emancipation, from the straight space outside, where abuse is real and where hierarchies of race and class continue to dominate people's lives.

Notes

Many thanks to Sabine Hake and especially to Leerom Medovoi for comments and critiques on previous versions of this essay.

1. Julia Knight, "The Meaning of Treut?" in *Immortal, Invisible. Lesbians and the Moving Image,* ed. Tamsin Wilton (New York and London: Routledge, 1993), 34–51.

2. While interest in queer theory and queer politics tends to be much more fully developed in the United States and Canada at the present moment than in Germany, I do not believe that fact makes it any less appropriate a category for the analysis of Monika Treut's films, most of which, though produced in Germany, are deeply interested in current sexual debates in the United States.

3. Alexander Doty, *Making Things Perfectly Queer. Interpreting Mass Culture* (Minneapolis and London: University of Minnesota Press, 1993), xv.

4. Judith Butler, "Imitation and Gender Insubordination," in *Inside/Out. Lesbian Theories, Gay Theories,* ed. Diana Fuss (New York and London: Routledge, 1991), 21. See also *Gender Trouble* (New York and London: Routledge, 1990).

5. This is precisely how "queer theory" is used, for example, in the following passage by Judith Halberstam:

The postmodern lesbian body as visualized by recent film and video, *as theorized by queer theory,* and as constructed by state of the art cosmetic technology breaks with a homo-heterosexual binary and remakes gender as not simply performance, but also as fiction. . . . The end of identity in this gender fiction does not mean a limitless and boundless shifting of positions and forms, rather it indicates the futility of stretching terms like lesbian or gay or straight or male or female across vast fields of experience, behavior, and self-understanding. (my italics) Judith Halberstam, "F2M: The Making of Female Masculinity," in *The Lesbian Postmodern*, ed. Laura Doan (New York: Columbia University Press, 1994), 210–28.

6. Butler, "Against Proper Objects," in *Differences*, special issue: *More Gender Trouble: Feminism Meets Queer Theory* 6 (summer-fall 1994): 1–26.

7. *The Lesbian and Gay Studies Reader*, eds. Henry Abelove, Michele Aina Barale, and David M. Halperin (New York: Routledge, 1993), xv.

8. In this context, Butler gives considerable attention to Rubin's seminal essay, "Thinking Sex: Notes for a Radical Theory of the Politics of Sexuality," in *Pleasure and Danger: Exploring Female Sexuality*, ed. Carole S. Vance (London: Routledge, 1984), 267–319.

9. As cited by Knight, "Meaning of Treut?" 38.

10. *The Taboo Parlor* was released, along with other erotic shorts by Lizzie Borden and Clara Law, under the title *Erotique* in 1995.

11. For an excellent discussion of Monika Treut's refusal of (and dependence on) the genre of the coming-out narrative, see Chris Straayer, "Lesbian Narratives and Queer Characters in Monika Treut's *Virgin Machine*," *Journal of Film and Video* 45 (summer-fall 1993): 24–38.

12. Catherine Saalfield, "*The Seduction of Monika*," in *Outweek*, 12 November 1989, pp. 40–43; and Colin Richardson, "Monika Treut: An Outlaw at Home," in *A Queer Romance: Lesbians, Gay Men, and Popular Culture*, eds. Paul Burston and Colin Richardson (London and New York: Routledge, 1995), 167–85.

13. Leopold Sacher-Masoch, *Venus in Furs* (New York: Zone Books, 1991).

14. Der Sklave vergöttert die Substanzen, die in unserem Kulturkreis als die denkbar Übelsten gelten. Seine unterwürfige Seele klammert sich an Sie und an alles, was Sie umgibt, sogar und paradox genug, an das, was Sie am wenigsten achten. . . . Überwinden Sie jetzt Abscheu und Ekel. Sagen Sie sich, meine Ausscheidungen sind das Normalste von der Welt, weder besonders schön, noch besonders furchtbar. Stehen Sie zu Ihrer Scheisse! Ein letztes Wort noch: . . . verwöhnen Sie Ihren Sklaven nicht zu sehr. Das Beste ist doch für beide, ihn in einem Zustand eines dauernden Verlangens zu erhalten.

15. Marquis de Sade, *Philosophy in the Bedroom*, in *The Complete Justine, Philosophy in the Bedroom and Other Writings*, trans. and eds. Richard Seaver and Austryn Wainhouse (New York: Grove Press, 1965), 219–21.

16. Treut describes how the film was made in an interview with Colin Richardson, published as part of the article, "Monika Treut: An Outlaw at Home," in *A Queer Ro-*

mance, 167–85. Treut's dissertation was published as *Die grausame Frau: Zum Frauenbild bei de Sade und Sacher-Masoch* (Basel, Switzerland: Stroemfeld/Roter Stern, 1984).

17. The reason the sex industry is so desolate is because women have so little say in it.

18. This description is not intended as a full discussion of the gender politics of horror films; for a more nuanced development of the topic, see Carol J. Clover, *Men, Women, and Chainsaws. Gender in the Modern Horror Film* (Princeton: Princeton University Press, 1992).

II

Triangulations of Ethnicity, Gender, and Class

5

"It Takes Three to Tango" or Romance Revised: Jutta Brückner's *One Glance and Love Breaks Out*

Barbara Kosta

Someday, he'll come along, the man I love. And he'll be big and strong, the man I love. And when he comes my way, I'll do my best to make him stay. He'll take my hand and smile. I'll understand. And in a little while, he'll take my hand. And though it seems absurd, I know we both won't say a word. Maybe I'll meet him someday. . . . He'll build a little house, just meant for two. From which I'll never roam, who would. Would you? I'm waiting for the man I love.

—Billie Holiday

To write about dance, desire, and gender calls for preparing a stage upon which the intricate relationships of cultural arrangements can perform. In contrast to the free dancing since the late 1960s, that celebrated nonhierarchical, unconfined self-expression, couple dancing prides itself on a series of tightly choreographed patterns, steps, and figures. This type of dancing, I will argue, is anchored in a script of social arrangements that are culturally coded in terms of class, gender, and race. With precision, the dancers adhere to the prescribed patterns which, in their aesthetic formulations, conceal structures of power. Each of their gestures reflect hierarchies and reinstate a relational system rooted in inequalities. Even though the dance may be individually inflected, the dancers remain within the boundaries of a tradition that they aspire to carry out flawlessly.[1] In Jutta Brückner's film *Ein Blick und die Liebe bricht aus* (One Glance and Love Breaks Out, 1985), it is the tango whose power and energy vitalizes these arrangements. The tango provides a backdrop for the exploration of passion and romance as they are negotiated within heterosexual relationships of a Western variant. Moreover, the tango functions as the receptacle for the expectations that arise from the powerful fantasy of romantic love and the longing with which Western culture has infused its subjects. In the tango, the play of desire and seduction is enmeshed in a struggle of sexual conquest and recognition. The rhythms of the tango eulogize these practices, while its songs often lament being deserted, neglected, or abandoned.

In the following discussion of *One Glance and Love Breaks Out,* I intend to choreograph a number of subtexts that converge in the tango's cortes (the halt or interruption of the dancing trajectory at which the tango figures take place). On stage here are the pulsations of romantic love, the longing gaze, and female desire, specifically within a traditional heterosexual context. The film centers around the denigration of female protagonists in the name of a phantasmagoric love that they spend their lives in search of. No matter what gains women have made since the 1960s, Brückner explains, women still seem to be enmeshed in the dream of romantic love that holds them captive. Even despite the sexual revolution of the 1960s and 1970s, patriarchy remains deeply embedded in women and men's psyches and social relations. This makes the women, who move within the theatrical spaces and on the stages Brückner constructs, tragic personae precisely because of their obsession with love and their ravenous desire to be desired. Most significantly, the women figure as accomplices in their own oppression. Their fantasies collaborate with the cultural scripts that disempower them. Thus, the site is the imaginary, in which the longing for romantic love is expressed by gendered subjectivities whose idioms differ even though the figures move to the same music. For as in the tango, the cultural text calls for women to follow, to be the ones who embody desire, while their male counterparts elegantly guide them through the movements.

One Glance and Love Breaks Out opens with ghostlike shadows that perform the tango. The dancers melt into each other to obscure the boundaries between bodies while the social arrangements they perform demand an intricate choreography of gender. These shadows are then fleshed out in the collage of tableaux Brückner constructs to explore women's subordinate positions within the traditional economy of love. The accompanying sound track of wind recalls the uncanny atmosphere of horror films. It is a horror film of sorts, which casts women as masochists with an alleged inventory of lack and men as the progenitors of desire. Under the present system of heterosexual coupling, it is men, who function as the agents of desire, while women embody desire much like the figures that the tango prescribes.

The tango sets the stage in Brückner's film; its throbbing rhythms punctuate the asymmetrical power structures that define traditional heterosexual love relationships. Marta Savigliano describes the sensuous struggle that takes place in the throes of the tango's passion. While the male leads and establishes his identity, the female's identity is continuously destabilized and renegotiated in relationship to his movements. The female is the effect of his motion and his gaze, for it is "she (la Otra)," as Savigliano explains, who "will be dragged into the dance, be led through it, and be held while performing unstable/excessive footwork. Her "instinctive" passion can never be totally subdued, and she passionately resists and is comforted by the male embrace/control. But her passion is aroused by the male desire. He instigates her passionate outburst by that thigh of his, insistently seeking to slip it between her legs throughout the whole musical piece."[2] It is this eroticized ritual that naturalizes gendered roles. For the female, her identity depends on being desired, on being the one to be looked at, instead of the one who actively looks. Savigliano claims, "The female dancer's role is one of legitimizing the need for external intervention and leadership."[3]

The male gaze initiates the dance, much like in the opening scene in the café, when the camera follows the gaze to a female partner. The scratched recording of a tango song with its refrain of *volver*, to come back or return, ironically comments on the persistence of these practices over time. In the voice-over, the singer not only nostalgically mourns the loss of his first love and the impossibility of ever returning to the remembered nest of love, but he simultaneously expresses a fear of engulfment. The underlying tension in the song results from the contradictory desire to surrender, while maintaining boundaries. In Kristeva's words, love erases the borders of the self: "in the rapture of love, the limits of one's own identity vanish, at the same time that the precision of reference and meaning becomes blurred in love's discourse."[4] The blending of self with other hints at a complex relationship between the willingness to relinquish oneself and the wish to fulfill individual needs. Brückner observes: "In romantic love, women always want physicality and closeness and what is often understood as physical passion. For men, romantic love calls for distance."[5] According to Brückner the perpetual tug-of-war between the desire for proximity and the fear of engulfment enacted in heterosexual love relationships is, all too often, gender specific. The pull between these two points manifests a struggle for control and power. This struggle, as I will show, reflects the dynamics of the early phases of identity formation which lays the emotional foundation for future love relationships and provides a memory of phantasmatic love. The encounter with the first love object (first sight of the love object) prepares the ground for the terms of desire in the future. In the traditional nuclear family setting, the first love object to fall within the visual field is the mother with the father soon to follow.

The film's title, *One Glance and Love Breaks Out*, playfully recalls the saying of love at first sight. In this one moment of visual encounter, love and desire are allegedly unleashed. It is the promise of the combined fulfillment of narcissistic as well as complex ideological wishes that seduce the eye. Brückner accurately describes the mechanisms at stake: "What allegedly appears 'at first sight' is a combination of emotion, sex, and a bourgeois desire for marital security."[6] It is through vision that the wild fantasy of love begins. The power of fantasy must not be underestimated in this equation, for fantasy is at the center of beliefs, perceptions, and actions; it acts as an organizing force both within psychic life and within a variety of cultural forms. Unconscious wishes, and the fantasy they engender, are as immutable a force in our lives as any material circumstance. In Brückner's film, fantasy is represented through the mise-en-scène of large, vacant rooms derealized with mirrors that emphasize the imaginary quality of the spaces in which the various vignettes take place. The perspective is that of the female protagonists, who project the fantasies that shape their emotional life onto the surface of men who embody their desire. Hence, it is the gaze that initiates romance, or at least the fiction of romance. At the same time, the title's perversion of the saying Love at First Sight suggests that romantic love is like a disease that afflicts its participants.

Brückner investigates the emotional returns that fuel women's willingness to lock in an embrace with their partners, despite their subordination within the configuration of traditional romances. The question of women's willingness to surrender themselves in the name of love, in fact, preoccupies many of Brückner's films that analyze the structures of emotion and especially the politics of love as they currently exist. Such film titles as *A Thoroughly Neglected Girl* (1977), *Colossal Love* (1983–91), and *Do You Love Brecht?* (1993) unequivocally signal Brückner's interest in questions of identity and love, and in the emotional transactions that leave women powerless. *A Thoroughly Neglected Girl* features a young woman who realizes a need for change but who dreams of a "prince" to rescue her from the monotony of her daily life; in *Colossal Love*, the figure Rahel Varnhagen struggles with her intense desire for love and recognition; in *Do You Love Brecht?* the protagonist Margarethe Steffin, the lover and colleague of Bertolt Brecht, is portrayed as his caretaker who surrenders to Brecht's "genius," despite her own creativity and literary talent. *One Glance and Love Breaks Out* investigates the obsessive pursuit of love unmindful of the cost to women themselves. In this film, Brückner recounts "the story of love as it is conveyed to us by our culture, and as it is written onto the bodies of women. . . . They are stories of remembrance, expectation, projections, images and the physical reactions to them, and a restless wandering through empty spaces in search of something. This something has to do with identity, with their own identities, which they still seek in the mirror of the male gaze."[7] According to Brückner, her litany of mute images symbolically represents the classic stages of a traditional woman's life: courtship, marriage, infidelity, and abandonment. The film includes scenes of a bride on her wedding night who seems to be raped by her husband; of a housewife poised at a sewing machine, frenetically sewing, while her husband peruses a pornographic magazine; of a man who smugly watches as two women grovel at his feet vying for his attention only to see him turn to a third woman, a servant; and of women who eat or clean to compensate for their frustration and emotional pain, in addition to filling the vacuum of their unfulfilled fantasies. Nurtured on the narratives of ecstatic love, the women are left pining for romantic love and for the actualization of the figments of their imagination.

At the beginning, a solitary woman reflectively sifts through an array of photographs strewn about her on the floor. As she walks about the wreckage of romance and gazes upon its memorabilia, a female voice-over recites a letter to love. The letter reveals a wish for identity, sexual experience, and merging with the love object, all of which are the promise of romantic intimacy. Interspersed throughout the following montage of filmic images, the epistolary to love progressively turns from a beckoning to love to a rejection of its deceptive promises and a bidding farewell. The letter begins:

> Love, you sneering angel, look at me. Show me who I am. Deliver me from the loneliness of my body.[8]

The photographs, the shards of memory, imply that this figure, too, participated in amorous fantasies. Just like the tango singer who croons *volver* on the accompanying sound track, the woman, too, seems to have fed off the memory of a first love and has longed for its return. Scattered among the photographs that she reviews is one of a wedding. The image comes to life with newlyweds who pose before a mirror, pleasurably constructing themselves for their own as well as for the public gaze. The happy event turns sour when the groom begins to manhandle the bride. Under his touch, she transforms into a prop that endures the sexual advances sanctified by their union. The nondiegetic sound of tearing and of glass breaking, repeated throughout the film, comments on the shattering of the bride's illusions. Once in their "Himmelbett," a canopied nuptial bed whose fabric resembles clouds, the groom fulfills his sexual needs while the bride is sacrificed on the altar of her dreams. To degrade her and to incite his arousal, the groom calls her La Puta. Virility depends on imagining the bride as a prostitute, whose body is coded as pure sexuality, in contrast to the dichotomous (m)other. Tango music animates the scene while the female voice-over in the letter to love intimates the hidden passion that remains unannounced: "I adorned myself for you. There are gulfs of desire between these blood red lips that I dare not think about." The articulation of female desire remains contained within the realm of fantasy, and the contract she imagines to have entered remains unhonored.

Although the articulation of women's desire hardly gains center stage in Brückner's film (except for frustrated desire), it is manifested in the disembodied female voice-over and reveals itself, if only fleetingly, in images that counterpoise the representation of women as impassive objects of sexual encounters. For instance, the same figure that portrayed the bride observes herself, this time alone, in a mirror. Seductively dressed, she douses herself wildly with champagne. This sensual fantasy, accompanied by a sound track of waves and ocean, contradicts the representation of the mute and violated body of the previous scene. In another scene, a festively dressed woman sits alone on the floor between two place settings. Seemingly abandoned, she tenderly kisses her hand and arm. These scenes suggest autoeroticism as an outlet for female desire while exhibiting the longing for their version of love.

The notion of identity, love, and female masochism are held in close proximity in *One Glance and Love Breaks Out*. Scene upon scene displays aspects of female masochism in which pleasure and anguish stem from the attainment of, and longing for, recognition. The topic of female masochism has only recently gained the critical attention needed to dispel long-held beliefs of female masochism as an innate reflex of femininity and are thus normative. Interpretations of late have moved to an understanding of masochism as a manifestation of cultural training, while ascribing to female masochism its rightful status as perversion and pathology. In other words, women are taught masochism through social, economical, and cultural designs. Sandra Lee Bartky proposes: "Feminine masochism, like femininity in general, is an economical way of embedding women in patriarchy through the mechanism of desire."[9] In *One Glance and Love Breaks Out*, Brückner challenges the assumptions that tend to naturalize women's masochistic impulse. By de-eroticizing the sexual encounter, she tears away the veil that hides the internalized forms of oppression that turn women into social actors who are complicit in the structures that disadvantage them.[10]

There have been a number of contemporary readings of female masochism that cite its occurrence and investigate its origins. To explain the masochistic tendencies that Brückner investigates in her film and that have come to be associated with femininity, I will draw upon Jessica Benjamin's provocative study entitled *The Bonds of Love: Psychoanalysis, Feminism, and the Problem of Domination*. In her study, Benjamin outlines a psychogram of desire based on recognition and on a strict division in the psychic development of male and female children largely influenced by the relationship to the mother. Using object relations theory as her framework that essentially is based on white, middle-class European family structures, Benjamin outlines the process of gender-specific differentiation and sees a disposition cultivated in girls toward blurring subject boundaries, because they often are denied the experience of separation. In Benjamin's own phrasing: "The girl requires no shift away from her mother [like the male child]. This makes her identity less problematic, but it is a disadvantage in that she possesses no obvious way of disidentifying from her mother, no hallmark of separateness. The feminine tendency, therefore, is not to emphasize but to underplay independence."[11] She sees in this tendency toward merging and relinquishing independence, a "fertile ground for submission."[12] In other words, the relationship to the mother, who does not encourage separation, results in a fatal attachment for the daughter. Benjamin speaks of a pervasive willingness in women to yield agency and to deny the self precisely because they paradigmatically lack the possibility of exploring the boundaries beyond the mother. Female masochism, consequently, is linked closely to the denial of women's autonomy, the inhibition of separation in girls as well as of an understanding of themselves as active subjects.

Women's lack of agency, Benjamin explains, results in an inclination in women to fantasize an "'ideal love'—a love in which the woman submits to and adores another who is what she cannot be."[13] Benjamin persuasively outlines the complex cultural training that sparks the need to produce an idealized figure. She sees it rooted in the relationship of the child to the all-powerful mother, who threatens to smother the female child and to discourage separation. Within the mother-father-child dyad, the ideal typically is the father who represents a sphere outside of maternal rule. In contrast to the Freudian paradigm of female lack and subsequent penis envy, the phallus provides escape from maternal power and becomes a symbol of disconnection in a girl's efforts to individuate. Yet, mobility is restricted within this traditional triad whose tangos are strictly plotted. For the girl, the father remains inaccessible for identification, since it would mean a disruption of traditional gender boundaries, not to mention a potential threat to male identity. "Thus the girls are confronted," Benjamin notes, "more directly by the difficulty of separating from mother and their own helplessness. Unprotected by the phallic sign of gender difference, unsupported by an alternate relationship, they relinquish their entitlement to desire."[14] A return to the mother leaves the girl to identify with a lack of agency; it means to be led through the tango's figures and to perform the sentadas that land women in the lap of patriarchy.[15] The longing for adventure outside of the realm of the engulfing mother is displaced onto the significant male in the girl's life or onto the "missing father" who stands for desire. Evolving from this triangular configuration then, the notion of an ideal love emerges from the desire to have agency, even though it is by proxy, and to experience the fulfillment of desire. The male thus becomes a phantasm or ideal.

Brückner astutely explores these structures in her cinematic exposé of female masochism. The ideal man, dressed in a tuxedo and prominently set off from the men in gray suits, periodically appears as a mirror image upon which women project their needs and desires. He stands for the phantasm of ideal love, "the missing father," who is sought obsessively, but who remains unattainable. When a well-to-do woman peeks through the blinds to gaze upon the "ideal" man, another woman enters the reflection and grovels at his feet. The woman who submits represents the masochistic impulse that the ideal demands. Frustrated by the inaccessibility of her ideal love object, the gazing woman commands her maid to clean the kitchen—to wash away desire while exercising power over a person of the lower class. It is the maid, a direct symbol of subservience, who is most violated in Brückner's exploration of love relationships and who bears the greatest burden of its inequalities.[16]

Even though the man in the tuxedo functions as the ultimate projection, the men dressed in gray are also sketched by patriarchy. They wield their power through their commanding gaze and through their sexual prowess. Within the film's logic, they serve to demonstrate the asymmetry of power in the relationship between men and women and to emphasize the vast disparity between the so-called reality of interpersonal relationships and the expectations attached to them. For the women, these men represent the sites at which the tale of romance is to take place. It is the women, as Brückner notes, who "fasten their silent and boundless longing for romance on the men, as if they were coat stands."[17] To pronounce the obsessive search for the ideal, a group of women is shown journeying through the warehouse of fantasies, visually alluded to by empty rooms and mirrors. Even though their frantic pace appears purposeful, they remain directionless in their pursuit of the unobtainable. They only pause to perch themselves like mannequins on a rooftop patio while the men dressed in gray stroll about and intently gaze upon the women who have adorned themselves to arouse the consumer's desire. The women do not return the gaze, but they direct it by constructing themselves to appeal and surrender to the feasting eye. The power relationship implied in this configuration lays the groundwork for masochistic tendencies whose pleasure lies in submission to an idealized figure. It stems from the desire to be recognized by someone who represents power, and within traditional gender arrangements, who stands for the possibility of slipping into a subject position by association. While the women delight in their desirability, their subjectivity, however, merges with male subjectivities that women absorb as their own. The internalization of the gaze reminds one of Foucault's description of the workings of the panopticon in which the prisoners themselves identify with the surveillant gaze of the guard.[18]

As Brückner shows in her film, women construct themselves to spark male desire and surrender themselves in hopes of having their images of romantic love fulfilled. The repertoire is all too familiar and only a few cultural representations offer a counterimage. Here too, the camera denies the viewer an alternative image. Instead it outrightly exposes the traditional interplay of gendered love relationships in order that they may deconstruct themselves. Thus, Brückner rids masochism of its potential pleasures, which are derived from recognition, and thereby challenges the legitimacy of such forms of desire, which in the scheme of the film, sustain the status quo, as opposed to subverting convention.[19] Brückner's women endure men's advances, the penetration of their bodies, and abandonment; they detach themselves inwardly from the sexual act yet continue to hold onto a dream. Their dispassion speaks through the muteness of their bodies. In the stairwell of the subway station, a girl stands patiently while a man has sex with her. Her thoughts of "I am a little whore," disclosed in a voice-over, reproduce the internalized conscience of patriarchy that narrowly casts women as virgins or whores. Her detachment undermines the notion of "the feminine taste for fantasies of victimization," which Bartky notes, "is assumed on virtually every page of the large pulp fiction literature produced specifically for women."[20] The lack of visible pleasure suggests submission in the name of the desire for love that becomes entangled with the fantasy of the penetration of boundaries, of violation, that is, the rapture of love. In a similar scenario, a young woman screams out "*te quiero*" (I love you) which seems to assault the man who consequently retreats from the opportunity for sex. In contrast to the men who appear in the film, the women are unable to translate their own fantasies into tangible experience.

Brückner calls attention to the civil institutions that organize relationships, encode gender assignments, and foster masochism in women. Among these institutions religion plays a prominent role in the film (given that the film was produced in Argentina, the iconography suggests Catholicism). Footage of a procession of girls who appear as miniature brides in their communion dresses and who carry candles to the altar conjures up associations with sacrifice; surrender; the suppression of female sexuality; the exclusive sanctification of monogamous, heterosexual relationships; and the glorification of virginity and the desexualized mother. To represent the continuity of such traditions over time, the wandering group of women join in the procession. Although these values may seem out of step with the progress made in the wake of feminism, they still wield their power within most of Western culture and widely influence cultural and social practices.

The structures of emotion, in fact, have changed little since the women's movement, Brückner contends. This further explains why her finely crafted images in *One Glance and Love Breaks Out* relentlessly replay the ways in which women are situated within the Western paradigm of love relationships. The film's repetition of scenes, in which traditional gender relationships are played out in various settings, self-reflexively reenacts the cultural script. The women's relationship to the men hardly changes; this frustrates a viewer's wish for narrative progression. Instead, the spectator bears witness to the persistence of masochistic subordination without the sense of pleasure or of power that a masochist may derive. It is the repetition of these structures that seal women's secondary status.

Even though the complex structures of hegemony seem impenetrable at times, Brückner does offer a glimmer of hope for a change in the social construction of women's position. Toward the end of the film, the woman, who was alone at the beginning and who initiated the letter to love, intervenes in the cycle of female submission integral to the film's structure. Punctuated by the rhythms of the tango, she resists the advances of a man dressed in gray who enters her sphere and who expects her to acquiesce to his desire. She struggles against his advances and eventually walks out on him. Her defiance does not resemble the seductive resistance of the tango, but rather a refusal to comply with the structures plotted in its steps. Rejected by the solitary woman and unable to maintain erotic domination, the man in gray regresses into a fetal position. In the following scene, he is held by a mother (the corroborator of male omnipotence) in a parody of the Pietà.

In the epistle to love that underscores the scene of struggle, the female voice articulates the wish to exorcise the parasitic demands of love and to escape its humiliations: "I am expelling you from my body, homeless beggar. I want to remain alone and to lock my windows and doors so that I cannot hear your howling. I do not want to see my disgrace, and I no longer want to taste the saliva of your kisses." Individual images of what was once the group of women who paraded through the film fade in and out. They pause in their pursuit of love and are implicated in the message of the voice-over. This scene is soon followed by the image of a faceless woman whose head and face are bandaged and who is seen attempting to walk. Uncertain and afraid, she cautiously proceeds into unknown territories. This image evokes the title of Brückner's earlier film, *Laufen lernen* (Learning to Walk, 1980) in which a housewife attempts to change her life after seventeen years of marriage. In *One Glance and Love Breaks Out*, the mummified woman is juxtaposed with the brigade of women who pass through the room, oblivious of the mummified woman's travail. At the end, the roaming women sit outside in the drizzling rain overlooking a courtyard, disheveled and exhausted from their pursuit of love. Their journey is over once they exit from the realm of the imaginary, the house in which the hallucination has taken place. "They [the women] are looking down," Brückner describes this scene, "into a courtyard that almost looks like a prison yard, and they see people who are still dancing the tango. But the music is percussion now, and the dance steps no longer fit the music. This is how I see the concept of love that we have today. We continue to go through the motions that have no basis anymore."[21] With the rhythms of the tango changed, the protagonists can no longer effectively follow the patterns mapped out in the tango. Their steps are in tension with the music that they will not be able to perform according to tradition. The change, however, seems so subtle that only few will be able to recognize the challenge.

Overall, Brückner denies her viewers a happy ending and a narrative resolution befitting the conventional structures of story telling. Instead, the gaze moves full circle and it returns (*volver*) to the site of the tango. In the courtyard of a tenement building, men and women perform the tango. They are the ones who originally cast the shadows that were seen in the first shots. Once again, each person dances the steps to precision and plays his or her role with fatalistic dignity. The transfer into a documentary mode serves to translates the imaginary into the realm of daily life.

The last image of the two men dancing returns the tango to the site of its origin, to patriarchy and to its culture of displayed virility that secures the proper place of the male in the configuration of desire and sexuality. Women are dismissed from the scene altogether. The men who dance together also reflect the narcissism of the tango for men, intimated by the use of mirrors. It marks a space in which the men can produce themselves to publicly solidify their identities. Traditionally, the men of the lower classes danced with each other because women did not have access to the streets and bars and the social spaces that belonged to men.[22]

What remains open in *One Glance and Love Breaks Out* is the cultural specificity of the tango. Even though tango dancers metaphorically glide over cultural borders, the tango, as well as the visuals, remain rooted in Argentina, where Brückner, along with a crew of actors and cameramen, made the film. The structures portrayed in the film could be read as specific to the geography of origin that could unwittingly reinforce stereotypes and cause a dismissal of the wider implications of the tango's popularization. Indeed, the tango has become a cultural icon that has crossed numerous borders, east and west, and has been colonized by its participants and admirers. Its international audiences use its rhythms overwhelmingly to dream about romantic love and to watch and revel in the erotic negotiation of power. The tango serves to unfold the structures that pervade Western culture, nuanced differently within various settings.[23]

As the dance of passion, it is important to note that the tango relies not only on the gaze of its performers but also on that of the outside. In fact, it is predominately the gaze of patriarchy that determines the relationship between genders. As Marta E. Savigliano eloquently observes,

> It actually takes three to tango: a male to master the dance and confess his sorrows; a female to seduce, resist seduction, and be seduced; and a gaze to watch these occurrences. The male/female couple performs the ritual, and the gaze constitutes the spectacle. Two performers, but three participants, make a tango. However, the gaze is not aloof and static; rather, it is expectant, engaged in that particular detachment that creators have toward the objects of their imagination.[24]

The gaze, informed by ideology and guided by the narrative of romance and immense longing, imposes itself upon the tango's tensions. In contrast to many films in which the viewer is able to participate in a dreamlike romantic intimacy, the camera in *One Glance and Love Breaks Out* denies the spectator entrance into an illusion. The gaze here is critical; the visuals brush against the grain of the tango's beats. As the film title suggests, love will not be aroused in the gaze of her camera. On the contrary, the camera's gaze interrupts the dance and probes the mechanisms that sustain a culture of abuse in the name of love.

Notes

1. Within a German context, it may be the waltz that was first danced by nobility and then later by the upper middle class, until the middle and even lower middle class began to send its sons and daughters to the Tanzschule.

2. Marta E. Savigliano, *Tango and the Political Economy of Passion* (Boulder, Colo.: Westview Press, 1995), 78.

3. Ibid., 80.

4. Julia Kristeva, *Tales of Love*, trans. Leon S. Roudiez (New York: Columbia University Press, 1987), 2.

5. Jutta Brückner, interview with Barbara Kosta and Lilli Limonius, *Berliner Filmfest Journal*, 1986, "Die Frauen klagen in der romantischen Liebe immer Körperlichkeit an und Nähe, und das, was man unter körperliche Leidenschaft verstehen kann. Für Männer beruft die romantische Liebe gerade auf Distanz."

6. Ibid., 363.

7. Brückner, interview with Barbara Kosta and Richard W. McCormick, *Signs* 21, no. 2 (winter 1996): 362.

8. All quotes are taken directly from the film, *One Glance and Love Breaks Out* (1986). All translations are my own.

9. Sandra Lee Bartky, *Femininity and Domination: Studies in the Phenomenology of Oppression* (New York: Routledge, 1990), 51.

10. Bartky mentions an interesting aspect that is missing from Brückner's film, namely that the relationship between erotic domination and sexual subordination may offer women some form of excitement. She writes: "Surely women's acceptance of domination by men cannot be entirely independent of the fact that for many women, dominance in men is exciting" (ibid.).

11. Jessica Benjamin, *The Bonds of Love: Psychoanalysis, Feminism, and the Problem of Domination* (New York: Pantheon, 1988), 78. For an excellent discussion of literature's construction of female masochism, see Michelle A. Massé, *In the Name of Love: Women, Masochism, and the Gothic* (Ithaca, N.Y., Cornell University Press, 1992).

12. Ibid., 79.

13. Ibid., 86.

14. Ibid., 109.

15. The sentada is a tango figure in which the female dancer sits with her legs crossed on her partner's thigh.

16. She is the only one in the narrative to have an abortion. A man in gray defers to her (the body that serves) while the women of the middle class fight for his attention. Thus, it seems that the sexual politics mapped out in the film are defined by an ideology that shapes the middle class. Even though the beliefs and longings spill over into other classes, its steps, poses, and figures are different, much like in the tango whose variations are class-bound. In other words, the ideal image, the object of desire, and the "love" ignited by the glance has various contours.

17. Brückner interview, *Signs*, 363.

18. Michel Foucault, "The Eye of Power: A Conversation with Jean-Pierre Barou and Michelle Perrot," in *Power/Knowledge: Selected Interviews and Other Writings*, ed. Colin Gordon (New York: Pantheon, 1972), 146–65.

19. Other interpretations of female masochism highlight its subversive potential, particularly when masochism is staged and masqueraded. Masochism can wield its own power over those to whom the masochist surrenders.

20. Bartky, *Femininity and Domination*, 46.

21. Brückner interview, *Signs*, 363.

22. See Savigliano, *Tango and the Political Economy of Passion*, 146–47.

23. Even though I have looked at the tango as a dance that reenforces traditional gender roles, it may also serve to subvert them and even to challenge bourgeois patriarchal culture. In *Some Like It Hot* (1959), the Austrian émigré Billy Wilder stages the potential for subversion when Jack Lemmon (Daphne) dressed as a woman with a rose in his mouth dances the tango with a slight man a head shorter. Momentarily forgetting her role in the dance, Daphne's partner reprimands her: "Daphne, you're leading again!" This scene is intercut with a "true" heterosexual relationship between Tony Curtis and Marilyn Monroe.

24. Savigliano, *Tango and the Political Economy of Passion*, 74.

6

Interview with Jutta Brückner:
Feminist Filmmaking in Germany Today

Ingeborg von Zadow

Jutta Brückner is the director of the Filminstitut Hochschule der Künste in Berlin. She has been making films since 1975, and is recognized as a successful director in the national and international film world.

In the early 1970s, Brückner began working with some of the people who founded the New German Cinema—among them Alexander Kluge and Volker Schlöndorff. Initially influenced by the auteur approach, Brückner later began to make her own kind of essay film, which explored individual and group experiences, and that examined questions of autobiography and film. Taking themes that she found in her own, her relatives', and her friends' lives, she began portraying conflicts that were specific to her generation of women. After her first film, *Tue Recht und scheue Niemand* (1975), which is composed entirely of filmed photographs, Brückner made two essay films, *Ein ganz und gar verwahrlostes Mädchen* (1977), and *Hungerjahre in einem reichen Land* (1979), which were set in realistic situations. She then began to concentrate on the development of a different aesthetic approach relating to questions of time, space, and narrative. Realizing that "we all live in many different spaces at the same time" she began altering her film style to combine realistic with nonrealistic images. Films such as *Ein Blick und die Liebe bricht aus* (1985), *Kolossale Liebe* (1983–91), or *Lieben Sie Brecht?* (1993) confront her audience with various, often contradictory images, to which her imagination, her experience, and her thorough control of old and new film techniques have led her.

Brückner never seems to get tired of exploring new aspects of life. It is the constant, almost restless search within herself and history, within societal structures and human interactions that fascinates the listener. As she transposes this search into film it does more than keep her alert and open for the things to come.

This interview, held in July 1995 in the Filminstitut der Hochschule der Künste in Berlin, strives to give an insight into her work and personality. It was held for the most part in English; I translated short passages from German later.

Zadow. Why did you start making films?

Brückner. From the very beginning I saw that filmmaking would help me to get out of the dead end I was stuck in with my writing. I saw that films allowed me to do what I needed most: to reinvent, to refigure myself, not only conceptually but also as a physical body. Filmmaking is the only art that permits you to do that. The bodily image of myself had been destroyed in the course of my youth, which I depicted in *Hungerjahre in einem reichen Land.* My adolescence wasn't very special; in fact it was very ordinary. Significant for me was the fact that I lost my words. When you lose your words it means that you have lost your body. They go together. So I had to reinvent myself as a body. I could not do that through writing.

Zadow. Do you think that many women-filmmakers of your generation had similar reasons to start making films?

Brückner. No, I think there were many different starting points. We had in common what we had learned from the feminist movement: that we had desires and longings, goals to achieve in life. We wanted our lives to be different from what they had been. Nearly all of those who belonged to my generation of feminist filmmakers in West Germany started making films after they were thirty years old. They were not very young and not students anymore.

I think it was the feminist movement with all its demands that pushed us to open ourselves to an art that is made for a large audience. We got the power to do this and also the questions, the ideas from the feminist movement. We hadn't dared to do this before, because of a lack of self-confidence. We thought that the problems we had in our lives were private ones. We thought we were isolated. We then discovered that our problems were social and historical. From the feminist movement we also got the power to demand the means, the money, television slots, positions in the filmmaking industry, and runs in the cinemas. We declared that we had the right to be there and that what we wanted to show was important.

Zadow. How do you see the situation of new women-filmmakers in Germany now? A feeling of collectivity like you had when you started twenty-five years ago doesn't exist in that form anymore. Have the new women-filmmakers been able to benefit from your work and from the feminist movement?

Brückner. Yes, they have. It is now generally accepted that women can make films even if it is not the norm as yet.

Young women now could benefit more from what we did but every generation has to fight its mothers and fathers. We are the "mothers" now. What we did is regarded as old-fashioned. I don't think it is.

We made films about the difficulties of being an "emancipated" woman in this still very patriarchal society. The new generation of women does not find a lot of things dear to them in our films. Whereas we talked about breaking out of normality for the sake of an inner and outer freedom, they want to have that freedom as part of their normal lives. They want to show that it is normal to have a career as a woman and nevertheless a life that includes men and children.

Zadow. Are you talking about young women-filmmakers now or about young women in general?

Brückner. Both. Young women want filmmaking to be a job, like other jobs. I think there is a split. Women at the university who learn feminist film theory are very dependent on what their theoretical mothers have worked out. They try to build their own research on existing studies and texts. The split between the generations is not as profound there.

In filmmaking there is a considerable rejection of past achievements. Feminist film practice has been influenced largely by German women. We had so many opportunities compared to women in other countries to develop a style of feminist filmmaking. The new West German auteurs' films are very distinctive, so this is true of the feminist branch as well. Women's filmmaking defines itself not only against what their "mothers" did, but also against what German "mothers" did.

Young women want to do something else now. The period of West German feminist filmmaking, as a period of auteurist filmmaking is very clearly over now. That does not mean that the women who began working during this time have stopped. I work; others do. But we or those of my generation are all developing in very individual ways now.

Zadow. Is it possible to say in what direction the new German women-filmmakers are going?

Brückner. There is a trend toward comedies. The German mainstream right now makes what we call Beziehungskomödien (comedies about relationships) In comedies the difficulties of life are obscured by the mechanism of misunderstanding. This is the way young women now convey their feelings about being cheated in or by life. Other women try to continue a more feminist way of filmmaking by continuing to work with experimental films. The kind of auteurs' filmmaking that we, the feminist women of the first generation did, is no longer possible. They are not funded anymore. There has been a big shift in film-funding since at least 1983.

Zadow. Let's switch gears a bit now. I'm interested in finding out how you work. How you deal with actors. In your film *Ein Blick und die Liebe bricht aus* you portray both men and women. Many of the men are portrayed in a very negative way. I sometimes got very angry at them while I was watching the film. On one hand you are the director who has a working relationship with these actors and you are the author who creates the scenes. On the other hand, you are a woman watching these men do what they do. How did you deal with this conflict?

Brückner. It was actually very difficult at that time. It was only possible because I made this film in Argentina at a moment when Argentina opened to the world after the dictatorship around 1983–84. My presence and what I wanted to do was something rather new. Not only for the men, but also for the women. Since people in Argentina were—and still are—very polite, and they were curious to see what they had missed throughout these years of dictatorship.

It went fine for a while. They were very patient. They watched and collaborated. I had no problem directing the male actors. But then, after some time, they got a little angry with me. They didn't show it really, but a woman on the set told me that one of the young men had said "What does she think, she just comes here and she tells stories about us. I think she needs"—and this is a very crude expression—"a good fuck." It was a very typical macho way of resisting. I didn't really feel it on the set though.

They asked me what image I had of men. I answered that that is of no importance for the film. I told them that this film is not about men; it is about women. I said to them, "You are only there as hooks on which the women hang their feelings. You are not in this film as individuals. Look at what you are wearing. You wear these gray suits and these red ties; you are just hooks, nothing else." They accepted it, somewhat reluctantly, but they accepted it nevertheless.

It was a little more complicated with the women, because the women really had to play roles. I had to explain to them that they should be individuals and stereotypes at the same time. This is somewhat hard to understand and maybe they only understood it because their roles had no lines. It would not have been possible if they had had text. Since they had no text, they had to exaggerate; they couldn't be nuanced and differentiated. Their roles were like wood carvings, just showing the outlines.

Zadow. In very simple situations?

Brückner. Yes, just very basic human reactions. The film is composed of seven different stories. I wanted to show the basic feeling of being a bride; of being a married woman in an unhappy marriage; of being cheated on by your husband; of being alone with a dream man and then seeing that there is another woman kneeling beside him; of being "on the market" and seeing all the others, being alone; of longing for the dream man and meanwhile being raped by four other men; of having an abortion; and of being a very young girl who thinks love is just like having a glass of water, and who allows a man to use her. The last situation is about leaving. About throwing dirty water from a bucket into a man's face and walking away. The film is like a whole life, seven situations come together. Seven very basic situations. To be able to show that, I used very slow and very stylized movements; I did not allow natural movements; that would not have worked. It had to be like in a dream or in a dance. Both are abstractions of reality, or condensed reality. I also used nonrealistic settings, non-realistic light, nonrealistic space, and many mirrors.

Zadow. This brings me to my next question. You use mirrors in all of your films. They seem to be very important for your work. How did your use of this device start?

Brückner. It started in the first version of my film *Kolossale Liebe* because I needed it. This film was shot in one room, in a studio. So I said, we will use at least three mirrors, so we can get more interesting shots in this one room. I then learned that working with mirrors and especially with mirrors in one room, is very complicated. But it can lead to fine pictures and I liked it very much.

Zadow. How did your use of mirrors change over the years?

Brückner. This is a very interesting question. You are the first one really to ask it. I started using mirrors to improve my films. I learned that the better picture for me is also the more real picture. Making visible what is normally regarded as an invisible inner reality. Not more realistic but more real. All my films revolve around the question of identity. The tool that provides us with an impression of our identity is the mirror. It is the essential tool for reflecting the identity of a person. Using these mirrors in the first version of *Kolossale Liebe* showed me that my films, in which I want to reveal something about identity, should depend more on mirrors. I knew that when I went to Argentina. I then met Marcello Lamorino, a very young cameraman. I was quite surprised when he said to me, "If you experiment, I'll experiment, too—I will use mirrors and colored light and smoke." I said, "OK, do it, we are in a workshop." I hadn't planned to make a film when I went to Argentina. It was initially a workshop situation. I was stunned when I saw the results. I discovered that I had met the very cameraman, the very operator I needed, because he used mirrors in an unconventional way. He made a real room into an unreal one. This was exactly what I needed. He helped me to discover what I really wanted to express. He helped me to find the real subject of this film, which is not these seven love stories but the search for one's own identity through love.

Zadow. In other words *Ein Blick und die Liebe bricht aus* was the first time when you, or the cameraman and you, used mirrors to convert a real space into a nonreal space.

Brückner. Yes. And it was essential for everything I now do. The people in my films live as much in a real space as in an unreal one. They live their lives in a very specific moment and at the same time they live in their thoughts. We all live in many different spaces at the same time. Not only in one. Remembrance is only one of the different spaces in which we can live. Projections, wishes, and hopes are other spaces in which we can live.

Zadow. Your work with mirrors was the first visual step into this unreal world. You are now working on a project to develop new pictures. You have a new theory and innovative technologies. Is the next step coming up?

Brückner. I have already taken it. After my experience with the mirrors in *Ein Blick und die Liebe bricht aus*, I got a lot of practice with video postproduction. You can see it in *Kolossale Liebe*. I have two main approaches to finding nonreal worlds, and I now have all my tools ready—the real ones and the nonreal ones. I will combine them in my next films.

Zadow. What would a dramaturgy that uses these new technological possibilities look like? Does every filmmaker have to find her own or is it possible to find one that is generally valid, like the Greeks developed in ancient theater?

Brückner. That is very difficult to talk about. You can see the first step of what is now possible in some Hollywood films. But they concentrate on genre films, for example, science fiction and fantasy films and then it is easy. You just use techniques like morphing. To show nonreal people in nonreal worlds. But it would be important to use these techniques to show all the levels of reality that come together in any single moment of a person's life.

Zadow. It is probably very good for a filmmaker to have all these possibilities now, but how do you choose?

Brückner. It's very difficult. We have the technical capabilities now, but we lack an understanding as to what they can accomplish in the portrayal of individuals and in story telling. Before these techniques were developed it was pretty simple. The camera was an instrument that served to depict real objects, and objects gained an added significance through montage. All films were realistic, but now you can and must decide which images should be juxtaposed to the realistic ones, and what the unrealistic ones look like. This decision is made only after earnest reflection about aesthetic and philosophical principles.

Zadow. You said, "Women have to take action now, so that the split between body and soul won't be inscribed once again within the new technology in the split between picture and word." Is this the chance for a film language for women?

Brückner. Of course there is not simply one female aesthetic or film language. The various aesthetic solutions are always individual. But I do think that the new technology opens tremendous opportunities for women and for their creativity. For one thing, they dislodge frozen power-relations that are inherent in the process of creating images; power games are still played in this area. Sometimes a female director can work well on the set, but often she cannot, especially when she wants to do something out of the ordinary. Those women who want to go beyond simply proving that they know the rules of the film business, still have a hard time getting others to work with them in supportive and creative ways. In addition, women facilitate the depiction of simultaneous realities, in which they move much more often than men do.

Zadow. These new possibilities in filmmaking depend a lot on machines. Will the main impulse for the films of the future come from machines? How important will actors be?

Brückner. Actors have been very important in the past and they will be very important in the future. Because they are human. Their roles will not really diminish. But the film will not only depend on actors to create a special emotional climate and to tell something about psychological processes.

Zadow. How important are words or the text now that you have these new visual possibilities of filmmaking? Will the picture become more important?

Brückner. No, I don't think so. The distinctions between what used to be a fiction film and what used to be a documentary film or an essay film are much more fluid than they were before. We are also going back to old techniques. A lot of the things that you can do now with little effort because of modern machines were also possible with the camera before but they required a lot of energy and time.

Zadow. That means that the old techniques, like your use of photos, will stay?

Brückner. Oh yes. They work. My aesthetic approach in its deepest sense is the combination of new and old media. Images of actors and images in which actors don't play any role any longer. Real world and nonreal world.

Zadow. What fascinates you about photos?

Brückner. First of all they are historical moments. They concentrate on one specific historical moment and I'm fascinated by that. It's not just that it was very important for me in my first film. Photos are something wonderful. They capture the moment between two heartbeats. It's like holding your breath before continuing to breathe. The moment when you hold your breath you realize that time is passing.

Zadow. How would you describe yourself as a director? The script you wrote for *Lieben Sie Brecht* is very different from the finished film. There are changes; many things were added. A lot of the work on the script must have happened in rehearsal.

Brückner. My way of filmmaking has meanwhile become very complex. I now write a detailed script when I make a feature film. I didn't do that during *Lieben Sie Brecht*. I was experimenting during that shoot.

Zadow. Do you mean "detailed" also in the delineation of the image?

Brückner. Yes. I have to do that now. When you work with a rather large amount of money that some institution gives you, you have to be very precise. You have to know exactly what you are doing. I still make changes on my way from the script to the film, though. If I find out that one of my fictional images should change after the script is finished it is probably a result of a lot of things that happened during the shooting, on the set, with the actors. But I believe that the meaning will not change from what I originally wrote in the script. Just maybe the way I want to express it.

Zadow. For your new Brecht project you are working with a professional producer that is something you haven't done before. So now you write the script, you show it to him, and he reads it. Doesn't he say—wait a minute, what's this—

Brückner. Oh yes, he does.

Zadow. What happens when your opinions clash?

Brückner. This is a very difficult situation. But it is so much better to work together with someone who has professional experience in filmmaking than to be left alone as a screenwriter and to not really know whether what you have written and want to show is clear or not.

Zadow. Is this your first film with such a detailed script?

Brückner. No. Another one that had a very detailed script was *Hungerjahre in einem reichen Land*, my first feature film. If I had shot everything that was written in the script, it would have been a five-hour film. In *Hungerjahre*, I realized that I react totally differently as a scriptwriter than as a director. I wrote the script and then I directed it in a totally different way. I had to go through this experience. Now I know when I write a script at which moment to slow down and when I want to speed up the rhythm. It represents a certain kind of editing. I didn't know these moments when I made *Hungerjahre*.

Zadow. You made a lot of films using your biography. What problems do you encounter in being a public and a private person at the same time?

Brückner. There are very few problems. I could not have survived if I had not had the opportunity to change into a public person. The only way to survive is to be a filmmaker who expresses these difficulties. You can ask me anything and there is only a small area of questions where I would say, no, this is really intimate and I don't want to talk about that right now. But maybe you will find the answer to your question in a film five years later.

Zadow. So you found self-confidence through openness?

Brückner. Yes. Exactly. The experience of my generation was that all the really vital things were hidden. The only chance of surviving was to make them public.

7

Observing Rituals:
Ulrike Ottinger's *Johanna d'Arc of Mongolia*

Julia Knight

Alongside such filmmakers as Wim Wenders, R. W. Fassbinder, and Margarethe von Trotta, Ulrike Ottinger has become one of German cinema's established auteurs. Although the notion of an auteur is somewhat problematic and has to be understood within the wider socioeconomic context,[1] Ottinger's films appear to constitute a highly distinctive and unified body of work. Her early fiction films—*Madame X—An Absolute Ruler* (1977), *Ticket of No Return* (1979), *Freak Orlando* (1981), and *Dorian Gray in the Mirror of the Popular Press* (1983)—have, for instance, been repeatedly noted for their lesbian "content" and for their "elaborate costumes, painterly shot composition, antirealist performances, and eclectic and abundant musical and sound quotations."[2] These recurring features—also evident in varying degrees in her later work—combined with Ottinger's much noted background as an artist, her self-declared lesbian sexuality,[3] and the high degree of control she exercises over her work,[4] make it difficult not to read her films as the product of a highly coherent and singular authorial "vision."

China, The Arts, Everyday Life (1985) initially seemed to represent something of a departure from her earlier works.[5] Variously described as a documentary film with a difference, an ethnographic film, and a travel account, *China* is a four-and-a-half-hour journey through Chinese life filmed in a distinctly "observational" style. After *China* Ottinger made *Countdown* (1990), a film about the ten days before currency union in Germany, and the epic eight-and-a-half-hour *Taiga: A Journey to the Northern Land of the Mongols* (1991–92), both filmed in a similar manner. Unsurprisingly, Bérénice Reynaud made the following observation: "Ottinger's career as a filmmaker may be divided in two: before and after *China*.[6] And on the strength of *China* and *Taiga* in particular, she has started to win recognition as an ethnographic filmmaker.

However, given her reputation as an auteur,[7] critics have tended to construct her ethnographic work as a logical progression, an extension of former interests rather than anything fundamentally different. Reynaud, for instance, also argues that Ottinger's fiction films were "anchored in a single project: 'how to represent Difference as something positive in a repressive society.' Confronting the Oriental Other was the next step."[8] In interviews Ottinger has similarly suggested that her concerns have remained entirely consistent throughout her filmmaking career. On the one hand, she has pointed out that her interest in the East is nothing new: "If I hadn't made films, I would probably have become an ethnologist. On top of that there was an early fascination with travelling in the East."[9] Even before making *China*, she had already set her 1977 film, *Madame X*, on the China seas and the idea for her 1989 film *Johanna d'Arc of Mongolia* had originated in the late 1970s.[10] On the other hand, she has also repeatedly stressed her interest in challenging the viewer's perception of reality, in bringing "the seemingly familiar into new and surprising contexts,"[11] in "finding new visions and new possibilities,"[12] when she has discussed both her fiction and her documentary work. Thus, the director's ethnographic filmmaking has functioned to reenforce her status as auteur status.

It is tempting therefore to similarly read *Johanna d'Arc of Mongolia* as a product of Ottinger's authorial "visions," especially since the film fuses the antirealism of her fiction films and the ethnographic interests of her documentaries in a staged meeting between Western travelers and Mongolian nomads. But it is possible to argue that such a reading delimits the film's meaning and obscures other equally productive ways of reading it. Indeed, several critics have observed that all of her work is rich in complex layers of possible meanings and Ottinger herself has argued that there are multiple levels to her films.[13] Although critics have noted this dimension of Ottinger's work with specific reference to *Johanna d'Arc*,[14] some aspects of the film have not yet been fully explored. The aim of this essay is to argue that the film can usefully be read in relation to some of the questions raised by ethnographic filmmaking in particular and by the nature of filmmaking in general.

The Dilemma of Ethnographic Film

A major criticism of ethnographic film is that, like ethnographic writing, it is "one of the means by which the West has objectified non-Western peoples."[15] Since making *China*, Ottinger's interest in ethnography, together with her self-professed "yearning" for Eastern cultures, has been well-documented in a number of interviews and articles. Although she acknowledges that she never studied it "in any scientific way,"[16] she has nevertheless demonstrated some awareness concerning issues of representation in ethnographic filmmaking.[17] One such issue, for instance, is the use of sound. Brian Winston has described how technological developments in the 1950s and 1960s facilitated the inclusion of speech in ethnographic film, giving a voice to native peoples that seemed to offer a more "genuine" or fully rounded image of those represented.[18] In discussing *China*, Ottinger has stressed the importance of using original sounds for similar reasons: "Everyday life on the streets of Beijing is quite different from our own European cities; even the sounds are different. I insisted absolutely throughout the trip on original sound."[19]

Ottinger has also expressed her intention to avoid exploiting or exoticising the cultures she films and claims to have done so by means of both her attitude toward the people she is filming and the filmic strategies she employs to represent them.[20] Thus, her documentaries have been characterized by their absence of a contextualizing commentary and by her camera's "respectful" distance as if to suggest that she is simply an onlooker rather than interpreting, colonizing, or appropriating.[21] Until relatively recently, there has also been a tendency on the part of some ethnographic filmmakers to claim—by way of their use of particular filmmaking conventions and by their editing decisions—"to offer pictures of uncontaminated cultures and to disguise their own presence."[22] Such an approach tries to conceal the fact that a particular representation has been constructed from and thus mediates a particular viewpoint. As if in recognition of this problematic, in *Johanna d'Arc* Ottinger effectively renders the Western "gaze" visible by incorporating a group of Western travelers into the Mongolian setting and by making one of them an anthropologist.[23]

Furthermore, Ottinger is at pains to point out that her films are based on extensive research and that she has made every endeavor to immerse herself in the culture she is going to represent, as if to suggest that this will allow her to better keep faith with the subjects of her films.[24] In discussing the preparation for *Johanna d'Arc* she has, for instance, made the following statements:

> *China* . . . is a preliminary study in the sense that it gave me experience filming in China, which was instructive in several respects. Not only was I able to experience and observe other cultural forms and another way of life, living there also helped me revise and enrich my own extensive theoretical preparation.[25]

> I read a lot about these countries and visited quite a few East Asian museums and collections. After the documentary [*China*] I traveled a few more times to China, and finally to Mongolia in order to begin preparing for this film.[26]

Although Ottinger is sensitive to the issues raised by ethnographic filmmaking, she nevertheless remains a Western filmmaker who is effectively packaging a non-Western culture for "our" consumption. She describes *China* as an "encounter with the foreign,"[27] but the film is *her* encounter with *them*, not theirs with her. This is very apparent in the way in which she describes her approach to filming it as "a method of noting and recording whatever seemed *to me* worthy of attention" (my emphasis).[28] Furthermore, as Winston has stressed, the camera is "a culturally determined artifact":

> Although influenced a millennium ago by Arab scientists, for the last five hundred years the lens has been a prisoner and a product of the West. It is ground to produce images with single-vanishing-viewpoint perspective according to Western representational codes. The camera to which it is attached has a viewfinder so small that it works . . . most easily if individual faces are privileged. Indeed . . . filming interactions is quite difficult, especially if you are as low as you need to be to shoot most non-Western domestic scenes. The machine is produced by Western individuals to photograph Western individuals.[29]

As if to counter these arguments, Ottinger has asserted that what she attempts to do is carry on a visual discourse "about exoticism as a question of point of view."[30] When asked to explain what she meant by this, she commented that

> When an African comes to Germany, he or she finds the Bavarians very exotic—a lot of people all over the world do. This is not automatically a bad thing. Clichés are not necessarily bad—only when you use them against people and rigorously generalize the view. My films don't do that. I work with prototypes, but always in connection with the broader structures of the films— topic, imagery, and so on—so that the characters, again, only become part of the whole.[31]

While her assertions are to a certain extent valid, they ignore the context in which her films are shown and consumed. And as Peter Ian Crawford and David Turton have argued, what is equally important with regard to ethnographic film, is who is doing the viewing: "whose 'desire' is being satisfied?" If it is "ours," if "we" are doing the viewing, then ethnographic film has to be regarded as a Western project, "something *we* do to *them*,"[32] and consequently "[t]he subject of ethnographic film will always be object."[33] Although Ottinger asserts that "I am not a colonizer,"[34] her films have predominantly been screened and distributed in Western Europe and in the United States.[35] Furthermore, *China* won the German Film Critics Award in 1986, while *Taiga* met with critical acclaim in both Germany and North America.[36] But according to James C. Faris, it is not just a matter of where the films are shown, since "[t]he West is now everywhere, within the West and outside, in structures, minds and technologies."[37] In this context, the central dilemma in ethnographic filmmaking has become how to "obliterate otherness while preserving difference."[38]

Exposing the Construct: *Johanna d'Arc of Mongolia*

In view of its apparently overt mixing of fictional and documentary material *Johanna d'Arc of Mongolia* does not conform to what is traditionally thought of as ethnographic filmmaking. But, given its subject matter, it has to a certain extent been incorporated into Ottinger's body of ethnographic work. The director herself has repeatedly linked this film to *China* (as, e.g., in her comments just quoted) and it has also often been referenced in reviews of *Taiga*.[39] Yet rather than inevitably functioning to satisfy Western "desire," *Johanna d'Arc* can instead be read as addressing and working through this dilemma.

The film follows four Western women—the anthropologist Lady Windermere, the schoolteacher Frau Müller-Vohwinkel, the American musical star Fanny Ziegfeld, and the young adventurer Giovanna—traveling on the Trans-Siberian and Trans-Mongolian railways. In the first half of the film, the train on which they are journeying is a stylized studio construct, where they meet other passengers and exchange stories. In the second half, filmed entirely on location in Inner Mongolia, they are abducted from their train by a Mongolian princess and by her band of female warriors and invited to stay in their camp for the duration of their summer festival. Indeed, Ottinger has described the film as showing "what happens when two extremely different cultures meet."[40] As well as "documenting" various rituals of the Mongolian nomads, *Johanna d'Arc* offers narrative development by establishing a relationship between the princess and Giovanna. Finally, the four Western women return to the train to continue their journey.

In terms of dress, language, customs, modes of transport, life-styles, and so on the Western women and the tribe of Mongolian women are clearly delineated as different. The Western women are traveling as a recreational pursuit, whereas the film presents the Mongolian women's nomadic existence as a way of life. Fanny, for instance, says that she's traveling simply because she wants to see something different, whereas when the Mongolian women hold up the train, Lady Windermere tells Giovanna: "I know only one thing: *this is no game.* They are carrying their weapons as if for battle. It's serious" (my emphasis). Similarly, the Westerners travel by train, while the Mongolian women go on horseback and by camel. Frau Müller-Vohwinkel is appalled at the prospect of eating the slice of animal fat offered to her by the Mongolian princess as a delicacy and gesture of hospitality. On the train the Westerners sit on chairs and at tables to eat their meals, whereas the Mongols sit on the ground to eat theirs. And predictably, on occasions these differences cause misunderstandings and moments of humor, which function to further emphasize the two groups of women as different. The most frequently cited example is when Frau Müller-Vohwinkel finds herself chased around the encampment for unwittingly threatening the Mongolian sky spirits by hanging washing on a clothesline.

However, in terms of the film's narrative structure it is possible to argue that the two cultures do not meet on an equal footing, but rather in a way that privileges a Western perspective and hence appears to "objectify" the nomadic women. The film introduces us to the Western women first, naming them individually in the opening credits sequence, and the first third of the film is taken up with their experiences and stories as they travel toward Inner Mongolia on board the Trans-Siberian Railway. Hence, we as viewers "enter" the film's narrative by sharing *their* journey. Similarly, at the end of the film we as viewers "leave" with the Western women when the Mongolian princess and her tribe take them back to the train to continue their journey. The final sequence is shot predominantly from the viewpoint of the departing train, as it speeds the Westerners on to their next destination and leaves the Mongolian nomads behind. And as the image fades to black, a voice-over informs the audience how the encounter influenced the fictional character's future exploits. The second part of the film, set in the steppes of Mongolia, may comprise two-thirds of the film's running time, but it is framed within and thus becomes part of a journey undertaken by a group of Westerners. Lady Windermere and her fellow travelers are effectively tourists, explorers, observers of something "foreign." Indeed, both Fanny and Frau Müller-Vohwinkel refer to themselves as "tourists" when they go to take their seats in the Trans-Siberian dining car, while Giovanna is described as a "backpacker." Their role as "observers" is repeatedly emphasized via Lady Windermere's role as an anthropologist and by showing how the women *watch* Mongolian rituals from the sidelines, or by representing them *looking at* strange new sights. For instance, The Kalinka Sisters, a singing trio from the train, are shown watching a wrestling competition staged by some Mongolian men who attend the summer festival, and later we see Lady Windermere translating for her Western companions as they watch the acting out of popular folktales.

The two cultures are also filmed very differently. When the group of Western women meet in the first part of the film, it is filmed on a studio set. The characters are frequently shot in close-ups and the camera is extremely mobile, roving around the sets to point up or zoom in on various artifacts, objects, details of decor, and so forth. Once they enter the Mongolian women's terrain in the second part of the film, however, it is shot entirely on-location. The camera becomes far more static and medium and long shots become much more the norm, together with durationally long shots. Although these filmmaking strategies further mark the difference between the two cultures, viewed from a Western perspective, the Mongolian tribe is also constructed as something that can only be looked at from a distance and that can never be fully understood. Hence they seem enveloped in an aura of mystery. Although Lady Windermere explains certain things (e.g., the misunderstanding about hanging washing on a clothesline), there are also long sequences that are merely "observed" (when, e.g., another tribe encountered en route sets up camp or when the nomads gather for the summer festival). Consequently, on at least one level, the film appears to exoticise the Mongolian people, to reenforce their "foreignness," their "otherness."

Such a reading, however, somewhat simplifies the film's narrative complexity, visual richness, and multiple cultural references.[41] Although it is impossible to address all of the film's different levels here, certain aspects are particularly pertinent since they function to expose the film—and hence any reading of it—for what it is: a construct. By using different modes of filmmaking for the two parts of the film, *Johanna d'Arc* plays with notions of realism and representation, documentary and fiction; and it does so in such a way that any previously perceived distinctions start to break down. Indeed this is flagged as one of the film's concerns in the opening credits sequence when a voice-over says: "Must imagination shun the encounter with reality? Or are they enamored of each other? Can they form an alliance? Does the encounter transform them? Do they exchange roles?"[42]

The first part of the film—the Western women's journey on the Trans-Siberian Railway—can be characterized by its excessive artificiality. This is most apparent at the level of set design—not only is the train clearly shown to be a constructed, specially built set, complete with obviously fake scenery rolling past the windows, evoking old-fashioned fairground rides, but the "stations" at which the "train" stops are two-dimensional, painted cardboard cutouts. And in constructing these sets, Ottinger has deliberately tried to create a mode of travel that no longer exists: she refers to her railway carriages as "a miniature museum on wheels," something from "bygone days."[43]

This is then juxtaposed with the location shooting of the second part: suddenly bright natural light, blue skies, and expansive rocky landscapes, complete with wind howling on the sound track, replace the enclosed and constructed studio sets. Filmed using the conventions of observational documentary filmmaking, it provides a dramatic and breathtaking contrast to the earlier artificiality—a contrast that is reinforced through exterior shots of a *real* train. Even though the fictional Western characters inhabit this very real environment and interact with the Mongolian women, it is virtually impossible not to read the Mongolian section of the film as some kind of "record" of an "authentic" Eastern culture.[44] Indeed, there are several long sequences from which the Western characters are entirely absent and the camera appears to simply "observe" the Mongol's way of life. But reading this second part of the film as some form of "documentation" depends primarily upon the viewer's *understanding* of filmmaking conventions rather than the subject matter presented (although the two are of course interdependent). Or as Dai Vaughan has succinctly expressed the point:

> If it has proved notoriously difficult to define documentary by reference to its constantly shifting stylistic practices, it is because the term "documentary" properly describes not a style or a method or a genre of filmmaking but *a mode of response* to film material. (my emphasis)[45]

Thus, according to Vaughan, what Ottinger is effectively doing is persuading us, as viewers, "that what appears to be *is*."[46] Only it isn't. The inclusion of fictional characters in what otherwise appears to be an "authentic" Mongolian community starts to problematize what is "real" and what is not, since it reveals that the supposedly "real" is in some way staged. This is apparent, for instance, in the way in which the film represents a growing friendship between the princess and Giovanna: at one point during the summer festival the princess talks to and giggles with Giovanna, then affectionately takes her arm and leads her over to a group of performers. The princess has the appearance of behaving "naturally," yet we know Giovanna is a fictional construct. And this blurring of the "real" and the "imaginary" is compounded at the end of the film. After the Mongolian women have returned the Western travelers to the train to continue their journey, the final sequence shows Lady Windermere sharing the luxury compartment of a wealthy Mongolian woman who is on her way to Paris. When Lady Windermere thanks her for her hospitality, she tells Lady Windermere that many Mongolian women return to the steppes in the summer months "in order to preserve in some measure the illusion of the free nomadic life." [47]

Hence we, the viewers, have been duped: what the film persuaded us was "authentic" is in a sense as artificial as the first part of the film. [48] And we are left wondering what it is that we have been watching. At one level, the use of such a strategy—making the fictional look "real"—simply places the film within a tradition of filmmaking that stretches right back to the earliest days of cinema when the Lumiere cameramen would reconstruct newsworthy events they had been unable to film live. But in *Johanna d'Arc*, the strategy is used to overtly challenge the assumed "authenticity" of what we have been watching and to expose the film for the construct it is. Once the whole film is revealed as an elaborate fiction, it has the effect of making—or at least encouraging—her to acknowledge that any privileging of a Western perspective, or reading of the Mongols as signifying "otherness," is equally constructed.

Enacting Rituals: Parallels between Cultures

Indeed, by representing both cultures as artificial constructs, the film effectively draws a parallel between them. That is, both cultural groups indulge in a form of theater or role-playing—the fictional Western characters play the role of tourists and recreational adventurers, while the Mongols play at being nomads and abductors. This parallel is underscored through the film's frequent focusing on the performing or acting out of "rituals" within both cultures—be they rituals of eating, socializing, entertainment, competition/sport, greeting, departure, or story telling.

After boarding the train at the beginning of the film, for instance, the Western women meet and greet one another in the dining car where they are entertained by the Kalinka Sisters, and encounter a Russian officer, his adjutant, and a Yiddish-American tenor. After ordering their meals, they pass the evening exchanging folktales, experiences, and family histories until Fanny and the tenor join the Kalinka Sisters on a small stage at the end of the carriage to perform for the gathered group. The following day, all the travelers meet again in Lady Windermere's "apartments" for afternoon tea, before the gentlemen politely take their leave to go their separate ways. This whole sequence performs little narrative function, other than to mark the passing of time (and by implication movement through geographic space), and functions primarily to establish a range of markers of Western culture by means of the performance of certain "rituals."

Similarly, in the second half of the film we see the Mongols make offerings to their gods at holy trees; undertake ceremonial greetings when two tribes meet; offer Mare's milk to the earth before they drink it; set up their summer camp; embark on a hunt; stage a summer festival; and indulge in story telling, sports, ceremonies, and so on. There are narrative developments of a kind in this second part of the film—for instance, Fanny expresses fears for Frau Müller-Vohwinkel's safety when she fails to return from a plant-gathering expedition by nightfall, and Giovanna's growing friendship with the Mongolian princess tempts her to stay when the others return to the train—but these are not developed. Frau Müller-Vohwinkel is found and Giovanna boards the departing train at the last minute to rejoin her traveling companions. Just as the first part of the film marks out a Western identity, the primary function of the second half appears to be the "documenting" of some of the rituals that signify Mongolian cultural identity.

Differences between the two cultures as represented in the film clearly do exist. In addition to those of dress, mode of transport, and so forth, cited earlier, a very marked difference is suggested when we see one of the Mongols undertaking the disemboweling of an animal while it is still alive. For most Western audiences, this represents an unnecessary act of cruelty, but it is clearly not understood in this way among the Mongolian nomads. They simply gather round, singing while watching, and appear entirely unmoved. But by establishing parallels between the two cultures, the film locates the various rituals represented—whatever their actual "content" is—as different ways of doing *similar* things. In doing this, the film highlights how both cultures articulate their respective cultural identities by "acting out" rituals, via—effectively—forms of "performance." And viewed in this way, *Johanna d'Arc* can be read as a film about *how* or by what means cultures—*any* culture—articulate their identities and whether the actual rituals are "authentic" or not becomes unimportant. At the same time, reading the film in this way, makes it virtually impossible to view the Mongols as signifying "otherness." Thus, on one level the film can be regarded as addressing and working through the dilemma of ethnographic filmmaking: it can be read as representing difference while obliterating "otherness."

Such a reading also offers a rationale for what is effectively the "road movie" structure of the film. The performing of rituals takes place in time and the passing of time is very easily visualized or represented in film via a journey. Thus, the movement through geographic space, both on the train and via the nomadic life-style, can be viewed as echoing or underpinning the process of constructing an identity. And given that the "journeys" of both the Western characters and the Mongolian women are "fictional," it also suggests that as the filmmaker Jean Rouch once observed: "Fiction is the only way to penetrate reality."[49]

Notes

1. Much of Germany's film subsidy system, for instance, actively promotes the notion of an Autorenkino by identifying the director as a film's creator and by structuring production loans on this basis. This situation emerged in response to the critical decline of German cinema in the 1950s and in the resulting campaigning work of Alexander Kluge and others for government aid. For a discussion of these issues, see Thomas Elsaesser, *New German Cinema: A History* (New York: MacMillan/BFI, 1989) and Julia Knight, *Women and the New German Cinema* (Verso, 1992).

2. Patricia White, "Madame X of the China Seas," *Screen* 28, no. 4 (autumn 1987): 81.

3. In her earlier films she collaborated with her then lover Tabea Blumschein who, for instance, acted in and designed the costumes for both *Madame X* and *Ticket of No Return*.

4. In addition to directing, Ottinger is frequently her own writer, art director, and camera operator as well.

5. See, for instance, Roy Grundmann and Judith Shulevitz, "Minorities and the Majority: An interview with Ulrike Ottinger," *Cineaste* 18, no. 3 (1991): 40.

6. Bérénice Reynaud, "Ottinger in Mongolia," *Cinemaya* 17–18, (autumn-winter 1992): 55.

7. See, for instance, Brenda Longfellow, "Lesbian Phantasy and the Other Woman in Ottinger's *Johanna d'Arc of Mongolia*," *Screen*, 34, no. 2 (summer 1993): 124, where Longfellow states that "Ottinger's influence at all levels of production results in films with a very strong and idiosyncratic authorial signature." See also Ulrike Ottinger, "The Pressure to Make Genre Films: About the Endangered Autorenkino (1983)," in *West German Filmmakers on Film,* ed. E. Rentschler (Holmes & Meier, 1988), 90–93, for Ottinger's own espousal of the Autorenfilm.

8. Reynaud, "Ottinger in Mongolia," 55.

9. "Ulrike Ottinger im Gespräch mit Karsten Witte über ihren Dokumentarfilm China, die Künste, der Alltags," from the program notes for the 16th International Forum of Young Film, Berlin 1986, unpaginated. All translations from German language sources are my own unless otherwise indicated.

10. See "Die heilige Johanna der Bahnhöfe," in *Berlinaletip*, 10−15.2.89, p. 9.

11. English translation of the *Johanna d'Arc of Mongolia* press information, 15.

12. Therese Grisham, "An Interview with Ulrike Ottinger," *Wide Angle* 14, no. 2 (April 1992): 33.

13. See, for instance, "Encounter Between Two Cultures: A Discussion with Ulrike Ottinger Introduced by Annette Kuhn," *Screen* 28, no. 4 (Autumn 1987): 74; and Erica Carter, "Interview with Ulrike Ottinger," *Screen Education* 41 (winter/spring 1982): 37.

14. See, for instance, Longfellow and Therese Grisham, "Twentieth Century Thearum Mundi: Ulrike Ottinger's *Johanna d'Arc of Mongolia*," *Wide Angle* 14, no. 2 (April 1992): 22−27.

15. Peter Ian Crawford and David Turton, eds. *Film as Ethnography* (Manchester: Manchester University Press, 1992), 166.

16. Grisham, "Interview with Ulrike Ottinger," 31.

17. For more details of some of these issues, see Crawford and Turton, *Film as Ethnography* .

18. Brian Winston, *Claiming the Real: The Documentary Film Revisited* (London: BFI, 1995), 195. However, Winston stresses that the inclusion of native people's voices did not necessarily improve previous modes of filmmaking that had excluded their voices.

19. Kuhn, 75. Although it should be noted that Ottinger doesn't use it in its original form, but rather layers it and also uses music on the sound track.

20. See, for instance, her comments in Grundmann and Shulevitz, "Minorities and the Majority."

21. Indeed, with regard to *China* one reviewer noted: "Ottinger herself does not pretend to know much about what's going on before her scrutinising eyes, she's content to take the pulse of life and let it go at that." See Ronald Holloway, "Journeys to the East: German Directors on Asia," *Cinemaya* 17−18 (autumn-winter 1992): 54. However, Holloway's assertion actually contradicts Ottinger's own claims made elsewhere. See, for instance, the English language press information for *Johanna d'Arc* and in footnote 10.

22. Winston, *Claiming the Real*, 191.

23. It should be noted that Grisham analyzes the film as preventing the viewer from identifying Lady Windermere as the film's narrative authority (24). Similarly, Longfellow argues that the primary gaze in the second half of the film is not aligned with Lady Windermere (132). Nevertheless, Lady Windermere's occupation as an anthropologist cannot be entirely dismissed, given the subject matter of the film.

24. For a discussion of this issue, see Dai Vaughan, "The Aesthetics of Ambiguity," in Crawford and Turton, *Film as Ethnography*, 99−115.

25. English press information, 21.

26. See footnote 10. From an English translation extract, "Saint Joan of the Train Stations," published alongside the German original.

27. English press information, 21.

28. Kuhn, 75.

29. Winston, *Claiming the Real*, 180. Hence the problem is not solved by putting the camera in the hands of those being filmed (see, e.g., Crawford and Turton, *Film as Ethnography*, 165).

30. Quoted in Claudia Hoff, "Ulrike Ottinger," in *Cinegraph: Lexikon zum deutsch-sprachigen Film*, ed. Hans-Michael Bock (Munich, 1984), Lg. 11, E1.

31. Grundmann and Shulevitz, "Minorities and the Majority," 41.

32. Crawford and Turton, *Film as Ethnography*, 166.

33. James C. Faris, "Anthropological Transparency: Film, Representation and Politics," in *Film as Ethnography*, Crawford and Turton, 178.

34. Grundmann and Shulevitz, "Minorities and the Majority," 41.

35. It should be noted that *China* was shown at the 1987 Hong Kong International Film Festival and that *Taiga* has been shown in Asia. Nevertheless *China, Taiga*, and *Johanna d'Arc* have been picked up for distribution only in Europe and in the United States, and the majority of festival screenings have also been in "Western" countries.

36. For the critical response to *Taiga* see, for instance, *Frankfurter Rundschau*, 24 February 1992; *Berlinale-Journal*, 21 February 1992; *Süddeutsche Zeitung*, 26 February 1992; and *New York Times*, 22 February 1992.

37. Faris, "Anthropological Transparency," 178.

38. Quoted in Crawford and Turton, *Film as Ethnography*, 166.

39. See, for instance, *Frankfurter Rundschau*, 24 February 1992; *epd Film* (May 1992); and *Tip* (April 1992).

40. English press information, 11.

41. For other ways of reading the film that address other aspects of the film's complexity and multiple levels see, for instance, Longfellow, "Lesbian Phantasy and the Other Woman in Ottinger's Johanna d'Arc Mongolia," 124–36; and Grisham, "Interview with Ulrike Ottinger," 22–27.

42. Quoted in Grisham, "Interview with Ulrike Ottinger," 24.

43. English press information, 11.

44. Albeit one exposed to the influences of the West, made apparent through the inclusion of the Western characters, but also via the inclusion of a shot of one nomad family using a camel to tow a motorbike and a sequence when Frau Müller-Vohwinkel stumbles on an underground shrine where foreign currency has been stuck to the wall by its many visitors.

45. Vaughan, "Aesthetics of Ambiguity," 101.

46. Ibid., 102.

47. Quoted in Grisham, "Interview with Ulrike Ottinger," 26.

48. In this context it is interesting to note that in the English press information pack Ottinger explains how she had to "manufacture" the scenarios she filmed in Inner Mongolia.

49. Quoted in Winston, *Claiming the Real*, 182.

8

Community and Its Contents
Race and Film History in Percy Adlon's *Bagdad Café*

David J. Levin

Percy Adlon's 1988 film *Bagdad Café* doesn't start off happily, except, perhaps, in form. The opening scene of two characters berating each other in German over Bavarian oompah music in the midst of Wile E. Coyote country comes very much out of the blue. There are no titles announcing the film or subtitles translating the harangue; the establishing shot establishes nothing so much as our disorientation. The form, however, is comically overwrought: the editing is extraordinarily jarring, the camera angles are oblique, and the lighting is heavily filtered. Eventually it will dawn upon us that we have witnessed the end of Jasmin's marriage. It is a familiar structure in Adlon's films: an end that starts the film will only make sense in retrospect.

This retrospective structure signals the film's claim to cinematic hipness and offers a pithy statement of its pedagogical aspiration: if we, like the film's main character Jasmin, can see our way through the initial disorientation and the diegetic aggression, then, in the end, everything will fall into place. And, in a certain sense, it does. But as the film moves forward in time, it moves backward in form. At the outset of the film, our pleasure derives from unusual representational form (which operates in striking contrast to the pain of the protagonists); at the film's conclusion, the pleasure has been wholly literalized, relocated to the level of content: everyone on-screen is awash in harmony and joy—and the film's form has become utterly banal. Like the sentiment it records, the concluding scene is designed to be reassuring, and nowhere does the film offer more assurance than in its pat form.

In a number of ways *Bagdad Café* presents itself as a quirky film—a quasi-modernist feel-good movie; a feminist, interracial, and international buddy

117

movie; a film, then, that thematizes what would appear to be intractable cultural and racial differences only to depict their resolution in a scene of saccharine harmony.[1] That harmony is hard won—not because Jasmin has to endure much before assuming her metaphoric and literal place, center stage at the Bagdad Café. Rather, the harmony takes its toll in representational terms. For as the film rushes headlong from the atomization and loneliness of its protagonists to a newly vibrant and dynamic community (with Jasmin in the driver's seat) it veers off into a region of film history that it doesn't mean to revisit: the 1940s entertainment film. In this essay, I want to examine this odd spectacle.

Before we examine the film, let me offer a thumbnail sketch of the plot:[2] Jasmin (Marianne Sägebrecht) is a big and big-hearted woman from Bavaria who happens upon the Bagdad Café and takes up residence there after abandoning her very Bavarian husband in the middle of the Mojave desert. The café—and for that matter, the town of Bagdad itself—consists of a ramshackle complex including a café/restaurant, a motel, and a gas station. Brenda (CCH Pounder) runs the place: she's an African-American woman whose golden heart will eventually (and oh so formulaically) emerge from behind an exterior of unabashed abrasiveness. In her first appearance, Brenda bids good riddance to her husband Sal (G. Smokey Campbell) who is apparently a lazy good-for-nothing. When Jasmin arrives shortly thereafter—alone and on foot—Brenda is suspicious and unfriendly. For her part, Jasmin tries desperately to befriend Brenda: she cleans up Brenda's office with the intensity of a German hausfrau, cuddles Brenda's grandson, and introduces Brenda's daughter to Lederhosen.

Bagdad Café is a spin-off of the Hollywood "fish-out-of-water" scenario: the German woman takes up residence in the middle of the American desert in a quirky community of African Americans, Native Americans, and white truckers whom Brenda describes as "sort of" or "almost" family. Jasmin, however, does not belong—not yet, anyway. Soon enough, Brenda realizes that Jasmin is actually OK, and even allows her to start working in the café. Jasmin immediately livens up the place by performing impromptu magic tricks to everyone's immense amusement: business booms and the place comes alive. When the sheriff shows up to point out that Jasmin's tourist visa has expired, she is forced to return to Bavaria, and with her, the magic and newfound spirit at the café disappear. The pathos of the film is such that we can divide it into distinct eras— before and after Jasmin is accepted into the fold of the café community. When the law intervenes and she returns to Bavaria, the café returns to what we might, with some irony, term the *dark ages*; the ages, that is, when the film was not graced by Jasmin's enlivening, enlightening presence. But sure enough, Jasmin comes back, and with her, the magic returns as well.

Jasmin's return is publicly celebrated with a grand "magic show" performed to a full house at the café. Jasmin stars in the magic show, assisted by her erstwhile sidekick Brenda and Brenda's kids: Phyllis, a libidinally overcharged teen

CCH Pounder as Brenda, an African-American woman whose golden heart will eventually—and oh so formulaically—emerge from behind an exterior of unabashed abrasiveness. Percy Adlon, Bagdad Café; *photo courtesy of the Museum of Modern Art/Film Stills Archive.*

with an incongruous Valley Girl accent, and Sal Jr., a sort of African-American incarnation of Charles Schulz's Schroeder who has been obsessively practicing Bach on the piano for much of the film. In the magic show, Phyllis serves as emcee and Sal Jr. provides the musical accompaniment. Other café regulars play "supporting" roles: among the two (white men) manning the lights is Rudi Cox (Jack Palance), a Hollywood artist whose eyes have been on Jasmin ever since she set foot in the café. Although Mr. Cox's appearance in the scene is fleeting, it is, like his name, heavily overdetermined: for in lighting the multicultural spectacle, the film aligns him with the apparatus that enables our gaze, inflecting it as white and male.[3] And sure enough, he will rise to the narrative occasion (in the most formulaic sense): standing in for the spectator's desire, he will seek the hand of its leading lady after the magical success of the magic show. The film ends with Jasmin's ambiguous response: "I'll talk it over with Brenda."

Although it is not necessarily clear from the preceding account, *Bagdad Café* clearly takes up the tradition of the German-American road movie, asso-

ciated most famously with Wim Wenders. In a number of his films, Wenders
takes his characters and viewers onto the road in a largely futile search for freedom, identity, and meaning. Where Wenders finds poetic, even tragic futility
(en route to Paris, Texas, or earlier, to Wuppertal), Adlon finds function (in Bagdad, Arizona)—indeed, he and his protagonists find function, family, and fun.
But *Bagdad Café* is less of a road movie than a roadside one: Jasmin has abandoned her husband, her car, and her travels in order to blaze a different trail
within the confines of the café. Off the road, she sets out on a journey for a different community and family, and the film charts her travels, which take her
from a literal and figurative place outside of the café and its community, to the
center of that community. Once she has reached the center and has become
"just like family," the law reasserts itself and she has to go, but only in order then
to come back, to retrace the same route from Bavaria to the Bagdad Café, albeit
in a very different affective context. When she returns to the desert café from
Bavaria, she is desired. Indeed, her absence is sorely felt—by the on-screen
community and by the film's audience, for it quickly becomes clear that nothing happens without Jasmin: she is, or more precisely, has managed to *become* the
absent center; her second coming marks the return of the magic. But what is
that magic and how is it that this German woman comes to embody it?

At the outset of the scene, we hear (but don't immediately see) the assembled crowd chanting, in unison, insistently, rhythmically: "Ma-gic, Ma-gic,
Ma-gic." Their unanimous chant reiterates the film's thematic goal of univocal-
ity as it emphatically intones the means to that end: magic. It is evidently show-
time at the Bagdad Café, but what exactly is being staged? The explicit magic is
in the monotonous and magical circling of Jasmin (and eventually, Brenda's)
magic-wands: after the two magicians wave the wands about for a bit, they
"magically" circle about on their own: it is as embarrassing to spell out as it is to
watch—*they are in sync with one another.* But the visual track also alerts us to a
different sort of magic, the magic, that is, of the interracial community: neither
black magic nor white, it will—magically—add up to more than its parts. Of
course, the magic of the interracial community won't be restricted to the stage.
Thus, we don't just see Jasmin and Brenda and company working together: the
audience, too, is unmistakably multiracial. And yet the terms of "mixing" here
are hapless. In one shot, we are shown a group of African Americans in the audience, grinning and clapping with effusive glee. They stand out just when the
film would assure us that they're merely joining in. Their effusiveness is telling:
where Adlon would have the sequence simply mark community, it instead be-
speaks an anxiety about the place of cultural and racial difference within the
community. For where and how can the film "place" difference? By devoting a
shot to the Happy Negroes (indeed, a shot without any explicit narrative justification beyond the sheer registration and thus reproduction of pleasure), the film
singles them out. But it does so in order to suggest that they are not at all sin-

Performing the magic of interracial community. Percy Adlon Bagdad Café; *photo courtesy of the Museum of Modern Art/Film Stills Archive.*

gular, but are instead an integral and fully integrated part of the larger group. The problem can be traced to a tension between intention and rhetoric: the intended meaning (to show the integrated café where everyone gets along) conflicts with the logic of the images that would record that integration. The sequence would deny the importance of difference at the very moment that it registers it quite forcefully.

There is something troubling in this inflection of racial, familial, and cultural community as a kind of magical immersion in fun, and something equally troubling about the role these characters—white and black; in the audience and on stage—play in its production. The problematics of community played out here recalls a similar scene that Freud presents in *Civilization and Its Discontents*.

Near the outset of his essay, Freud expresses his uneasiness with what Romain Rolland had designated an "oceanic" feeling—an impression of something limitless and boundless.[4] Freud admits to his unfamiliarity with that feeling, thus implicitly positioning himself as a "discontent" among—or more precisely, outside of—the community that shares Rolland's feeling. (Indeed, Freud notes that Rolland portrays this community as immense, numbering in the millions.) It is this shared experience of vastness and limitlessness or, indeed, his lack of that experience that impels Freud's analysis. Here is how Freud terms his reservation: "The views expressed by the friend whom I so much honor [Rolland], and who

himself once praised the magic of illusion in a poem, caused me no small
difficulty. I cannot discover this 'oceanic' feeling in myself" (11).

In the course of his allusion to Rolland's work, Freud proposes a character-
istically revealing association: the sense of the "oceanic" is linked with Rolland's
evocation of "the magic of illusion." In this case (as in many of his literary allusions), Freud is not specifically interested in questions of literary form. Thus, it
is of no particular importance to him how Rolland praises the magic of illusion;
he is simply interested in the fact of the allusion. For Freud, the link is clear
enough: a belief in the "oceanic" is as remote and—more to the point—as *regressive* as a belief in that magic.

It is just such a link—between magic and community and regression—
that is forged in the culminating scene of *Bagdad Café*. The scene's magic, of
course, will inhere as much in the consolidation of community as in the myste-
rious twirling of wands. But one crucial aspect of the magic goes largely overlooked (which is, of course, a precondition for magic to succeed): in this case,
not the invisible strings that make the wands dance, but the disappearance of the
film's claim to an unusual cinematic form. In the following, I want to determine
whether and how we might discover *within the film's form* the resolute absence of
"discontents" (and the preponderance of "contents") that we're presented with
on-screen. It is here, in the space opened up between *contents* (as opposed to
form) and *contents* (as opposed to discontents), that I want to situate the rest of
my discussion.

In his canonical essay "Entertainment and Utopia," Richard Dyer observes
how song and dance routines ("entertainment") in film musicals tend to produce the impression or sensibility of utopia. "Entertainment offers the image of
'something better' to escape into, or something we want deeply that our day-to-
day lives don't provide" (222). In the case of our magic show, that image of
"something better" involves an envisioned community associated with a sense
of togetherness, and belonging.[5] One question we might ask is whose vision
produces the image (and for whom)?[6] I am posing a different if related question:
namely, how can we read this particular vision of community in terms of film
form and film history? For the scene, it seems to me, ends up doing the opposite of what it thinks it is doing. The vision of community presented here suggests a problematic relationship to racial and cultural difference—one that the
film in general and this scene in particular are undoubtedly designed to combat.

On the most obvious level, the community represented here reflects a
utopian racial and social cohesion. In keeping with Dyer's observation, the film
repeatedly figures that cohesion in and around song. Indeed, the singing starts
long before the magic scene gets underway. Thus, in the preceding scene, we see
Jasmin's surprise return from Bavaria to the café and her reunion with Brenda,
but we do not hear it. Instead, the sound track erupts into song as Brenda and
Jasmin recognize each other, embrace, and sit down to laugh and talk. For the

moment, song engulfs and marks the utopian restoration of friendship. Initially, the utopia of Jasmin's return is private (between Brenda and Jasmin); then, it turns familial (Brenda's kids heartily welcome Jasmin back, too).

Before Jasmin's return is celebrated publicly in the communal magic show (which is, as I just suggested, also a magic show of community itself), the film takes a detour into self-consciousness. Debby (Christine Kaufmann), the tattoo-artist, has packed her bags. When the café regulars (now, once again, including Jasmin) come running to ask why she is leaving, she responds crisply: "too much harmony." The film does not follow Debby (the European) as she heads down the lost (high?) road to discord—a road that the film set out from and has long-since abandoned.[7] Instead, the film cuts directly to the harmony: in this case, not just (harmonious) song, but a combination of song and magic.

Without a doubt, the utopia presented in *Bagdad Café* is a racial and national utopia, a proto-Schillerian vision of universal brotherhood, both the particular reconciliation of the two "sisters" (Brenda and Jasmin) and the general harmony of the community. The sensibility is explicitly (if also quite awkwardly) one of interracial harmony: here, whites and African Americans and Native Americans don't just come together to attend the performance, but in fact perform the harmony that they are supposed to embody. Thus, during the course of the musical number preceding the magic show, the camera and the characters shuttle between the stage and the audience: a trucker from the audience ends up singing on stage, while Phyllis, the emcee, leaves the stage in order to sit in the audience (indeed, she sits on the lap of one of the white truckers). In thus repeatedly traversing the line separating audience and performers, the film figures its programmatic (utopian) determination to dispense with difference itself. Bavarian, white American, African American, Native American—the scene aims to suggest that insofar as they (and by extension, we) all laugh and sing and dance and clap and have fun together there *is no difference*. Although this may strike the viewer as naive, it is not in itself problematic: after all, the scene proposes a utopian vision of community. But in the course of denying difference in the vision of utopia, the film unwittingly refigures it.

I have already noted that the utopian vision proposed here is organized around the stars of the magic show—Jasmin, Brenda, and her family. But it is not only organized around them, it also could be said to organize them. Thus, by the end of the film, Brenda and her family will end up someplace very different than Jasmin. According to the terms of the magic show, Jasmin has not only arrived at the center of the café community, she has become its feature attraction. It is the ultimate narcissistic fantasy: she has moved from the viewer to the viewed, from wistful "outsider looking in" to desired center of attention. Having experienced exclusion from the community, Jasmin is now its greatest attraction; having traveled from the margins of the café to its center, she now acts as a magnet attracting others and thus expanding the sense and experience of community. In resorting to this utopian song and dance, the film produces another type of utopia, a regressive, negative, and, no doubt, unintended one. This dystopia is registered in the visual track as it is signaled on the audio track.

It is not hard to notice that the visual and sound tracks of the magic show are out of sync with one another. We can read the lack of synchronicity as bespeaking a disjunction between the diegetic and ideological articulation of utopia in the film; a disjunction, that is, between the utopia explicitly proposed and depicted in the film, and another, related utopia that is articulated in the process of that depiction. What is at stake here is a kind of psychic gentrification, a conflict between diegetic narcissism (the fantasy of Jasmin's centrality) and the suppressed traces of the aggression that underlies it. Thus, we might ask, who or what has to move out in order to facilitate that centrality? In the magic scene, those suppressed traces emerge as cinematic and diegetic effects. That is, the scene played out here does not just stage Jasmin's return to the café in all of its narcissistic splendor, it also stages a much more subtle and problematic return: the return of Brenda and her family to a long-outdated role of African Americans as entertainers in film.[8] For as Jasmin is inflected as the star, the film reassigns Brenda and her family to supporting roles as entertainers, roles to which African Americans were assigned with particular (and particularly overdetermined) frequency in the 1940s.[9] According to Donald Bogle, the forties saw the heyday of what he terms "the entertainment syndrome":

> In almost every American movie in which a black had appeared [in the 1930s and early 1940s], filmmakers had been trying to maintain the myth that Negroes were naturally rhythmic and natural-born entertainers. With their cast of darkies singing and dancing, *Hearts in Dixie* and *Hallelujah* had obviously presented blacks not only as jesters but as uninhibited entertainers, too. Even as Bessie Smith cried the blues in *St. Louis Blues*, she was at heart an entertainer. (118)[10]

In *Bagdad Café*, Brenda is the effervescent backup singer and magician's assistant, Phyllis is the sexy, melodious emcee, and Sal Jr. is the happy, grinning, versatile piano man. (The fact that he is jamming on a theme by Bach merely makes him that much more eclectically charming: he loves to improvise on the master's tune.) Jasmin's return allows things to fall into place: her accession to a position that we might label the "*Über*-other" (the German outsider who is now an insider) is built upon a regressive, nostalgic fantasy that requires an "*unter*-other" (the African-American insider who is marginalized) on-screen. It is as if there is a Manichaean split in the representation of alterity, with Jasmin catapulted into a newfound centrality, while Brenda, Phyllis, and Sal Jr. are jettisoned into an outmoded, if still vibrant marginality. It is, after all, a familiar scenario (both structurally and historically): for the German to emerge as central; the other needs to be identified and duly marginalized. This film seems to want to abandon precisely that structure: thus, the German is cast, at least initially, in the position of the powerless outsider;[11] and the traditional other is cast in the position of power. But the film can't help itself. When Jasmin assumes center stage, Brenda and her children assume their more traditional and familiar places. Thus the film reestablishes, through the vocabulary of film history, a very traditional hierarchy of cultural and representational power—with the German on top, or at least at center stage, and the African Americans having so much fun by helping as best they can: with music, song, and dance.

This scene of Jasmin's accession and Brenda's marginalization is not merely incidental to the plot. For if Brenda was running the show at the Bagdad Café, it has now become Jasmin's show, and the film needs to mark that shift. One of the ways it does so is in a rearticulation of family. At the outset of the film, Brenda's family, like the café/motel/gas station grounds, is in a shambles: she kicks out her husband, repeatedly berates her son (for playing the piano and neglecting his infant son), and is constantly running after her daughter (who keeps running off with various men). Things start to improve as we move into the After Acceptance era. And when Jasmin returns from Bavaria, she is not just reunited with Brenda's family, but the film shows us that the family is reunited with itself: the whole family (with the exception of Sal Sr., the still-absent, deadbeat dad) comes out to greet Jasmin, and they appear as a family unit on stage. Indeed, Sal Sr. returns during the course of the magic show and joins the audience. Here Jasmin's return produces the magical return of the nuclear family.

The magic of the family's reconsolidation is augmented by the fact that their disparate talents have been so effectively channeled here. Thus, Sal Jr. is no longer practicing but performing, showing off his keyboard talents and assisting the show. Likewise, Phyllis's sexiness has been domesticated and commercialized. For her part, Brenda's rage has been transformed into happy artistry—and subordination. That is, she and her family are positioned as Jasmin's assistants— and they are clearly having *so much fun.*

The fantasy being played out here is not just a fantasy of social inclusion— for instance, the loner, accepted, becomes one of the gang. Beyond that, I think the film works as a parable (indeed, a relatively transparent and familiar parable) of *national* inclusiveness, a parable, namely, of getting a kinder, gentler German(y) to matter, to be essential. It does so counterintuitively, quirkily, off the beaten track. Thus, it's not as if Jasmin conquers New York or L.A.—the aspirations here are explicitly smaller. Jasmin is presented as a nobody and Bagdad is presented as a no place: "magically" they will turn out to be very special indeed. And although the film lampoons her manic cleaning campaign, it also shows us that the café—and its boss—are much better off for her intervention.

Thus, while the trajectory would appear to be different, the ultimate terms are quite familiar: thanks to her magical charms (which is also to say, her magical efficiency), the German will save the day, in this case bringing order, charm, and appeal to the lonely American outpost.

Thus if the film could be said to envision a road to racial and domestic harmony, it does so, finally, in order to reserve a place on that road for the good German—indeed, it's an important place. After all, without the good German, the magic is gone. Since the community dissolves in her absence, then surely the solution to the problem of community will be the good German's return. But the terms of return here are downright perplexing. The logic here is reminiscent of the Palmolive dishwashing liquid commercials that ran in the 1970s and 1980s where Madge the beautician is soaking her client's hands. The client mentions that her dishwashing liquid is particularly abrasive and Madge recommends that she try Palmolive: "after all, you're soaking in it now." Her client recoils in horror: "dishwashing liquid!?" "Relax," says Madge, "it's Palmolive." Here the dishwashing liquid is not just *not* a problem, it is the solution to itself: in order to heal the effects of soaking your hands in dishwashing liquid, it's best to soak your hands in dishwashing liquid. In terms of the logic of the film, racism is not just not a problem, it is the solution to itself: in order to heal the wounds inflicted by a history of the abjectification of African Americans on-screen, it's best for the natives to reassume the very abjection that marked their subjugation to begin with.

If Wim Wenders shows us Alice—and with her, paradise—lost in the cities, Percy Adlon shows us community—and with it, paradise—regained in the little town of Bagdad. But the terms of retrieval mark the determination and its representation as particularly suspect. The desire may be laudable, but the execution is shoddy, for the representation of the manically happy community consolidated in Bagdad is overwhelmed and undermined by the bad-faith happiness of its supporting musical staff. The magic show, it seems, not only shows us sticks flying through the air with the greatest of ease; it shows us just how powerful the diegetic effects of alterity can be. In reproducing these traditional structures, *Bagdad Café* mistakes the problem for the solution to the problem, and thus celebrates as a repudiation of racism what is, in fact, merely its restatement.

Notes

My thanks to Michel Chaouli, Jonathan Elmer, and Jack Zipes for their helpful comments and suggestions.

1. Hollywood produced a number of biracial buddy movies in the 1980s, including *Stir Crazy* (1980), *48 Hours* (1982), and *Running Scared* (1986). Robert Stam has noted

that "the box-office appeal of such films suggests that they touch something within the American Unconscious, a kind of wish for an easy and low-cost racial harmony." In *Bagdad Café*, the low-cost harmony will exact a high price in terms of representational politics. See Stam, "Bakhtin, *Polyphony*, and Ethnic/Racial Representation," in *Unspeakable Images: Ethnicity and the American Cinema*, ed. Lester D Friedman (Urbana: University of Illinois Press, 1991), 260.

2. A more complete plot summary (and a list of major reviews) can be found in Frank N. Magill, ed. *Magill's Cinema Annual 1989: A Survey of the Films of 1988* (Pasadena, Calif.: Salem Press, 1989), 28–31.

3. There are two spots lighting the show: the second is manned by Eric (Alan S. Craig), a young white backpacker who has been camping on the café grounds.

4. Rolland invokes the "oceanic" to explain religious feeling. See Freud's discussion in chap. 1 of *Civilization and Its Discontents*, trans. James Strachey (New York: Norton, 1961).

5. The terms are taken from Richard Dyer's table categorizing entertainment's utopian sensibilities. See Dyer, "Entertainment and Utopia," in *Movies and Methods*, ed. Bill Nichols (Berkeley: University of California Press, 1985), 2:225.

6. This question is addressed with precision and rigor in Konstanze Streese and Kerry Shea, "Who's Looking? Who's Laughing? Of Multicultural Mothers and Men in Percy Adlon's *Bagdad Café*" in *Women in German Yearbook*, eds. Jeanette Clausen and Sara Friedrichsmeyer (Lincoln: University of Nebraska Press, 1993), 8:179–97.

7. Here the film echoes the trajectory of Kaufmann's own career, since she abandoned Hollywood to return to Germany.

8. The midseventies saw a large number of books and essays on the position(s) of African Americans in cinema. Among the better known of these studies, see the recently expanded edition of Donald Bogle's 1973 study *Toms, Coons, Mulattoes, Mammies, and Bucks: An Interpretive History of Blacks in American Films* (1973; reprint, New York: Continuum, 1989) as well as two books by Thomas Cripps, *Slow Fade to Black: The Negro in American Film 1900–1942* (New York: Oxford University Press, 1977) and *Black Film as Genre* (Bloomington: Indiana University Press, 1978). Recently, the study of minority representation has been the subject of increasing critical attention. For a polemical account (and endorsement) of the place of theory in the study of minority representation, see the opening pages of James Snead, *White Screen/Black Images*, eds. Colin MacCabe and Cornell West (New York: Routledge, 1994) as well as Robert Stam and Louise Spence, "Colonialism, Racism, and Representation: An Introduction," in *Movies and Methods*, ed. Bill Nichols (Berkeley: University of California Press, 1985), 2:632–49.

9. For a discussion of African Americans as entertainers in American films of the 1940s, see Bogle, *Toms, Coons, Mulattoes, Mammies, and Bucks*, 5:117–35.

10. According to Bogle "the entertainment syndrome, endured a bit past the mid-1940s; ultimately it wore itself thin and died" (ibid., 132).

11. A number of theorists, including Eric Santner and, in a very different register, Henryk M. Broder, have shown that this is a position with no small allure for the elaboration of a post-Nazi German identity. See chap. 2 of Santner's *Stranded Objects* (Ithaca: Cornell University Press, 1990) and see also Broder's "Der Täter als Bewährungshelfer, oder Die Deutschen werden den Juden Auschwitz nie verzeihen," in *Der ewige Antisemit: Über Sinn und Funktion eines beständigen Gefühls* (Frankfurt/Main, Germany: Fischer, 1986), 125–64.

9

Interview with Seyhan Derin: *ben annemin kiziyim*
(I Am My Mother's Daughter)

Henriette Löwisch

Seyhan Derin belongs to the very young generation of highly ambitious German filmmakers who are independent-minded and pragmatic in achieving their goals. Little links her to the well-known names of the New German Cinema; she is used to searching for and finding her own way. Born in Turkey, brought to Germany at a young age, and raised there, she left home as a teenager to avoid being sent back to her homeland. Since then, she has been living with the challenges of a dual cultural heritage. This connects her to many of her contemporaries, especially young women of Turkish descent, who are unwilling to follow the family traditions of rural Turkey. It is not surprising then, that life on the boundaries between Germany and Turkey is an ongoing theme in her work.

Derin's first full feature film *ben annemin kiziyim* (I Am My Mother's Daughter), a project that came out of the prestigious Munich film school, premiered at the 1996 Berlinale and won a second prize at the Munich documentary film festival in the same year. In this film, she attempts to portray a close-up of her mother, who throughout her life, stood in the shadow of the dominating father to whom Seyhan was the favorite child. Derin's current project is the story of a German woman who is invited to a funeral and only then finds out that her father was a Turk.

When I met Derin in Munich, I was startled by her youth: she looks incredibly young, and that makes the fact that she is really older than stated in her passport all the more ironic. When she was born twenty-nine years ago in rural Turkey, no one had time to go to the next town and register her birth. Only when her father returned from Germany did the family start the obligatory pro-

cedures. At that point, Derin's parents would have risked an inquiry, had they admitted that their baby girl was already two years old. As this story illustrates, social conventions and cultural differences crisscross Derin's biography even in such prosaic ways as mistaken entries in her passport. What follows is my conversation with Derin on 25 August 1996.

Löwisch. How was *I Am My Mother's Daughter* conceived?

Derin. It came about quite by coincidence; my film school, HFF, Hochschule für Film und Fernsehen, H.L., cooperates with a school in Turkey; exchange projects exist that are sponsored by the European Union. They really wanted a project on the theme "three generations of women." A daughter born in Turkey and growing up in Germany, a mother who came to Germany as a guest-worker, a grandmother who never left Turkey—those were the conditions, and I fulfilled them.

Löwisch. The film shows you questioning your mother, shows you as a little girl on a journey, shows the places of your childhood in Turkey. Which parts are realistic and which are fictional?

Derin. The film isn't fictional at all; it is absolutely realistic. That's really the way it was. I didn't know much about my mother, I hesitated in the beginning; what should I say about my mother? I really didn't know anything about her. And then I realized that this could be the theme of the movie, that I knew nothing, yet wanted to learn about her.

Löwisch. Was it easy to convince your mother to participate in the film?

Derin. When I first called and told her that my professor had proposed this project to me, she hesitated a bit. Then she said—well, if it's going to help you, then it's OK. Later, when things became more concrete, when I arranged for the shooting and called her to get ready, she said, "I can't do this." And then I heard my father in the background, saying, "Of course you can." The funny thing was that she didn't end up having any of the difficulties she anticipated, quite the reverse: I was the one who had difficulties with the situation.

Löwisch. She seems a born actress.

Derin. Yes, it's quite amazing. I think for her it was in a way a welcome thing, that this was about her, that she got the opportunity to tell her story.

Löwisch. What made you want to become a filmmaker?

Derin. Thinking back, it had to do with my father as well. He organized a cinema for the guest-workers, showed Turkish films on Sunday afternoon. So I sat in the movie theater when I was five years old and watched Turkish movies. Later, I started making movies myself, with a super-eight-camera, just for fun. I didn't think about becoming a filmmaker until just before I finished high school.

Löwisch. Was it an advantage for you being a woman and a foreigner when you applied to film school? Or is it easier for men to be accepted there?

Derin. Whether it's easier for them I can't say, but there are always more men; that's true for our school as well. Some years there are classes where only one of thirteen students is a woman. In my class, we were four of thirteen.

Löwisch. Why is that?

Derin. Since among the professors who are on the selection committee, eight are men and only one is a woman, then this really isn't a mystery. I remember, in the year I applied, I was able to talk to one of their students beforehand, and he said, "Oh well, you're a woman and a foreigner as well; your odds look good," and I thought, "Excuse me?!" Then, when I was interviewed, I really got the impression that they made an extra effort with a female. However, I think it was just some kind of fashion trend then. It's not my sense that overall this had led to professors becoming more women-friendly.

Löwisch. Do you have role models?

Derin. Not really, but there always were people who gave me courage, people of various nationalities. Take the Turkish cinema, for example. I still find Yilmaz Güney very, very interesting: he actually also comes from a rather poor family background and has made a very realistic cinema. The realistic cinema is really what I like. I also enjoy the work of Maya Deren, she has made a very extravagant super-eight-movies. I can relate to her very well, it's a perfect match: just wanting to go out, wanting to tell, use the simple realities that exist around you, that was her goal, as she said, "I could only claim a tiny piece of their visions, if my images do that to them, then I have achieved everything I could achieve."

Löwisch. What do you think about German cinema?

Derin. Interestingly enough, so far, German filmmakers have preoccupied me least. When I think about role models, I get to Andrej Tarkovskij, Carlos Saura; right now I'm quite interested in Bertolucci. I do like Wim Wenders's film *Himmel über Berlin*, but his other films don't really tell me much.

Löwisch. If current German cinema as such is criticized for being boring, uninspired, do you feel pressed to defend it?

Derin. Absolutely not. My problem right now is rather that they are trying to put me into the Turkish corner, which sometimes makes me almost angry when I'm confronted with it. In the end, I really don't care whether I am German or Turkish. I just try to make and develop my own kind of film.

Löwisch. Are there any great actresses in Germany at the present time?

Derin. I can't think of anyone off the top of my head. But of course, there are actresses that I'd like to work with one day, real stars, some of them.

Löwisch. For example?

Derin. Of the women there is Juliette Binoche, for example. I really would like to work with her; I find her very interesting. And of the men that she has already worked with, Jeremy Irons, Daniel Day-Lewis. With these three my mind is made up; I'll work with them one day.

Löwisch. It appears that women from Turkey have become more prominent in the German public lately, as actresses, in the media. What do you think is the reason for this development?

Derin. There simply has grown a new generation, who, after their parents were the workers' generation, don't want to follow this path, but want to go a different way. The options they see are either to be workers or to do something entirely different. I think that it's quite inevitable that this entirely different thing will be art. You don't want to live what your parents lived, for your own sake as well as for the parents' sake.

Löwisch. Do you dream of making a blockbuster?

Derin. Yes, of course.

Löwisch. What do you have to do to achieve that?

Derin. Well, it's certainly important to know the right people, to tell them, "Read this, tell me what you think of this." It's hard to call somebody to say, "I'm dreaming of telling this story." But in reality, people are just waiting for you; they are happy to be asked, to be able to help.

Löwisch. And yet, to make movies that are successful with a big audience, don't you have to compromise, to make faster-paced films, for example?

Derin. Yes, I guess that would be a major source of conflict. A friend of mine who is interested in my newest script and who keeps on saying, get going with it, he's already starting with that: it shouldn't be too long, it shouldn't be too boring; the narration shouldn't be too slow. That puts pressure on me, makes me question my own style, my own way of narrating. And yet, all I want is just to start out with my own way of doing things. But those fears stay with me, fears like who might want to see this anyway.

Löwisch. Is your mother, are your parents, proud of your success as a filmmaker?

Derin. I remember my mother saying in the old times: artists always have a bad life, no stability, they die before they're fifty, it's exhausting, and most of them end up doing strange things, take drugs, and so forth. But my parents had patience with me; they went through three years when I was doing only internships. They were relieved when I was accepted at the film school, because school for them means education; you end up having a diploma, and that's something that counts in Germany. Today my mother quite likes the fact that I do something I like to do, even though she keeps complaining that I'm over-worked. But in the end it's something that she knows about. She always says that she can't do otherwise, that she just has to work. She wouldn't know how to do nothing; she would die if she couldn't work.

Löwisch. What is your relationship with Germany?

Derin. It is quite ambivalent, really. On the one hand, I very much like to live here, there is no other country where I feel so safe. Very banal things: if you order something, you get it, if you make an appointment, the appointment is kept. That isn't at all the way things work in Turkey, where they tell you "to-morrow," "day after tomorrow," and still what you wanted hasn't arrived. I experience this unreliability as very difficult, something I don't like to be con-fronted with. On the other hand, here I often miss spontaneity and change, and that can make me angry as well.

Löwisch. The Germans don't consider their country a country for immi-grants, with citizens of various cultural and ethnic origins.

Derin. That's true, but I think they will have to get used to it. The con-frontation is there and I don't shy away from it. In a way, I've maybe been too lucky, unlike some people, I'm not constantly confronted with being a for-eigner. It probably has much to do with the fact that I know how one lives here, how to assert myself, to get on with my own thing. It would be different if I didn't speak the language as well as I do, if I just wasn't aware of certain things, then this might be a bigger problem.

Löwisch. Would you say that your are politicized?

Derin. I certainly am political, but not in the sense that I feel part of any political group, that I would work in a political group; that's out of the question. But I do take sides, reflect on daily political matters and on the way we deal with each other.

Löwisch. The Kurdish question in the southeast of Turkey that concerns also the Turks and Kurds that live in Germany; does that interest you at all?

Derin. Yes, absolutely; this will be one of the themes of the next project I want to do. And then I'll have to be on guard. There are certain trends or ten-dencies that always get me into trouble with the Turkish consulate, the Turkish state. Once, I even spent a night in a Turkish jail. These things usually happen entirely by chance—that I get involved in such things, as I don't belong to those that take to the streets, waving flags.

Löwisch. Will this topic always stay with you or can you also see yourself making films one day that have nothing to do with this cultural conflict?

Derin. Well, there are quite a lot of sketches, treatments, that I write and then put aside for a while. About a third of them have to do with Turkey, but most of them are actually quite normal stories.

Löwisch. You try to reconcile Germanness and Turkishness.

Derin. For me and some of my friends that is in fact the way we live: trying to extract the best we can get out of everything and see what we can do with it. But we are in the minority. For my second youngest sister, for example, things are very different: she is married to a Turk in a very normal way, has two children, is a housewife; for her it is obvious that she is a Turkish woman. She lives the way my parents used to live. She would never even consider saying that she identifies with German culture.

Löwisch. Reconciliation of cultures and generations seems to be the leitmotif for your film *ben annemin kiziyim.*

Derin. Exactly, that was what mattered for me personally. Normally things remain clichés: bad parents on the one hand, good children who try to find their own way on the other. I now learned from my parents what it all meant to them, that it was a loss for them, too. That was what I wanted, to show that things always have two sides to them.

Löwisch. After this exceptionally tough and open conflict with your parents, how did your family achieve reconciliation?

Derin. Sometimes I think that it isn't such an exceptional story after all, if one looks at the family history as a whole, which is full of children-against-parents situations. In the end, my father did the same thing; he revolted against his father. What is novel in this generation is that this time it's the girls. We have four generations about whom is told that the sons revolted against the father who then fought back. Somehow there is this readiness to accept your children, your own children, your own flesh and blood, and to try time and again to find the way back to them. This doesn't mean though that one is understood in the reasons why one does things, that conflicts are resolved, not at all. And—today my parents feel at ease. In the beginning, they had this great fear that we might end up on the street. Now they see that we have an entirely normal life, that there is nothing they would have to be ashamed of before their own people.

III

Images of Power and Pleasures

10

Narcissism: The Impossible Love

Kaja Silverman

At first glance, *Bildnis einer Trinkerin* (1979) seems to provide an extended illustration of two of the most accepted tenets of feminist film theory. Like the theories of Laura Mulvey and Mary Ann Doane, it seems to suggest that there is a certain collapse between woman and the image,[1] and to propose as an alternative to this specular implosion the masquerade of femininity.[2] Its female protagonist is pathologically obsessed with her own mirror reflection; that reflection engrosses all other desire, and completely defines her relations to all of the other characters in the film. A long fantasy sequence in the second half of *Bildnis*, however, shows her assuming in succession a whole range of professional roles, and in the process manipulating the contours of her bodily image. Here, she seems to have achieved some distance from the mirror, to be detached from the identities that it figures forth. Because of the parodic aspect of the fantasy sequence, this detachment might well be taken for irony, and the images it inflects as a politically enabling masquerade of femininity.

I want to advance a very different reading of *Bildnis*, to show that, from the very beginning, Madame (Tabea Blumenschein) stands at an irreducible distance from the mirror, and that her pathological relation to her own reflection is the logical extension not of too complete a specular "captation," but of her inability to accept her exteriority to the idealizing image.[3] I also want to use Ottinger's film to challenge the assumption—which sometimes informs the equation of woman and spectacle—that the female subject stands outside lack, along with the particular reading of psychoanalysis from which it proceeds.[4]

Bildnis provides a wide-ranging commentary on what Jacques Lacan calls the imaginary, on the psychic register that is specific to identification and narcissism, and that the author of *Seminar II* places in the closest possible relation with the specular.[5] *Bildnis* tells the story of a woman who abandons her past, and with it her name, in order to dedicate herself uninterruptedly to the adoration and exhibition of herself-as-image. More precisely, it recounts the narrative of a woman who decides to take seriously the impossible mandate that is culturally imposed upon the white female subject: that she conform to the visual specifications of an ideal femininity. *Bildnis* brilliantly dramatizes the fantasy of bodily disintegration that haunts this project, and the consequent self-hatred into which self-love constantly threatens to devolve. However, it refuses to characterize the imaginary as a "feminine" domain, as a presymbolic space from which woman never fully emerges, or to which she easily regresses from the symbolic order.

Rather, like Lacan's early seminars, which will figure prominently in the following pages, *Bildnis* shows the imaginary to be fundamentally *reparative*, and, hence, unthinkable prior to the subject's symbolic structuration. It suggests, that is, that the images of an ideal unity within which the subject attempts to locate herself are not only always inflected by meaning, but are also conjurations against the void that is introduced by language. And if the imaginary cannot be thought apart from the symbolic, neither can the symbolic be "entered" without imaginary mediation; it is only through the coordinates of that necessary fiction, the self, as *Bildnis* shows, that the subject is able to apprehend the other. The theoretical gendering of the imaginary as "feminine" consequently represents a misrecognition of the part that it plays within all subjectivity. Finally, Ottinger's fourth feature film takes very seriously both the dangers and impasses to which the logic of the imaginary can lead, and its undeniable seductions, pleasures, and powers—seductions, pleasures, and powers that are at the heart of its own spectatorial appeal.

The white protagonist of *Bildnis* is introduced in terms not of her biographic specificity—we are in fact never given a single concrete detail about her past—but rather in terms of what might be called her mission. A disembodied female voice-over characterizes her as someone destined to embody the feminine ideal. It invokes this ideal by enumerating a number of the names with which it has been associated throughout the history of Western representation:

> She, a belle of antique grace and raphaelic harmony, a woman, created like no other to be Medea, Madonna, Beatrice, Iphigenia, Aspasia, decided one sunny winter day to leave La Rotunda. She bought a one-way ticket to Berlin-Tegel.

However, this proliferation of names attests to the impossibility of locating the feminine ideal within any individual woman, even within the realm of literature or art; it can only be conjured forth through the spectacle of swirling red fabric, and through the sound of high-heeled shoes tapping with exaggerated precision on a green marble floor.

These images demand to be read in relation to the project outlined in the opening monologue. There, we are told that Madame is leaving La Rotunda for

Berlin because Berlin seems to be a place where she will be able to devote herself uninterruptedly to a very singular goal:

> She wanted to forget her past, rather leave it like a ragged house. With heart
> and soul she wanted to concentrate on one affair. Her affair. To finally follow
> her destiny was her sole wish. Berlin, foreign to her, appeared to be the right
> place to live her passion undisturbed. Her passion was to drink, live to drink—
> a drunken life, life of a drunkard. Upon landing at Berlin-Tegel, her decision
> had become irrevocable. Inspired by a Berlin folder that was presented to her
> by a friendly stewardess, she decided to set up a drinking schedule. . . . She de-
> cided to do a sort of boozer's sightseeing, briefly, to use sightseeing for her very
> private needs. . . . Her plans for a narcissistic worship of loneliness have deep-
> ened and intensified to the point where they have entered a stage worthy to be
> lived, not to risk being lost in realms of fantasy. Now had come the time to let
> everything come true.

As this commentary makes clear, the object of the passion to which Madame
commits herself for the duration of *Bildnis* is only ostensibly alcohol. The consumption of wine and brandy is really a metaphor for another kind of incorpo-
ration, one much more difficult to effect. It is a metaphor, that is, for Madame's
attempt to assimilate or to become the specular ideal in relation to which she,
like all female subjects, is (negatively) defined. However, whereas for Doane the
dilemma of femininity is the excessive proximity of the mirror, for Madame the
problem is rather its irreducible distance.

Alcoholism functions as an appropriate metaphor for the project described
by the voice-over for two reasons. First of all, the consumption of alcohol leaves
behind no permanent "deposit" or residue. It results only in a very transitory
and delusory euphoria, which gives way to a sense of emptiness and loss, and
must consequently be endlessly repeated if its effects are to be sustained. Alcohol also lends itself to Ottinger's purposes because it is a fluid substance. Implicit
in the Narcissus myth, as in Ottinger's retelling of it, is an insistence upon the
impossibility of the lover's incorporative desire for the idealized self, and liquid-
ity assumes a privileged role in the articulation of this impossibility. Because the
image that engrosses him is reflected in a pool, he cannot embrace it without
shattering it.

Lacan provides an important definition of the fragmented body in *Seminar I*. He suggests that it is "an image essentially dismemberable from its
body"[6]—it provides the fantasy through which the subject acknowledges his
or her distance from the idealizing representation with which he or she would
like to find his or her "self." It could thus be said that any attempt to enter the
impossible frame of that representation leads inexorably, as in the Narcissus
legend, to the subject's "fall" into an image that is the very opposite of the one
that is desired: his or her headlong "plunge," that is, into an image of bodily
decomposition.

When Madame appears in the ornate double doorway of her hotel prior to leaving for the casino, dressed in an exquisite black evening gown and matching hat, and with a golden spiral hanging from each ear, she seems at least momentarily to approximate the image around which her desire revolves. The ensuing cab ride, however, already attests to a certain unraveling of this coherence. Initially, Madame is located firmly in the backseat of the car, but eventually she projects herself imaginarily into the driver's seat, in the guise of a young white man with a mustache and black leather jacket. Significantly, this masculine masquerade fails to alter the terms of her self-address. What this scene dramatizes is less the production of an ironic distance from the mirror than the conjuration of yet another ideal image of self, this time male rather than female. As is so frequently the case in *Bildnis*, either the image cannot be assumed, or it quickly loses its seductive luster. The fantasmatic cab driven by Madame in her capacity as male driver knocks over the cart of Lutze, a homeless white woman, and spills its contents all over the street. This accident dramatizes the inability of the self to contain the images out of which it is ostensibly composed. But here, at least, the specter of disintegration is successfully exteriorized.

As she leaves the casino, Madame once again encounters Lutze, who helps her into a cab and who washes one of its windows with spit and a rag. Lutze's actions serve to liquefy or destablize the image on the other side of the glass. Her face also functions as a kind of alternative mirror. As Lutze wipes the window with her rag, Madame stares intently at her features, even turning to look back when the cab pulls away. This scene clearly positions the wealthy woman in a narcissistic relation to her homeless counterpart. However, this relation differs markedly from that described by Lacan in "The Mirror Stage."[7] Lutze does not provide Madame with an idealized self-image, but with the opposite; she literalizes the fantasy of the body in bits and pieces, which constantly threatens to undermine that image.

Back in her hotel room at the end of her first day in Berlin, Madame resorts once more to alcohol as a device for closing the gap between herself and ideality. Her room has been transformed into a narcissistic shrine: two identical photographs of its occupant in masculine clothing hang on the wall above the bed, each lit by three lights in the shape of votive candles. Madame again positions herself in relation not only to feminine perfection, but also to what might be called "the man she would like to have been."[8] *Bildnis* thus equips its protagonist with both a female and a male ego-ideal. And, unlike the woman about whom Freud writes,[9] Madame reserves for herself the right to approximate each in turn.

The wine Madame consumes facilitates a series of extraordinary fantasies. Because these fantasies are "actualized" at the level of the image but not the narrative, they dramatize the resistance that the spectacle of woman can offer to the forward movement of the story. Each takes the spectator into what Mulvey calls "a no man's land outside its own time and space," and gives "the quality of a cut-out or icon, rather than verisimilitude, to the screen" (20). Of course, given its larger preoccupation with female specularity, and, most particularly, with those idealized images of femininity that can be neither temporally nor spatially localized, this quality inheres as well in many of the film's other images; this fantasy sequence merely represents its apotheosis.

In the first shot of the sequence, a dwarf (Paul Glauer) stands to the right of an elaborate granite fountain, bowing and gesturing to Madame to approach. She enters from the other side, sits down on the ledge of the fountain, and drinks from its contents. The hyperreal acuity of the sounds made by her approaching footsteps and by the placement of her glass on the ledge evoke the clink of ice cubes in a glass. This acoustic version of the alcohol metaphor surfaces again in the next fantasy, where it is given a visual analogue. Here, Madame and the dwarf slowly climb up a glass-enclosed stairway. This structure has the shape and the opaque consistency of the glasses conventionally used for iced tea or mint juleps. The third fantasy shows the dwarf, in extreme long shot, carrying a drink on a tray toward a pagoda, in which Madame sits. She raises the glass to her lips.

In the final, and most aesthetically compelling fantasy, Madame and the dwarf ceremonially cross a brook on the round steps provided for that purpose, again producing a sound evocative of ice against glass. Here, as in the other fantasies, her clothing, the music, and the general mise-en-scène connote "the Orient." The dwarf plucks an orange flower from the water and hands it, as if it were a glass, to Madame. She raises it to her lips, her head thrown back voluptuously. Three more shots repeat this gesture, emphasizing the contrast between the intense orange of the flower, the rich black and blue of Madame's dress, and the exaggerated pallor of her complexion.

Each of the first three fantasies consists of only one isolated shot, as if to insist at a formal as well as conceptual level on its status as "cutout" or "icon." The final fantasy, on the other hand, consists of four shots. Interestingly, however, this recourse to montage does not serve to advance the narrative; each subsequent shot merely works to reiterate the action shown in the preceding one. The final fantasy does nevertheless dramatize an "advance," but one that is spatial rather than temporal. Whereas the camera remains at a discreet remove from its human subjects in the first three fantasies, in the last one it abandons this principle. In each of its four shots, the distance between Madame and the camera diminishes, until her face is finally shown in an eroticizing close-up that isolates the activity of drinking from all else. I say "the distance between Madame and the camera," but what is really at issue here is the distance between the protagonist of *Bildnis* and her ideal imago. In the first three fantasies, that imago remains unapproachable, but in the final four shots, Madame moves closer and closer to the desired mirror, until she almost achieves in relation to it that proximity that Doane characterizes as the feminine norm.

Significantly, in the shot immediately preceding the fantasy sequence, Madame is shown lying with her back to the images that hang on the wall above the bed. Consequently, she is not overtly positioned as an external spectator in relation to the ideal she seeks to approximate, which presumably facilitates the imaginary approach to it dramatized by the flower-drinking shots. However, not only are all of the fantasy images marked by a high degree of "unreality," located in a "no man's time and space"—a place, that is, where no one can actually "be"—but each is emphatically displayed for an implied viewer, who can only be Madame. The final shot of her lifting the flower to her mouth gives way to two scenes in which the axis of vision is much more fully foregrounded, in ways that work to place her once again at an irreducible distance from ideality. Here, Madame is subordinated to the gaze, in her capacity both as spectacle and as look.

In the first of those scenes, Madame sits at a table in a coffee shop drinking brandy after brandy, the empty glasses ranged in front of her. Here, the ingestion of alcohol offers none of the narcissistic gratification it provides in the fantasy sequence; instead, it is manifestly desperate and obsessional. She faces a window, toward which she repeatedly grimaces and gesticulates. At first, she appears to be addressing someone on the other side of the window, but as the scene progresses, it becomes increasingly apparent that the window is important less for its transparent properties than for its reflective ones. Madame's gestures and grimaces are not directed to the world outside the restaurant, but to the body in bits and pieces, or—to state the case somewhat differently—to the principle of decomposition that now threatens to gain the upper hand. Significantly, the principle is once again represented by Lutze, who is now placed in an even more intimate psychic relation to Madame than in the cab scene. In the only shot that purports to show what Madame sees when she looks at the window, Lutze pushes her cart toward the restaurant from the rear of the frame, until she stands directly behind the reflection cast on the glass by Madame. This shot not only indicates that the window functions as a mirror in the coffeehouse scene, but it also incontrovertibly establishes Lutze as the image that that mirror shows.

Significantly, Lutze passes through the window that maintains her exteriority in the cab scene, and into the space where the other woman sits. Madame summons here inside the restaurant, in an explicit acknowledgment of the psychic affinities that link her to the "bag lady." The two women drink several double brandies, but the alcohol again fails to provide Madame with the desired *méconaissance*. Finally, in a reversal of the Narcissus legend, she attempts to shatter rather than to embrace the mirror. She tosses the contents of a glass of brandy onto the window, much as one might throw something into a pool of water to disrupt the image formed there. As she does so, two other patrons of the coffee shop quickly pull out their cameras. They point them not at Madame or at Lutze, who replicates the action initiated by her friend, but at the streaming surface of the window. They thus photograph Madame not as "herself," but rather in the guise of the image she attempts to efface.

The photographers' action serves as another potent reminder that self-recognition is never a purely imaginary transaction. That transaction involves not only subject and image, represented in the restaurant scene by Madame and by the window/ Lutze, but also the gaze, which is metaphorized—as it is in Lacan's eleventh seminar[10]—by the camera. The gaze, which can perhaps best be defined as the inscription of otherness within the field of vision, radically exceeds the human looks through which it often manifests itself. It impresses itself upon us phenomenologically through that sense that we all have at moments of acute self-apprehension of being seen from a position outside ourselves, a position that *Bildnis* inscribes through the flash of the camera. That experience of specularization constitutes a necessary feature of identification; we can only effect a satisfactory captation when we not only see ourselves, but *feel ourselves being seen* in the shape of a particular image.

I say "particular image" because the gaze does not photograph us directly, but rather through the cultural representations that intervene between it and us—representations that Lacan calls the screen.[11] Although we often treat these representations as simple mirrors, they do not so much reflect us as cast their reflection upon us. They are carriers—among other things—of sexual, racial, and class differences. For these reasons, the subject does not always occupy the field of vision happily. No image can be comfortably assumed by the subject unless it is affirmed by the gaze, but the gaze does not necessarily photograph the subject in ways that are conducive to pleasure. As is so clearly the case in this scene, the gaze often imposes upon the subject an unwanted identity.

Even before the actual cameras are pointed at the window within which Madame sees herself as a body in bits and pieces, the screen is firmly in place. It manifests itself through a conversation taking place elsewhere in the restaurant. At a certain point in this scene, three women in houndstooth suits enter, and order matching deserts. As they eat their sweets, they engage in a conversation about alcohol abuse. At the precise moment that Madame and Lutze are ejected from the coffeehouse, one of them provides a verbal gloss on the screen through which those figures have been "photographed": "Disgusting! Women getting drunk in public!"

This commentary serves an extremely important function. It suggests that the image of the fragmented body is no more "authentic" than those within which Madame more jubilantly apprehends herself. In other words, it disposes of any temptation on the part of the spectator to see the restaurant window as the mirror in which Madame discovers her "true" self. Like the spectacle of ideal femininity, that of corporeal disintegration is culturally produced, and projected onto certain bodies by the social gaze. Not surprisingly, then, when Madame apprehends the distance that separates her from that femininity, she visualizes herself in the guise of Lutze. In our culture, homeless bodies signify the unraveling of the bodily ego.

The next morning, an unseen hand pushes under Madame's hotel room door a copy of a newspaper with the headline "Wealthy Foreign Lady Raised the Roof at Coffeehouse *Möhring*." When Madame picks up the paper, she discovers that it also features one of the unflattering pictures taken of her the day before. She carries the picture to the mirror, ostensibly to compare it with her reflected image. But the dissatisfied expression on her face shows that she is unable to separate the two representations. After several more unsuccessful attempts to isolate the mirror image from the newspaper photograph, she throws the contents of a glass of wine against her recalcitrant reflection, in a repetition of the previous day's action, and looks at it once more. Again, *Bildnis* stresses that there can be no direct access to the "self," and that even the subject's relation to the literal mirror involves all kinds of cultural coercions.

The film cuts immediately from this shot to a scene which, although clearly fantasmatic, is nevertheless curiously embedded in the larger narrative, and that again draws attention to the gaze. This scene begins with the oblique image of a sexually ambiguous figure whistling and gesturing, as if signaling the opening of a circus performance. This is followed by an overhead shot, which shows a large auditorium, with a conspicuously empty orchestra space. Five women, all dressed in black, file ceremoniously down the aisle, and sit down in the front row. A second whistle is heard. Madame enters and is escorted to her seat by the androgynous figure. The camera cuts again to the black-clothed women, who turn around en masse to stare at Madame. Their faces have been dramatically made up, as if for a dumb show. The character presiding over this strange "event," who can now be seen to be an elderly woman, brings Madame a glass and a bottle of champagne. Madame takes a sip of the champagne, and gestures her enthusiasm to her server. Again, the camera cuts away to the five women in the front row, who continue to stare fixedly at the drinking woman. There is a final shot of Madam: she takes another sip from the glass, puts on her dark glasses, and adopts a theatrically spectatorial position.

This scene, which might be said to make a spectacle out of spectatorship, demands to be read in relation to the one that follows. This next scene begins with a close-up of the blue video monitor in Madame's room. It shows the dwarf carrying a large cooked turkey on a platter into the same room. He stands motionless for several moments, as if displaying the turkey, and then carries it over to the bedside table and bows. The camera then pans away from the monitor to the right, revealing the "actual" night table and turkey. Madame enters the frame, picks up the carving knife that accompanies the bird, and stabs with it violently around one of the two images of herself hanging on the wall. Again, that image is illuminated by a bracket of candle-shaped electric lights, as if it were a shrine. Madame is dressed in the same pink satin nightgown that she wears when tossing the wine against the mirror, suggesting that this scene is the continuation of that one.

Whereas in earlier scenes Madame lay with her back to the images on the wall, she is now manifestly a viewer of them. This unwanted exteriority promotes aggressivity; located at a stubborn distance from the figure standing in front of it, the idealizing representation becomes a threatening rival that must be destroyed. This scene thus dramatizes the "despair" side of what Mulvey characterizes as the "long love affair/despair between image and self-image" (18).

In the auditorium fantasy, the desire for the elimination of the hated rival finds dramatic fulfillment. Again Madame is positioned as spectator rather than spectacle, but now the stage remains conspicuously empty. This void permits her once again to make a narcissistic claim on ideality, this time from the position of spectatorship. She attempts, in other words, to retreat from specularity to vision, to position herself as gaze, and thereby to achieve the narcissistic gratification that is denied to her in her capacity as image. But this is an impossible aspiration. The subject always looks from a position within the field of vision. Even when adopting a spectatorial position, in other words, she is subordinate to the gaze, which remains outside. The impossibility of Madame's project is signified in this scene not only by the hyperbolic specularization of her look, but also by the fixed stare of the five black-clothed women.

Yet another fantasy sequence occurs immediately after Madame and Lutze visit the lesbian bar. In this sequence, Madame aspires to occupy not only the position of the gaze, but that of the spectacle "photographed" by the gaze. This sequence is initiated by an extreme long shot of Madame sitting in a sky blue dress on a decorative park bench, symmetrically positioned in front of a bridge over the Spree, and framed by trees. The dwarf enters from the left, places a picture of himself on the ground beside the bench, and exits to the left. A close-up of Madame's left eye follows, accompanied by the click of a camera. This image gives way to six more shots of her sitting in the same place. The camera moves progressively closer to its human subject, cutting back and forth between each shot to the close-up of her eye. The last of the eye images introduces a series of six "professional" fantasies. At the end of this series, the frame sequence is repeated in reverse, beginning with a close-up of Madame's eye, and concluding with an extreme long shot of her sitting on the park bench while the dwarf removes his photograph.

The close-ups of Madame's eye that are interspersed between images of her on the park bench are extremely brief, more like "flashes" than composed images. Like the sound that accompanies them, they suggest the opening and closing of a still camera shutter. Because of the metaphoric value afforded the camera in the restaurant scene, these shots make very evident Madame's renewed aspiration to occupy the position of the gaze. However, whereas the auditorium scene dramatizes her attempt to abolish the spectacle she cannot inhabit, the situation here is more complicated. The eye/park bench series does not dramatize Madam's ambition to become a transcendental gaze, outside spectacle, but rather her attempt to occupy the point from which she is "photographed." She seeks to safeguard the ideality of herself as spectacle by functioning simultaneously as the gaze, thereby imposing a purely imaginary logic on the field of vision.

Once again, *Bildnis* attests in all kinds of ways not only to the alterity of the gaze, but also to the unavoidable imbrication of imaginary and symbolic. To begin with, in each of the professional fantasies, Madame "performs" not for herself, but for the houndstooth women, Common Sense, Social Question, and Exact Statistics, who offer a parodic personification of the symbolic order. Moreover, although Madame never produces "embodied" speech in any of these fantasies, each depends in some central way upon a verbal text, whether it be the soliloquy from *Hamlet*, the outraged monologue a business owner directs toward his recalcitrant secretary, an advertising brochure for coffins, the words of a popular song, or the exclamations of onlookers during a tightrope performance. Sometimes these texts are spoken by a voice-over, and at other times they are spoken by a voice internal to the fiction, but we are never given images uninflected by language. The professional fantasies are also characterized by a certain degree of narrative elaboration, which, like the centrality of language, and the spectatorial role played by the houndstooth ladies, testifies to the omnipresence of the symbolic.

The first fantasy begins when the dwarf pulls back the curtain on the stage on which Madame will subsequently "deliver" Hamlet's most famous soliloquy. That gesture suggests that the scenes that follow are being ordered or "managed" from another "scene," and that Madame's desires are the desires of the Other.[12] The soliloquy from *Hamlet*, moreover, immediately introduces a topic that will resurface repeatedly in the professional fantasies, only to be subordinated each time to a concern with "appearances." The first words Madame "speaks" after appearing on the stage are "To be or not to be—that is the question." The subsumption of death to a narcissistic problematic indicates perhaps more strikingly than anything else that the fantasy sequence represents an imaginary displacement of a symbolic problematic.

In *Seminar XI*, Lacan proposes that his subject accedes to language only at the cost of "being." He allegorizes the entry into the symbolic as an old-fashioned highway robbery, in which the alternatives are not money or life, but meaning or life. The subject, of course, always chooses meaning, and hence speaks from the domain of death.[13] However, Lacan writes in "Aggressivity in Psychoanalysis" that "fear of death" is subordinate to "narcissistic fear of damage to one's own body."[14] He thereby underscores the reluctance of the subject to arrive at a conscious acceptance of his or her "being-for death"—his or her unwillingness, that is, to confront the nothingness or *manque-à-être* out of which desire issues. The ego represents the primary vehicle of this denial, that through which the subject procures for him or herself an illusory plenitude.

As is so often the case within the psychic domain, we are of course not dealing here with a simple denial, but with a simultaneous avowal and disavowal. The only ego capable of filling the lack at the heart of subjectivity is the one that affords a "jubilant" self-recognition, and this exemplary unity—which always assumes in the first instance a corporeal form—is impossible to sustain. It inexorably gives way to its antithesis, corporeal decomposition. The body in bits and pieces might thus be said to provide the imaginary construct through which the subject indirectly apprehends both her distance from the mirror, and her *manque-à-être*.

The eye/bench sequence enacts precisely the displacement I have just described. The *Hamlet* soliloquy offers yet another version of the old-fashioned highway robbery, only here the options are more starkly stated; the alternatives are, quite simply, life and death. But even as this grim choice is articulated, it undergoes an imaginary transmogrification. While listening to the famous monologue, Social Question, Common Sense, and Exact Statistics comment not upon the relative merits of the two possibilities it presents, but upon Madame's unsuitability for the role she plays. "The lead is totally drunk!" one of them exclaims. Another complains that Hamlet is a "breeches" rather than a female part. Again, attention is deflected away from death to the specular domain, or, to state the case slightly differently, from *manque-à-être* to the *moi*.

The subsequent fantasies subordinate death even more fully to a "fear of narcissistic damage to the body." Madame literally falls out of her assigned role in two of these fantasies, dramatically opening up that gap between the subject and its ideal imago that Lacan associates with the fantasy of the fragmented body. In one scene she loses her balance while attempting to walk a tightrope and plummets to the ground; in another, she rolls unconscious off the hood of a stunt car after the latter drives through a wall of flames. *Bildnis* shows the last fall three times, with virtually identical shots, as if to emphasize the loss of corporeal control. In the remaining fantasies Madame's fall out of the idealizing frame is more metaphorically rendered. In the scenes in which she represents an advertising consultant, a secretary, a singer, and a coffin salesman, she remains manifestly exterior to the roles she plays. This exteriority is perhaps most strikingly communicated through the sound track; the voices that speak "for" Madame are not synchronized or "married" to her body, but manifestly derive from elsewhere.[15]

In the penultimate sequence of *Bildnis*, Madame wears a dress composed primarily of silver foil. She has attempted to close the gap between herself and her ideal imago by literally "putting on" the mirror. However the dress does not entirely close in the back, and in the final moments of the film, this gap will become more and more pronounced. As before, the exteriority of the idealizing representation provokes violence; in asserting its independence from the desiring subject, the beloved imago becomes a hated rival, and must be destroyed. Madame stabs with a knife at her own shadow in the wall. Significantly, the sound of the knife striking the wall is connected acoustically to all the many variations on the theme of ice cubes clinking in glass; indeed, the ice cubes clinking can be heard in the knife stabs, and vice versa.

The final sequence of *Bildnis* is organized around a text by Peter Rosei. This text, titled "Drinkers," circulates among a series of narratively inconsequential characters, each of whom reads a passage aloud. Ottinger herself initiates this textual relay, in the guise of a derelict alcoholic. Sitting on a bench with a bottle of alcohol, she reads,

> Wondrous plan: to heighten a pleasure so much that it torments one to death. Lately I talked it over with Lipsky. He meant: "Our manias are nothing but Eryns in the theater of cruelty." I said: "So we hate ourselves." "Yes," Lipsky said, "It's not that bad."

This passage makes explicit the metaphoric connection between alcohol and narcissism. It also suggests once again that a libidinal economy organized entirely around the attempt to approximate an ideal imago could more justly be characterized as "self-hatred" than "self-love," since the demands it makes on the subject are impossible to sustain for more than a delusory moment. However, since the "intoxication" of that moment is so extreme that all other pleasures pale by comparison, there is nothing more addictive.

The final section read from the Rosei text also emphasizes the thrill that comes from being lifted even briefly into the rarefied atmosphere of ideality. It compares that experience to planetary travel; "drinkers are travellers," reads a businessman into whose open suitcase Madame has dropped the book, "they're . . . moved without moving. You pick them up, you give a lift. Can you see the galaxy?" The Rosei text stresses not just the pleasures, but also the life-threatening dangers of this situation. To identify with ideality is to refuse lack, and with it desire; consequently, it is to turn away from life itself. For this reason, the Rosei passage concludes, "self-sufficiency could only be 'ruin[ous].'"

The last diegetic shot of *Bildnis* shows Madame lying unconscious on a flight of stairs leading to a train station. Lutze finds her there, and attempts to lift her to a standing position. As she does so, a crowd of people rush down the stairs, obscuring the two women from our view. Lutze screams in terror, indicating that Madame has been trampled to death by the crowd. This shot must be read in relation to the one with which the film concludes. In it, Madame walks down a hallway constructed entirely of mirrors in her silver foil dress. As she proceeds, she crushes her own reflection underfoot. This shot, which has no narrative locus, repeats the one that precedes it at a metacritical level. Together, these two shots make clear that Madame's death is less literal than symbolic. The event outside the train station signifies not Madame's physical demise, but rather her full and final surrender to the morbid economy of narcissism.

Notes

1. I do not mean to suggest that the formulations advanced by these two theorists are in all respects commensurate. Laura Mulvey's concern is with the positioning of woman as spectacle within classic cinema (see "Visual Pleasure and Narrative Cinema," in *Visual and Other Pleasures* [Bloomington: Indiana University Press, 1989]), 14–26. Mary Ann Doane addresses rather what she sees as the psychic proximity of the female subject, and most particularly of the female spectator, to the image—her lack of symbolic differentiation from it (see *The Desire to Desire: The Woman's Film of the 1940s* [Bloomington: Indiana University Press, 1987]; and "Film and the Masquerade: Theorizing the Female Spectator," in *Femmes Fatales: Feminism, Film Theory, Psychoanalysis* [New York: Routledge, 1991], 33–43.

2. This argument derives primarily from Doane's "Film and the Masquerade," 24–26, although Mulvey also talks about female transvestism in her "Afterthoughts on 'Visual Pleasure and Narrative Cinema' inspired by King Vidor's *Duel in the Sun*," in *Visual and Other Pleasures*, 29–38.

3. For a longer reading of *Bildnis einer Trinkerin*, and for a much fuller discussion both of the dangers of self-idealization, and of the transformative potential implicit in the active conferral of ideality upon an other, see my *Threshold of the Visible World* (New York: Routledge, 1996), chap. 2.

4. Again, within film studies it is primarily Doane who has articulated the argument that woman stands outside lack. See, in addition to the texts just cited, "Woman's Stake: Filming the Female Body," in *Femmes Fatales*, 165–77.

5. In Book 2, *The Ego in Freud's Theory and in the Technique of Psychoanalysis, 1954–1955*, trans. Sylvana Tomaselli (New York: Norton, 1991), Lacan observes that "*Bildnis* [images] means imaginary," 137.

6. Lacan, *The Seminar of Jacques Lacan*, Book 1, *Freud's Papers on Technique, 1953–1954*, trans. John Forrester (New York: Norton, 1991), 148.

7. In "The Mirror Stage as Formative of the Function of the I," Lacan emphasizes the jubilation experienced by the child upon first seeing its reflection in a mirror (in *Ecrits: A Selection*, trans. Alan Sheridan [New York: Norton, 1977], 1).

8. For a discussion of the woman who takes as her ego ideal the man she would like to have been, see chap. 1 of *Threshold of the Visible World*.

9. See Sigmund Freud, "Femininity," in *The Standard Edition of the Complete Psychological Works*, trans. James Strachey (London: Hogarth Press, 1957), 22:132–33.

10. See Lacan, *Four Fundamental Concepts of Psychoanalysis*, trans. Alan Sheridan (New York: Norton, 1978), 106. For a general discussion of the gaze, see not only this text, but my book *Male Subjectivity at the Margins*, chap. 3, and chaps. 4 and 6 of *The Threshold of the Visible World*. In the latter text, I provide a fuller discussion of the metaphorization of the gaze as a camera.

11. See Lacan, *Four Fundamental Concepts*, 91–107; *Male Subjectivity*, chap. 3; and chaps. 1 and 4 of *The Threshold of the Visible World* for an account of the screen.

12. Miriam Hansen characterizes the dwarf as the representative of Madame's death wish, and as the "master of ceremonies" within the domain of her fantasies, in "Visual Pleasure, Fetishism and the Problem of Feminine/Feminist Discourse: Ulrike Ottinger's *Ticket of No Return*," *New German Critique*, no. 31 (1984): 100.

13. Lacan, *Four Fundamental Concepts of Psycho-Analysis*, 210–11.

14. Lacan, "Aggressivity in Psychoanalysis," in *Ecrits*, 28.

15. Synchronization implies above all else a unified subject. Its absence here attests yet again to the heterogeneity of Madame's bodily ego, as well as to her dependence upon the other. For an analysis of the cinematic norm of synchronization, and its implications for sexual difference, see my *Acoustic Mirror: The Female Voice in Psychoanalysis and Cinema* (Bloomington: University of Indiana Press, 1988), chap. 2.

11

Wanda's Whip: Recasting Masochism's Fantasy— Monika Treut's *Seduction: The Cruel Woman*

Barbara Mennel

"Controversial," Julia Knight concludes in a rare overview of the German filmmaker Monika Treut's oeuvre, is "the one term that has been used repeatedly in reviews and discussions of Treut's work—and hence appears less open to dispute."[1] Yet instead of deriving the term from the topics of Treut's films, Knight argues that it stems exclusively from her first feature-length film *Seduction: The Cruel Woman* (1985). Moreover, Knight believes that "the controversy has very little to do with any actual lesbian or sadomasochistic 'content' and much more to do with the film's production history and reception."[2] Treut herself describes audience reactions to the film's first showing in 1985 at the Berlin Film Festival "like a riot . . . a nightmare."[3] In an interview I conducted with her, however, she links both the production and the reception scandals of *Seduction*, which, according to Knight, produced her controversial fame. Treut recalls:

> And then we got the first rejections from the minister of interior, Fritz Zimmermann, a right-winger from the Christian Democratic Union. He personally rejected our script, after it had already been accepted, which created a scandal. Ultimately we received a smaller amount of money from two Social Democratic Party state grants. But this scandal created a problem for the film's reception later on in Germany, because this media spectacle gave the film a pathetic kind of fame, even before it was finished. . . When the film finally was produced, expectations were very high. People must have believed it to be incredibly radical, and projected absolutely different fantasies onto it. As a result, audiences were disappointed that this film is not pornographic, shows no genitals or genital sex. . . . People commented: "What is this? It is altogether harm-

less! How come Zimmermann opposes this?" We were criticized, and we had almost more reviews than viewers. From the right to the left, the consensus was, this film is useless and superfluous.[4]

Clearly, the production and reception scandals of *Seduction* are more closely linked to the film's topic of sadomasochism than Knight suggests. I want to maintain that the twin responses of censorship and outrage reflect the displacement and aggression that are publicly produced in reaction to representations of masochism and sadism. Knight avoids addressing the issue of masochism and S&M in favor of presumably "neutral" topics, such as financing and reception history.

In this essay, I demonstrate that the issue of masochism produces the film's controversial provocation and enables its potential productive contribution to current discourses on perverse desire. In particular, *Seduction*'s appropriation of historical models of sadism and masochism creates a space to investigate, rearrange, and reverse sexual and gender configurations.[5] I suggest that the film's recasting of the seduction fantasy undermines the heterosexual inscription of Freud's analysis of the Oedipal seduction scene. *Seduction* re-creates and complicates the interrelatedness of perverse desire and heteronormativity; transgression and commodification; traditional accounts of sadism and masochism and current formations of S&M. Furthermore, the film reproduces the aesthetics of perverse desire structured around suspense and fetishization. Through the integration of video into the film's narrative, *Seduction* constructs a polymorphously perverse gaze. The film portrays lesbian desire and fetishism without constructing a specific lesbian etiology. The collaboration of Treut and Elfie Mikesch inverts the male bonding of traditional masochistic texts, such as Leopold von Sacher-Masoch's *Venus in Furs* (1870), and the representation of lesbian desire decenters the heterosexual structure of traditional formations of masochism. The political and aesthetic significance of Treut's film lies in its resistance to the representation of a separate lesbian etiology and to its simultaneous insistence on the political and sexual transgressiveness that results from recasting traditionally gendered and heterosexual spectatorial and psychological models.

More than simply the topic of sadomasochism itself, *Seduction*'s reappropriation and reversals of those gender and sexual positions inherent in the traditional models of masochism and sadism led to the film's negative reception and to the label "controversial." For example, the public response to *Seduction* contrasts with the West German box office successes of that time, Carlos Saura's *Carmen* (1982) and Robert von Ackeren's *Woman in Flames* (1984). Both of these films address masochism and sadism explicitly, but advocate implicitly traditional gender politics. The consensus of the political Left and Right in their rejection of *Seduction* reflects male-dominated discourses on both sides of the political spectrum, embodied on the one hand by the right-wing minister Zimmermann, and manifested on the other hand by the left-wing magazine *Konkret*, which ran a lengthy negative critique of *Seduction*.[6] The dissolution of differences between the traditional political poles also points to the symptomatic difficulty of categorizing masochism politically. Masochism's inherent staging of domination and submission allows for a reading of subversion: performativity foregrounds and appropriates domination and submission in the existing system and therefore subverts it. Yet it also allows for a reading of conservatism: reenactment reproduces and reinscribes the status quo.

Seduction not only evoked male-dominated discourses on both sides of the political spectrum, but it was also positioned in opposition to the second wave of the German women's movement. While the women's movement figured female masochism as the ideological underpinning of patriarchy, more recent pro S&M rhetoric emphasizes both women's choice and playfulness in relationship to enacted roles and employed fetishes. It is precisely the aspect of staging within masochistic aesthetics that opens up the question as to whether a masochistic performance reproduces or subverts the status quo. I suggest, that instead of positing the problem as an either/or question, however, it might be more productive to discuss the potential and limitation of subversion through reenactment within specific historical and political parameters.

While *Seduction* never became a very successful film with West German audiences, its screenings at several film festivals abroad (especially in the United States and Canada), initiated Treut's international reception as a lesbian German filmmaker within a newly emerging queer cinema.[7] The resulting academic valorization of Treut's work in the United States, Britain, and Canada (both in film and queer studies), coincided with debates over the constructions and representations of queer identities and sexualities, in particular, lesbian desire. In this context, *Seduction* opens up possibilities to think through the relationship of lesbian desire and fetishism. The centrality of the fetish derives from a tradition of masochistic aesthetics, embodied by Treut's rereading of Sacher-Masoch's *Venus in Furs*, one of his many novels centering on the cruel woman.

Seduction cites and appropriates characters, aesthetic structures, and textual passages from Sacher-Masoch's *Venus in Furs* and Marquis de Sade's *Justine* (1787) and from *The Story of Juliette* (1797). In *Seduction*, Wanda, the heroine of Sacher-Masoch's novel, is an independent video-artist who heads an artistic community producing S&M performances. Instead of a conventional narrative, *Seduction* is comprised of sequences of dialogues, tableaux of S&M performances, and sexual scenes. Gregor, the male masochist from *Venus in Furs*, is disempowered and dependent on Wanda, who is coded as lesbian through relationships with Caren, a shoe store owner, and with Justine (later in the film called Juliette), a composite of two Sadean characters. Mährsch, a journalist, enters the masochistic universe to write an article on Wanda, but instead becomes her customer.

The film culminates in an elaborate staging of a costumed sadomasochistic ritual directed by Wanda, in which Gregor shoots at her, but only produces laughter by Wanda and the ensemble.

Widely read and well-received during its time period, *Venus in Furs* was generally forgotten until Gilles Deleuze recuperated it in his path-breaking essay, "Coldness and Cruelty." [8] Deleuze pointed to the literary basis of the concept of masochism, and outlined its aesthetic structure according to Sacher-Masoch's novel. *Venus in Furs*'s narrator is an unnamed man who receives a manuscript from his friend Gregor, which entails the actual masochistic narrative: Gregor's encounter with Wanda and the process of education through which he molds her into the dominant woman, adorned with fetishes. Their contract inscribes his absolute dependency on her and he changes his name to Severin. When Wanda brings in "the third term," the Greek, who whips Gregor, the masochistic relationship falls apart. In the final scene, we learn that Gregor has married and dominates his wife. The scenes of domesticity enclose the masochistic narrative staging of a gender role-reversal. The novel's structure therefore provides a blueprint for masochistic texts: a fantasy embedded in a frame portraying the status quo.

In *Venus in Furs*, the cruel woman embodies two interconnected features of masochism: fetishism and suspense. Arrested images of the cruel woman, adorned with fetishes represent the permanent delay of sexual gratification to the extent that the investment of pleasure lies in the suspense itself. *Seduction*'s stylization of S&M performances in staged tableaux quotes the stillness and coldness of the construction of the "original" dominant woman in *Venus in Furs* and creates the suspense that underlies the masochistic aesthetic. *Seduction* establishes fantasy from the beginning of the film as part and parcel of masochism. Yet the structure of fantasy radically departs from the structure of margin and center implied in the traditional relationship between frame and masochistic fantasy in masochistic narratives. In *Venus in Furs*, and in films (e.g., *Woman in Flames*) that take up these traditional structures, a traditional bourgeois home provides the frame for a reversal of roles in a masochistic staging. In contrast, *Seduction*'s opening quotes the formal structure of masochistic narratives while reversing margin and center. In the opening scene, the scene that frames the masochistic narrative, a sailor played by Georgette Dee, stands in the harbor, singing "Wenn ich mir was wünschen dürfte. . . ." (If I were granted a wish. . . .). Citing Marlene Dietrich in *Der Mann, der seinen Mörder sucht* (The Man Who Is Looking for His Murderer), the song conjures up the tradition of masochistic film texts.[9] To viewers familiar with German gay subculture, Dee connotes transvestism; Dee is also positioned in the harbor, a site of marginalized eroticism. This framing points to the significant difference between Treut's project and traditional cultural constructions of masochism.

The film cuts from this opening shot in the harbor to a camera movement through a tunnel underwater. The subterranean environment and the lack of suture address the subconscious. Heavy male breathing begins (nondiegetic), creating suspense and affecting the viewer's bodily responses. After the next cut, the sound is diegetically linked up with the image as we see Mährsch, the journalist, crawling on a ceramic floor, licking it.[10] Mährsch's body is fetishized, beginning with the old-fashioned women's shoes he is wearing. The slow camera movement from the women's shoes along his male body takes up the gender fluidity introduced by Dee. These early scenes present a different male masochist than the one constructed in *Venus in Furs*, who adorns the dominant woman with fetishes. Here, the male masochist has used the fetishized object to adorn his own body; he produces internal pleasure, because the integration of "female" fetishes heightens male submission and humiliation. After being crosscut with the subterranean space, we again see Mährsch crawling through what could be a whip or rolls of film hanging from the ceiling. The indecidability of these strips' signification adds another meaning to Dee's song. The desire for fantasy expressed in the opening shot not only quotes from the tradition of an enclosed masochistic world within a narrative of the real, but also enunciates the desire for the machinery of moving images, the body moving through images: the cinema.

After another sequence of establishing shots, we see the beginning of a sequence that indicates a temporal and logical flow: Wanda wakes up in her bed; the other side is empty. We see her female lover moving down a hallway, picking up clothes. A video in the mise-en-scène of Wanda's office plays a tape of Mährsch's movement, which we have just seen. The video is produced by Wanda and projected in the space between her and Caren. This sets up a triangulated relationship that is a reversal: the image of the male masochist projected between Caren and Wanda inverts the male bonding over the woman in Sacher-Masoch's novel. The doubling of the images, shown earlier as part of the film and later as video, self-reflexively points to the machinery of cinema and of the filmmakers themselves.

Specifically lesbian S&M became a central metaphor for transgressive sexuality as part of "the sex wars," a harsh debate between antiporn feminists and prosex lesbians.[11] While the dichotomy between the two positions was more pronounced in the United States, it nevertheless was introduced to Germany, mainly through the feminist magazine *Emma*, which endorsed the antipornography campaign of Andrea Dworkin and Catharine MacKinnon.[12] More recently, lesbian S&M has achieved a privileged status both theoretically and politically as transgressive and subversive in relationship to the status quo. Some scholars have engaged with the inherent connections between feminism and lesbian S&M.[13] Nevertheless, the majority of texts concerned with lesbian S&M presuppose a distinct uniqueness of lesbian S&M in relationship to any other form of masochism or sadomasochism.[14] Parveen Adams for example, argues that S&M lesbians are fundamentally different from both of the other two categories of masochists she cites ("the religious martyr" and "the male masochist"), as well as from "the lesbian who is not a pervert."[15] According to Adams, the sado-masochistic lesbian "appears not to be compulsive, . . . she constructs fetishes and substitutes them . . . [and] she has succeeded in detaching herself from the phallic reference."[16] In contrast to Adams's differentiation between S&M lesbians and lesbians who don't perform S&M, in *Seduction*, lesbian desire is neither subsumed in these relationships nor absolutely separate from heterosexual configurations of masochism.

Wanda's relationships with Gregor and Mährsch are simultaneously traditional in their citation of the paradigmatic relationship of male masochist and female dominatrix and radically different because Wanda directs the fantasies of submission. Lesbian desire is not reduced to either the bourgeois relationship, reenacted by Caren and Wanda, or to the S&M performance, for which Wanda educates Justine. Though all female characters partake in the S&M performances as either members of the audience or as participants, their relationships and sexual interactions are also portrayed outside of the masochistic universe. Lesbian sex acts literally take place outside the house: at the waterfront, on a boat, and in Caren's store. In addition to the spatial separation, sequences portraying lesbian sex are set apart through audio and rhythm, and are characterized by a repetition of movement and cuts. The resulting aestheticization connects the scenes portraying lesbian sexuality with each other, even though they are not connected through the narrative. For example, when we see Wanda and Caren embrace, the 180-percent rule is broken repeatedly, and we see a repetition of the embrace from different perspectives. The aestheticization of the dark shot is reminiscent of early cinema and denaturalizes lesbian sexuality and desire.

The question of cultural representations of lesbian perverse desire (e.g., in avant-garde cinema) and psychosocial development of lesbian identity are at the center of Teresa de Lauretis's book *The Practice of Love, Lesbian Sexuality and Perverse Desire*.[17] Basing her argument on the work of Jean Laplanche and Jean-Bertrand Pontalis on primal fantasies, she privileges Sheila McLaughlin's 1987 film, *She Must Be Seeing Things*, because of "the reinscription of the original fantasies, and in particular the recasting of the primal scene."[18] De Lauretis argues that the film constitutes lesbian spectatorship through a staged primal scene "recast in relation to the lesbian lovers" within the film.[19] Her approach suggests distinct boundaries between lesbian and heterosexual identities. Elizabeth Grosz, on the other hand, has argued that a specifically lesbian etiology can account neither for fluidity between sexual and gender identities nor for biographical moments of ruptures in identity formation.[20] Nevertheless, de Lauretis's argument about lesbian representation and identity is important on at least two accounts: one, she theorizes lesbian desire in terms of fetishism, and not in terms of the lack of the phallus. This distinguishes de Lauretis from other theoreticians, like Julia Kristeva, who represent lesbian desire as a regressive return to the mother. Instead, in de Lauretis's concept, perverse desire is mature desire that locates the lesbian in woman.[21] In addition, de Lauretis's approach intervenes in theorizations of lesbian desire, because she integrates both individual psychosocial development and production of cultural discourse in terms of content and aesthetics. In contrast to de Lauretis's argument about the construction of the lesbian gaze through the recasting of the primal scene in *She Must Be Seeing Things*, I follow her use of Laplanche and Pontalis to argue that Treut recasts the primal fantasy of seduction. Instead of the construction of a specific ideal lesbian spectator who must be defined prescriptively, *Seduction* employs video to self consciously reflect on cinematic representation and desire, and offers a polymorphously perverse gaze for multiple spectatorial positions.

The structures of the seduction fantasy are inscribed in Treut's film; however, the film's rearticulation of the seduction scene rewrites the traditional Oedipal and heterosexual structure of the origin of sexuality. Following Freud, Laplanche and Pontalis argue that the main primal fantasies are the primal scene (the fantasy of origin), castration (the origin of the difference between the sexes), and seduction (the origin and upsurge of sexuality).[22] In the seduction fantasy, Freud emphasized the seductive role of the mother. In the encounter between her and the infant, "certain chosen parts of the body itself . . . may . . . be a meeting place with maternal desire and fantasy. . . ."[23]

Seduction rearticulates the seduction scene in a sequence that takes place in the shoe store. Caren attempts to put shoes on a girl who refuses to conform. Shots of the girl are crosscut with shots of her mother trying to touch the girl's hair. Music begins when the girl gazes at Caren. This convention signifies the onset of the seduction scene. A sequence of stills of the daughter in seductive poses and clothes follows, while her mother, tied to a chair, is unable to move, touch, or speak to her daughter. Caren, who walks over to the mother and forces her to look at the daughter, tells the mother: "Du siehst, meine Liebe, wenn Dein Herz bricht, ist es wie Theater ohne Publikum" (You see, darling, when your heart breaks, it's like theater without an audience).

The relation between mother and daughter poses a stark contrast to Freud's description, because the mother has no access to the child. The stereotype of the seductive daughter, which is usually, according to feminists, employed to justify the father's seduction, is portrayed as Caren's fantasy, rearranging the Oedipal construction of the primal fantasy of seduction. In Caren's fantasy about the seductive daughter, the father is absent, and the mother impotent. The title *Seduction: The Cruel Woman* foreshadows that in Treut's reconstruction of the seduction scene, the cruel woman replaces the father and daughter as central subjects.

The representation of Caren's fantasy in the shoe store encapsulates the political ambivalence of Treut's film. On one hand, it reproduces a stereotypical visualization of the adolescent seductress similar to images found in heterosexist

erotica. On the other hand, the recasting of the seduction fantasy undermines
the fantasy's traditional Oedipal and heterosexual structure. In its rearticulation
of the seduction scene, the film reconfigures the traditional account of the origin of sexuality around the fantasy of the cruel woman.[24]

Because she is a video-artist, Wanda, the cruel woman, is also the producer
of fantasy, history, and discourse within the film. Her videos are integrated in
the mise-en-scène of *Seduction* in several scenes, comparable to video installations positioned in relationship to other objects and viewers. When Wanda leads
Mährsch through the house, she shows him a video in which she is speaking on
the history of obsession. Assuming Mährsch's gaze, we see Wanda at the right upper frame of the screen, while the video screen, which takes up most of the film's
frame, reproduces Wanda lecturing. The character Wanda is positioned at the
intersections of the projections of her own fictitious work (alias Treut's work)
and the camera (alias Mikesch's work).

According to Rosalind Krauss, in video installations, it is not only "the
artist-practitioner's" body but also "the body of the responding viewer" that are
central instruments.[25] In *Seduction*, however, these two bodies are collapsed. Because Wanda is both the artist and the addressee in these situations, the scene
marks Wanda's autonomy. That autonomous position contrasts with the Wanda
in *Venus in Furs*, who is indistinguishable from portraits of women in a tradition
of art history. The construction of Wanda as an independent artist in *Seduction*
relies on a medium that creates the "psychological condition of the self split and
doubled by the mirror reflection of synchronous feedback."[26] The formation of
subjectivity doubles Wanda's visual representation. Her occupation as video producer refers to Treut in two ways: first, as the actual producer of videos within
the film, and, second, as the creator of the history and fantasy of perversion,
whose authorship is shared with Mikesch. Toward the end of a second sequence
in which we watch Wanda watching herself on video, Wanda turns away from
her own image as if she is bored by her own production, a movement that undermines her narcissism with irony.

Seduction historicizes masochism, and consequently inscribes itself into
history. The film resists the commodification of perverse desire by breaking
with the traditional narratives, and by creating multiple identificatory and disidentificatory moments, and spectator positions. Through the deployment of
masochism—a differently organized pleasure—Treut and Mikesch demonstrate women's ability to sublimate and fetishize. While the film's political impact is limited—this limitation inheres in the subject of masochism—it is able
to represent autonomous female desire. In the historical context of West Germany in the eighties, for women to position themselves as fantasizing and desiring subjects in a film that could not be commodified entailed a radical stance.
The investigation of masochism involves, for women, a double transgression of
positing themselves as speaking subjects in a discourse that has traditionally po-

sitioned women as sublimated objects. *Seduction* works within masochistic aesthetics and simultaneously deconstructs the myth of feminine masochism.

Notes

I thank Amy Abugo Ongiri and Jeff Schneider for reading earlier versions of this essay.

1. Julia Knight, "The Meaning of Treut?" *Immortal, Invisible. Lesbians and the Moving Image*, ed. Tamsin Wilton (New York: Routledge, 1995), 40.

2. Ibid., 41.

3. C. Saalfield, "The Seduction of Monika," *Outweek* 12 (November 1989): 40–43. Quoted from ibid., "Meaning of Treut?" 41.

4. Interview with Monika Treut, conducted by the author, January 1995 in Hamburg. All translations by the author.

5. Treut wrote her dissertation on the "The Cruel Woman" in Marquis de Sade and Leopold von Sacher-Masoch's work. Monika Treut, *Die grausame Frau* (The Cruel Woman) (Frankfurt, Germany: Stroemfeld/Roter Stern, 1984).

6. Tilo Rudolf Knopf, "Die Grausame Frau: Verführungen," *Konkret* 4 (1985): 79–80.

7. B. Ruby Rich, "New Queer Cinema," *Sight and Sound*, 2, 5, 30–39.

8. Gilles Deleuze, "Coldness and Cruelty," *Masochism* (New York: Zone Books, 1989), 15–138.

9. From *Der Mann, der seinen Mörder sucht* (The Man Who Is Looking for His Murderer) (Germany, 1931). About Dietrich, cf. Gaylin Studlar, *In the Realm of Pleasure, Von Sternberg, Dietrich and the Masochistic Aesthetic* (New York: Columbia University Press, 1988). The song is also central in Liliana Cavani's *Night Porter* (1974). For Cavani, cf. Chantal Nadeau, "Girls on a Wired Screen, Cavani's Cinema and Lesbian s/m," in *Sexy Bodies, The Strange Carnalities of Feminism*, eds. Elizabeth Grosz and Elspeth Probyn (New York: Routledge, 1995), 211–31.

10. We are not introduced to the character, and because the image is dark and Mährsch moves through hanging stripes, it is hard to recognize him. However, within the narrative it is not logical that we see Mährsch crawling at the beginning of the film, because his character is only introduced later. Viewers would expect this to be Gregor as an embodiment for the male masochist, an assumption I held in an earlier essay, but Treut herself rectified my assumption.

11. Lisa Duggan and Nan D. Hunter, *Sex Wars, Sexual Dissent and Political Culture* (New York: Routledge, 1995). Within the German context, Treut's film predates the antipornography campaign. This sheds an interesting light on recent interpretations of

lesbian S&M as a response to feminism as the punishing mother. An in-depth comparative analysis of the S&M debate in the United States and Germany, however, is beyond the scope of this essay.

12. *Emma* 12 (December 1987).

13. Julia Creet, "Daughters of the Movement: The Psychodynamics of Lesbian S/M Fantasy," *Differences* 3, no. 2 (1991): 135–59; Mandy Merck, "The Feminist Ethics of Lesbian S/M," *Perversions* (New York: Routledge, 1993), 236–67.

14. On this issue, cf. Marcia Klotz's essay "The Queer and Unqueer Spaces of Monika Treut's Films" in this volume.

15. Parveen Adams, "Of Female Bondage," in *Between Feminism and Psychoanalysis*, ed. Teresa Brennan (New York: Routledge, 1989), 247–66.

16. Ibid., 262–63.

17. Teresa de Lauretis, *The Practice of Love. Lesbian Sexuality and Perverse Desire* (Bloomington: Indiana University Press, 1994).

18. Jean Laplanche and Jean-Bertrand Pontalis, "Fantasy and the Origins of Sexuality," in *Formations of Fantasy*, ed. Victor Burgin, James Donald, and Cora Kaplan (New York: Routledge, 1986), 5–34. De Lauretis, *Practice*, 84–85. Interestingly, Sheila McLaughlin plays Justine in *Seduction*.

19. De Lauretis, *Practice*, 89.

20. Elizabeth Grosz, "Labors of Love (Analyzing Perverse Desire: An Interrogation of Teresa de Lauretis's *The Practice of Love*)," in *Space, Time, and Perversion, Essays on the Politics of Bodies* (New York: Routledge, 1995), 155–73.

21. Biddy Martin, "Masochism in Feminist and Queer Studies" (lecture) DAAD, NEH, and CU Summer Seminar on Masochism (Sander Gilman) Cornell University, summer 1995.

22. Laplanche, "Fantasy," 19.

23. Ibid., 26.

24. This ambivalence came into play when this scene was used as an argument against the screening of *Seduction* at the Toronto film festival.

25. Rosalind Krauss, "Video: The Aesthetics of Narcissism," in *New Artists Video*, ed. Gregory Battcock (New York: Dutton, 1978), 45.

26. Ibid., 54.

12

Why Drag the Diva Into It?
Werner Schroeter's Gay Representation of Femininity

Ulrike Sieglohr

Introduction

Werner Schroeter, whose films have often outraged audiences and critics alike, is a seminal figure of the New German Cinema, and he gained an international cult following for his cinema of camp excess and artifice. His emotionally charged, performance-inspired mode of representation draws on opera, pop music, stage melodrama, contemporary dance-theater, and cabaret. Distilled moments of desire, loss and death are conveyed through intense stylization of gestures, postures, tableaux, and music, thereby relying predominantly on nonverbal affective strategies to involve the spectator. Although he is a gay filmmaker, homosexuality is rarely an explicit topic in his films. Schroeter approaches the problem of the construction of the subject from the position of an outsider by foregrounding female protagonists, who thus become figures for the displaced expression of a gay subjectivity.

Schroeter's career started in 1968 as a self-producing underground filmmaker and he made a number of experimental films. *Eika Katapa* (1969), a camp appropriation of nineteen opera scenes, provided him with a major international breakthrough and as a consequence he got taken up by television. With *Regno Di Napoli* (1977–8) (Kingdom Of Naples), Schroeter had shifted toward art cinema and it became his first commercial release. Working nowadays mainly as a theater and opera director, Schroeter had a brief comeback as a filmmaker with a big budget production, *Malina* (1990), starring Isabelle Huppert.

When I first encountered Schroeter's work, I was curious as to my own strong affective response to the sumptuous images and sounds. His highly stylized mode of narration depicts images of femininity in terms of artifice and emotional excess. How could I then as a feminist respond so emotionally to these artificial representations of femininity? An underlying aspect of my fascination with Schroeter's films is the more general significance of a gay filmmaker for feminist audiences and critics.

It is worth noting that his cinema shares certain characteristics with that of German feminist filmmakers who, like Schroeter, have turned to the performance-arts as an inspiration for their aesthetics. Unlike Anglo-American feminist countercinema, which during the 1970s had rejected emotional involvement as the manipulative pleasure of patriarchal mainstream cinema, German feminist filmmakers in the 1980s wanted to develop a mode of narration that could engage with female pleasure, fantasy, and desire in all its contradictions and thus represent an embattled female subjectivity. Ulrike Ottinger's work with its stylized theatricality and music is generally characterized by such preferences as are a number of other films like Jutta Brückner's *Ein Blick und die Liebe bricht aus* (One Glance and Love Breaks Out, 1995); Helke Sander's *Der Beginn aller Schrecken ist Liebe* (Love is the Beginning of all Terrors, 1984); and Pina Bausch's *Die Klage der Kaiserin* (Lament of the Empress, 1989). To construct films that are not predicated on a male Oedipal trajectory and resolution had a logical and "natural" appeal to feminist filmmakers who, moreover, shared with Schroeter an ideological awareness that in a heterosexual/patriarchal society a female and gay identity could be represented only through a process of negotiation. Indeed since Schroeter's films preceded them, it has been argued that his films provided prototypes for these women filmmakers. Like their work—although his films deconstruct conventional identification mechanisms—they still promote an emotional response by emphasizing those strategies that yield affect, for instance, music, pitch of voice, rhythm, and gestures.

Schroeter's hypermelodramatic and operatic films appear to be primarily concerned with female suffering and ineffable yearning. Yet, as I hope to illustrate, his representations of excessive femininity are in fact not representations of women. If anything, his performers would appear to be drag queens, irrespective of the fact that actually they may be transvestites or female actors. These representations invoke the drag queen through their flamboyant performance of "femininity." Not only do the transvestites wear "femininity" as a mask, but the female performers also flaunt their "femininity" with their accentuated makeup. The latter can be read as female drag queens by viewing Schroeter's cinema through a camp perspective. Paradoxically through exaggerating their "femininity" the female performers denaturalize their biologic gender. It is through this double take and turning round of "femininity" and by rendering appearance as artificial, that they invoke the drag queen.

More specifically, Schroeter's films raise issues concerning female representation in reference to gay identity, hence the cult of the diva in terms of role model. In my view, critics who all too easily dismiss his female figures as misogynistic representations miss the point. They may indeed be misogynistic if the performance of drag is considered as negative stereotyping of femininity. However, rather than imitating stereotypical female conduct, the extravagant behavior of the diva often provides an inspiration for the drag queen, and objections to drag fail to take into account a gay economy of desire whereby the construction of femininity is not an object for possession but for identification. Marjorie Garber's perceptive analysis about men in drag suggest that there are no straightforward answers.

> The politics of drag are complicated by persistent divisions within the gay male culture about the relationship of "dressing up" to gay male identity. Is the drag queen a misogynistic put-down of women, a self-hating parody, or a complex cultural sign that defies any simple translation into "meaning?" [1]

She continues by referring to and quoting Oscar Montero:

> [D]rag can also be an important destabilizing element that, in performance, "questions the limits of representation. The imperfection of her imitation is what makes her appealing, what makes her eminently readable. Foolproof imitations . . . are curious, but not interesting, There has to be some telltale [sign]." [2]

Although Schroeter insists on staging femininity as spectacle—in both senses of the word: *Schauspiel*, that is, vision and grandiose performance—the image of woman does not become the object of heterosexual desire. The spectacle of femininity does not seem to be motivated by fetishistic disavowal, but by the desire to depict a psychic reality of ineffable loss. In other words, Schroeter's exploration of femininity and emotional excess is often manifested through the performance of drag that becomes a trope for pathos and mourning.

Schroeter's female figures are driven by yearning, yet they do not represent psychologically defined women. In all of his films the actors/performers never strive for psychological realism; instead, the role is played as a role and through over-the-top acting and manneristic gestures, the actors embody a part rather than a psychologically fleshed-out character. Instead of offering coherent fictional characters, Schroeter's films promote dispersed imaginary identities, that is, they are about explicitly "artificial people." This is most obvious in some of the early Schroeter films such as *Paula—Je Reviens* (1968) and *Neurasia* (1968). These films are comparable to dream work insofar as different actors play the same character, and conversely the same actor plays various roles. In his key film, *Der Tod der Maria Malibran* (The Death of Maria Malibran, 1971) Maria Malibran, the nineteenth-century opera diva, is played mostly by Magdalena Montezuma, Christine Kaufmann, and Candy Darling, who all play different roles as well. Moreover, gender becomes a continuum when Malibran is played by Montezuma and Candy Darling, the famous transvestite of Andy Warhol's *Factory*. In *Der Tod der Maria Malibran*, the manner in which the performers parade the signs of hyperbolic femininity undermines seemingly uncontradictory manifestations of a biologically given sexual identity even when exhibited by female performers, who occasionally cross-dress as men. For example, Magdalena Montezuma plays the formidable Hugo in *Der Tod der Maria Malibran*, the shaven-headed Herodes in *Salome* (1971), and the eponymous hero in the *Rigoletto* sequence in *Eika Katappa*. As Garber explains, the figure of the transvestite is intolerable to many people because "gender exists only in representation . . . this is the subversive secret of transvestism, that the body is not the ground but the figure."[3]

Understanding transvestism or the performance of drag as a cultural phenomenon would suggest that to parade the hyperbolic signs of femininity, particularly in its transvestite version, is motivated by a desire to project an identity that is denied social validation. A film like *Der Tod der Maria Malibran* could therefore be said to become an experience of otherness, an impossible quest to strive for authenticity through self-alienation.

The Cult of the Diva

The cult of the diva, one of Schroeter's recurring preoccupations, is for me an obvious example of a gay encoding. With few exceptions within Schroeter's cinema, male homosexuality remains a subtext within an aesthetic sensibility and thematic encoding. Karsten Witte identifies Schroeter's "homosexual aesthetics" by pointing out how this works with "hidden signs and signals—allusions and secret figures . . . insisting it is from a gay perspective that one understands [Schroeter's] encoding as an aesthetic counter-strategy."[4] Wayne Koestenbaum traces the special appeal of the opera diva for gay men and provides an intriguing and detailed analysis of the diva cult.

> A love for opera, particularly on record, is a nostalgic emotion, and gay people are imagined to be a uniquely and tragically nostalgic population—regressive, committed to dust and souvenirs. A record, a memento, a trace of an absence, suits the quintessential gay soul, whose tastes are retro and whose sexuality demands a ceaseless work of recollection: because queers do not usually have queer parents, queers must invent precedent and origin for their taste, and they are encouraged, by psychoanalytical models, to imagine homosexuality as a matter of trauma adaptation.[5]

Many gay men cultivate their obsession with a diva (or a film star), and identify with these women as emotional subjects. Michael Bronski suggests that "gay men's identification with women stars is a celebration of their own sexual feelings and a means of experiencing them in an exalted context."[6] This obsession and identification with the diva, if expressed in the mode of camp, for example, the drag act, involves loving pastiche but also parody and irony. To imitate the extravagant behavior of the diva is also "to dramatize the problematic of self-expression"[7]—it allows gay men to invent an identity by staging it and by making fun of it. In the very mockery of sending up conventional forms (in Schroeter's case the grand operatic gestures), these emotional states are simultaneously celebrated and parodied, as, for example, in *Eika Katappa* when an exalted Carla Aulaulu throws herself into the arms of her male lover over and over again, or when as an aging diva she makes her farewell to the adoring young men.

Schroeter's formal choices, particularly his foregrounding of affective strategies, are made in order to convey emotional states, subjectivity, suffering, impossible desire, and aggression against the self. One crucial aspect that relates to Schroeter's quest for the representation of emotion is the figure of the operatic diva, personified and immortalized by the voice and myth of Maria Callas. All of Schroeter's female figures are versions of her. The explicit or implied presence of Callas provides the link between formal strategies and the particular camp sensibility that one can identify in Schroeter's work.

Narration as a Mode of Adoration, Maria Callas as a Figure of Inspiration

Callas is the historical reference point for Schroeter's formal narrational strategies and for his particular gay sensibility. The five 1968 experimental Callas films (see the next section) have the diva as their explicit subject. In the later films Callas is evoked more indirectly; for example, as the adoration of the idol in *Neurasia* (1968); or in *Eika Katappa*, where her presence is invoked through arias, photos, costume, and thematically through the aging diva episode, and in *Der Tod der Maria Malibran*, where the central theme of the opera singer engenders a dense network of allusions and references to Callas. The imagination of gay artists is said to typify both the melodramatic and the operatic in the way in which it represents female suffering and yearning, and from the very beginning of his career, Schroeter's films register an obsession with Callas, the diva. In fact, it could be argued that Callas's voice and performance embodied all those features that are central to Schroeter's own aspirations as an artist. In his obituary for Callas, he defined her artistic ambition as a desire:

> . . . to live to the limits of musical and gestural excess the few totally defendable emotions—life, love, pleasure, hate, jealousy and fear of death—and to demonstrate them in their totality and without psychological analysis.[8]

Schroeter explains that of all the female singers, it was Callas's expressiveness and the intensity of her performance that for him could momentarily halt time, keeping at bay fear—even fear of death—and thereby promoting a state of happiness and feeling of immortality.[9] In his words: "Callas embodied the most extreme feeling of yearning, yet simultaneously the fulfillment of this longing."[10]

Wayne Koestenbaum's examination of the Callas cult, which illustrates how she engages with gay subjectivity, is useful in talking about Schroeter's Callas films. One aspect of her appeal to a gay sensibility is the way in which she confounds distinctions between real and artifice. She remade her own body, transforming herself from a plump and awkward singer into a highly stylized diva; and to reinvent the body, not accepting the idea of a natural given, also has forceful resonances within gay culture, and specifically relates to the performance of drag. She embodied Oscar Wilde's dictum that life should be art. "Her operatic performances seemed real; her real life seemed operatic."[11] Koestenbaum also describes the forms whereby the "fan's" diva cult is ritually expressed through gazing at the photo of an adored diva, by collecting mementos, by lip-synching to the recording, by impersonating, by enacting famous moments, and by repeating over and over favorite musical pieces. These very precise strategies of the "fan" are deployed by Schroeter in a number of his films and his particular form of narration would therefore also seem to be motivated, at least in part, by the cult of the diva.

Narration as a mode of adoration is most clearly identifiable in the first films, which are studies of Callas, articulated most often through structural repetition, use of photos of the opera singer, reviews of her performance, and replay of recordings of her voice on the sound track. In *Callas Walking Lucia* (1968), he edits the production stills from the madness scene of "Lucia di Lammermoor" in such a way that Callas appears to be walking. *Callas Text mit Doppelbelichtung* (Callas Text with Double Exposure, 1968) superimposes photos from "Lucia" onto Leonardo da Vinci's *Mona Lisa* on one side of the frame, while on the other hand offering a projection of an enthusiastic Callas review. At the end, Schroeter screams silently. *Maria Callas Porträt* (Maria Callas's Portrait, 1968) represents another attempt to animate stills. The study, Mona Lisa (also 1968), consists of a thirty-five-minute-long contemplation by the camera of just three photos; Callas as Lucia, a publicity still of Callas, and a photograph of the Mona Lisa painting. Superimpositions and extreme details are supported by a complex sound track of Callas's voice, mixed with snatches of a Catarina Valente pop song.

Invoking the Maternal through the Female Singing Voice

Thus far I have discussed the specific attractions of the diva for gay men, and although these are compelling accounts, I want to turn finally to psychoanalysis since it yields a more nuanced and a multifaceted reading of Schroeter's female figures. For Schroeter, the female singing voice has the potential to achieve perfect fusion between an idea and its representation—a fusion that he can find equally in pop and high opera, which explains his juxtaposition of such a seemingly incongruous pair as Catarina Valente and Maria Callas. I want to finish therefore with a more speculative paradigm to try to articulate how the female figure, the diva, invokes aurally through the singing voice a yearning for a state of plenitude that in turn is conveyed as a state prior to sexual difference. As Kaja Silverman expresses it: "[The] maternal voice not only wraps the child in a soothing and protective blanket, but bathes it in a celestial melody whose closest terrestrial equivalent is opera." [12]

Arguably a discussion of the female singing voice could be considered a digression from issues surrounding the representation of women. However, not only has the emphasis on woman as image in feminist film theory been one-sided in general, [13] in Schroeter's case, to analyze woman just on the level of image, can easily lead to a misinterpretation regarding the function of femininity in his cinema. In many of his films, the visual and aural invocation of the diva are complexly imbricated and at times not without contradictions. *Macbeth* (1971) provides a striking example as to some of the ambiguities engendered by the diva cult. Annette Tierer who plays the role of Lady Macbeth wears a copy of Callas's famous "Tosca" costume while screeching discordantly her lines. In other words, whereas the image pays homage to Callas, the sound undermines this by representing her as a shrieking harridan.

Psychoanalytic theorization seems to me to be of some interest when considering the status of the female singing voice in Schroeter's films. Regarding the constitution of subjectivity, research in this field points to the inherent regression of aural perception and specifically in reference to the female voice. Auditory faculties form the first layers of subjectivity in the imaginary when the mother's voice acts like an "acoustic mirror," which Kaja Silverman has theorized as the auditory introjection of the maternal voice and "precocious vocalization," this being a decisive stage in the formation of subjectivity: "The child could be said to hear itself initially through that voice—to first 'recognize' itself in the vocal 'mirror' supplied by the mother." Subsequently, the mirror phase introduces the symbolic that splits subjectivity, and vision becomes associated with self-differentiation from the mother. Silverman identifies in *The Acoustic Mirror* a male fear of the prelinguistic because, she reasons, it is conceived as preidentity and as such it is also a fear of the irrational. Silverman applies Kristeva's idea of the "chora" [14] to analyze a range of conventional films in order to understand how the maternal voice is articulated within classic cinema. She demonstrates that this regressive anxiety of nondifferentiation is projected onto the female voice, and as a consequence in dominant cinema the female voice has to be contained textually. Silverman argues that only the male voice is given the authoritative and transcendental status of the voice-over while the female voice always has to be matched with a body. However, in Schroeter's films the female voice has a more contradictory function, insofar as it is poised between seduction and abjection. On the side of seduction, Schroeter foregrounds those non-verbal aspects of the female singing voice that yield affect—namely, pitch, rhythm, and grain—since they emphasize the more archaic and prediscursive dimension of communication. Thus, it could be suggested that more clearly than the speaking voice, the harmonious dimension of the female singing voice recalls a period of imaginary plenitude prior to the subject's differentiation. This fantasy of the maternal voice described by Guy Rosolato as a "sonorous maternal envelope"[15] manifests itself quite clearly in *Der Tod der Maria Malibran*. On the side of abjection, undermining the seductive pull of the female singing voice, is the struggle for synchronization. Incoherence is one of the effects of complete nonsynchronization between image and voice (even further compounded by the fragmentary structure of the respective tracks). When the performers move their lips to the borrowed harmonious voice of the prerecorded singer, this can be seen as an attempt to recover the "sonorous maternal envelope," while also illustrating that "reawakening . . . the voice always presupposes a break, an irreversible distance from the lost object."[16] Therefore, the permutations of (non-)synchronization, the break between image and sound engenders painfully nostalgic yearnings that can find no fulfillment, no object. However, death becomes a kind of fulfillment in *Der Tod der Maria Malibran* that finishes with the ecstatic death of the diva, singing "peace and content . . . at last." Crucially, this is also at the point when image and sound are in harmony, the voice is lip-synchronized. Perfection or creative fulfillment is in Schroeter's cinema, paradoxically only achieved with the knowledge of always imminent death, or in the moment of dying.

This "digression" shows that Schroeter's representation of femininity is constituted like a palimpsest insofar as there are several layers to the representation of women. On the level of the image: excessive femininity on the surface connotes the drag queen that in turn invokes the diva; and on the aural level—which is ambiguously poised between nostalgia and loss—one discovers the structuring core: whereby the seductive voice of the singer reevokes the fantasy of the maternal voice.

> In its fantasmatic guise as "pure" sonorous, the maternal voice oscillates between two poles; it is either cherished as an object—as what can make good all lacks—or despised and jettisoned as what is most abject, most culturally intolerable.[17]

However, to conceive of the maternal as the vanishing point of all subjectivity is highly problematic.[18] What Schroeter's use of the female voice demonstrates is that there is more at stake in representing women than just the female image.

Lack is not inscribed on her image; her visual representation is not fetishized, but both of these psychic structures manifest themselves in her voice. Nevertheless there is a sense of loss and nostalgia that is experienced by men and women. Although from a feminist perspective, Schroeter's representations of women as divas and drag queens remain ideologically ambiguous, from a gay perspective his construction of excessive femininity allows a different purchase on sexual politics. It should therefore come as no surprise that Schroeter's cinema has been influential not just with gay filmmakers and critics but with those feminist women, myself included, who can identify with an imaginary identity driven by the romantic impulse of all-pervasive emotionality.

To return to my question that I pose in my title why, indeed, drag the diva into it? An answer to this could be because it is the diva's exaggerated femininity, as opposed to ordinary femaleness, which is the desired effect of the drag queen's performance. The diva has to remain an unattainable role model since it is precisely in the self-conscious visual "failure" but perfect aural mimicry that the performance achieves its aim. Thus, what is important is the very gap between the diva and the drag queen, not in terms of authenticity and imitation, but as an expression of a desire for reinventing, negotiating, and even negating gendered identity through performance.

Notes

1. Marjorie Garber, *Vested Interests: Cross-Dressing and Cultural Anxiety* (Harmondsworth, England: Penguin, 1993), 149.

2. Ibid.

3. Garber, *Vested Interests*, 374.

4. Karsten Witte. "Versteckte Zeichen und Signale: Werner Schroeters Filme," *Frankfurter Rundschau* 5, no. 1 (1991): 3.

5. Wayne Koestenbaum, *The Queen's Throat, Opera, Homosexuality, and the Mystery of Desire* (London: GMP, 1993), 47.

6. Michael Bronski, *Culture Clash: The Making of Gay Sensibility* (Boston: South End Press, 1984), 94.

7. Koestenbaum, *Queen's Throat*, 133.

8. Werner Schroeter, "Der Herztod der Primadonna," *Der Spiegel*, no. 40 (1977): 261.

9. Ibid., 265.

10. Schroeter interviewed by André Müller, "Äußerstes Gefühl von Sehnsucht," *Die Zeit*, no. 13, 21.3.1980, p. 13.

11. Koestenbaum, *Queen's Throat*, 140.

12. Kaja Silverman, *The Acoustic Mirror: The Female Voice in Psychoanalysis and Cinema* (Bloomington and Indianapolis: Indiana University Press, 1988), 85. Her discussion at this point is a critical commentary on Guy Rosolato, "La Voix: Entre Corps et Langage," in *Revue Francaise de Psychoanalyse*, no. 38 (1974): 75–95 and further citations are all from Rosolato's article as discussed and referred to by Silverman.

13. Silverman, *Acoustic Mirror*, 80.

14. Kristeva's concept of the "chora" as the maternal locus of the semiotic (presignifying energy) explores the contradictory tension between symbiosis and psychosis. The "chora" is the site of the child's unmediated relation to the mother's body—an undifferentiated bodily space shared by the infant and the mother. Kristeva's theory of subject formation stresses the senses rather than vision (Lacan's concept of the imaginary), she claims that rhythm, intonations, and other paralinguistic features can reevoke earliest affective processes. In her theory these elements constitute the semiotic; they are an expression of primary drives and originate in the infant's symbiotic relation to the maternal body. See Toril Moi, ed., *The Kristeva Reader* (Oxford: Basil Blackwell, 1986); see especially "Revolution In Poetic Language," 113–36. Kristeva's own analysis, however, was developed in reference to the literary avant-garde text rather than to the audiovisual text.

15. Guy Rosolato quoted by Silverman, *Acoustic Mirror*, 85.

16. Ibid.

17. Silverman, *Acoustic Mirror*, 86.

18. See also Jacqueline Rose, *Sexuality in the Field of Vision* (London: Verso, 1986), 156.

13

Interview with Doris Dörrie:
Filmmaker, Writer, Teacher

Klaus Phillips

Doris Dörrie is among the tiny group of filmmakers who ever appeared on the cover of *Der Spiegel*, and the only woman featured in all of 1986. Dörrie is a phenomenon. Since her film *Männer* became the sleeper hit of 1986, soundly beating heavyweight competitors such as *Out of Africa*, *Rocky IV*, and *The Name of the Rose* at German box offices, she has established herself as a major power on several fronts: she continues to make films that make money and that are generally lauded by critics, many of whom clearly expected her to continue in the *Männer* vein and then chastised her for not doing so. Ironically, some of the same critics also have taken her to task for daring to appropriate the male gaze, since her narratives often favor the perspective of a male protagonist.

She is a shrewd businesswoman; she exerts considerable influence in the distribution and release of her films; her most recent feature, *Keiner liebt mich* (Nobody Loves Me, 1994), was distributed by the German branch of Walt Disney's Buena Vista and started in a larger number of theaters than many American blockbusters.

Doris Dörrie also is a passionate and prolific writer who jealously guards her daily six-hour writing sessions against interference; more often than not, her films are based on one of her own stories and she writes the screenplay; several short story collections and novels have been published by Diogenes Verlag, and more are on the way; the first two short story collections, *Love, Pain, and the Whole Damn Thing* (1989) and *What Do You Want From Me?* (1991), have been published in the United States, by Random House; a third is in preparation in Canada.

Less well-known is the fact that Dörrie loves to teach. In early 1990 she spent a month as a visiting professor at Colorado College. In the spring of 1992 she taught a semester of Screenwriting as Fulbright Scholar at Hollins College, where she usually warmed up her students with an aerobics session in preparation for the hard work ahead. The Hochschule für Fernsehen und Film (HFF) in Munich, of which she is an alumnus, offered her a teaching position for the fall of 1996.

In addition to her professional success, Dörrie found happiness and personal fulfillment with Helge Weindler, who was a fellow HFF graduate and her cameraman for *Männer*. They married in 1987; their daughter, Carla, was born in 1990. Weindler continued behind the camera in all of her films until his premature death in early 1996, during the initial shooting for *Bin ich schön?* (Am I Beautiful?)

Given the varied accomplishments just outlined, Dörrie obviously is not an easy fit for the territory inhabited by other German filmmakers, and some exasperated critics have lashed out at her with a vengeance uncommon even in Germany. They gleefully attack her films, for example: Rainer Finne: "Such disparate acting powers like Elisabeth Trissenaar's and Peggy Parnass' unite, thanks to Ms. [!] Dörrie's unstoppable desire for a cinematic flop, for absolute pointlessness."[1] They attack her writing, as did Franz Josef Görtz: "Really now, writing is not her forte, since clearly, she has only a passing acquaintance to language and its potency."[2] They attack her persona, as, for example, Sabine Pichlau:

"Everyone can be her pal Dörrie. She's cool and without mercy. But don't be flattered, her coolness is icy, and makes you want even more distance. She overdoes it, even with her perfume."[3]

Outbursts such as those illustrated by these samples are predictable, especially since Dörrie seems to encourage critics' perception of her as a nonconformist outsider who, for example, has little in common with the generation represented by Wim Wenders, another HFF alumnus. Moreover, her work abounds with sly, nagging reminders that Germans excel at making themselves and each other miserable instead of enjoying life, and that they continue to have particular difficulty accepting and adapting to Germany's multiculturalism.

In the following pages Dörrie explains how she perceives herself, Germany, and making movies today. The telephone interview was conducted in English on 13 July and on 24 August 1996.

Phillips. What's it like for you to make movies in Germany today?

Dörrie. What's it like for me? Well, for me it's a little difficult to tell, but I think I'm still in that very luxurious position where I can get movies financed very easily as opposed to everybody else because most of my movies have made so much money that people keep thinking the next one will make money, too; and especially because of the last movie, *Nobody Loves Me*, which was a big hit, the financing for the next one, *Am I Beautiful?* was very easy.

Phillips. Is there a danger inherent in this perception, then, a fear of failure, a fear that taking a risk, doing something that you believe in but that wouldn't necessarily meet audience expectations, could obstruct future funding?

Dörrie. Oh, you're always scared that nobody will want to see your movie, but I think, compared with the United States, the pressure is not as high because it's not quite as commercial here yet; it's going to get more commercial as we go along.

Phillips. A number of your colleagues decry the lack of support for women as opposed to male filmmakers in Germany. Have you found your gender to be a help? A hindrance? Has it mattered?

Dörrie. Well, maybe I've been very blind all along, but I think I've never experienced any difficulties because of my gender. In Europe, no. In Hollywood it was a different story; there it's really a "boys' business" because there's so much money involved; it's much more about power, not about art.

Phillips. Do you have any advice for fledgling female colleagues?

Dörrie. If you want to play the game in Hollywood, that takes a lot of stamina, and it's quite scary because you're going to be all alone; but as an independent filmmaker I don't think any woman would have any more difficulties than a man, raising money, getting the project off the ground. It's a little bit like any big industry. If you want to get to the top, it's the glass ceiling that's going to dawn on you at some point; it's the same in Hollywood.

Phillips. Beyond the power plays, Hollywood has influenced and inspired you artistically, hasn't it? I don't just mean the obvious links to the American work of émigrés such as Billy Wilder and Ernst Lubitsch, but, more generally, the Hollywood product.

Dörrie. The question of influences on my work is a little difficult to answer. Part of the reason it's difficult for me is that I'm a woman-filmmaker. Women in general have difficulty naming their influences, and that seems to be very different from men because men tend to feel much part of a tradition of artists, depending on their field, and it seems to be much easier for them to see themselves as a continuation of, let's say, John Ford, or whoever it is. As a woman-filmmaker I find it difficult to claim to be following somebody or to be in the same line as somebody. It would just feel strange to say, "I was heavily influenced by John Ford, or Billy Wilder, or Lubitsch, or whoever." And also I never felt I could adapt things that I had seen; I had to invent my own language. I could never quite understand people like, let's say, Wim Wenders, who would say things like, "I saw every movie by John Ford, and I try to set up every shot like John Ford did." It's never felt right for me to say that; not John Ford, but whomever I really admired. Among the many directors whose work I really like certainly would be Billy Wilder, Lubitsch, but also most of the directors of the nouvelle vague, Truffaut, Godard, Bertolucci! I really admire his earlier work. And then, of course, the new American cinema: Scorsese was a huge influence, I think, on everyone in film school in the late seventies. *Taxi Driver* had a great impact on everybody who went to film school in those days.

Phillips. Both you and Wenders went to the HFF in Munich, and both of you, presumably, grew up with a steady diet of American film that was served as part of America's cultural colonization of Germany.

Dörrie. Actually, I didn't. The nouvelle vague had already become so important by the time I started to go to the movies, far more important than American movies. Only when I went to film school, the new American cinema became important. It was different for us than for Wenders's generation; they felt much more connected to the old-time Hollywood guys: Hawks, Ford, Huston, those guys. Scorsese was a generation later. Cassavetes, Rafelson, those people.

Phillips. You've inspired a new generation of filmmakers yourself. I'm thinking of people such as Dani Levy, possibly Katja von Garnier, certainly others who have come up through the HFF since you finished there.

Dörrie. I guess my movies, especially *Men*, inspired a lot of people because *Men* made so much money. That definitely was new, I guess, because before *Men* not too many German films made a lot of money. It was simply unheard-of that a German film could gross a lot of money. And, after 1945, another thing that was new was that a movie could be funny, entertaining, and not completely shallow, maybe, at the same time. But I see this inspiration also as quite difficult, or at least ambivalent right now, because certainly it has led to many, many very shallow German comedies that still make some money, even a lot of money. Right now it seems to be the only genre in German film that can make money.

Phillips. Which of the newer German films are your favorites?

Dörrie. I find some of the really young guys quite interesting, people like Martin Enlen, M. X. Oberg's *Unter der Milchstraße*, some people from Berlin, such as Matthias Glasner, who made *Die Mediocren*. There are a lot of people out there now who try to make interesting, quite personal films with not very much money, but they have tremendous difficulties getting their movies on the screen because right now the big trend seems to be that only comedies get to be seen. And that's why I'm quite ambivalent about my influence on the German film market altogether because if it means that nothing can be seen other than German comedies it's a quite disastrous situation.

Phillips. What have been some of your favorite films from outside Germany during the past few years?

Dörrie. One movie that stuck out during the last, let's say, five years, was *Short Cuts* by Robert Altman, also *The Player*. I really like those two films because they are different. They try to achieve something different. And also a few movies, such as *Shattered Sky* by Bertolucci, which was not very successful but that I like because they try to pick up on an epic rhythm that's not done very much anymore. Also cheaply made American movies, such as *Drugstore Cowboy* or *Grand Canyon*, movies which, unfortunately, didn't turn out to be commercially successful but that try to tell stories in a manner that is not completely formalized and predictable.

Phillips. In addition to being a successful filmmaker and an author of note, you are an effective teacher, having taught at Hollins College and at Colorado College. When you teach Screenwriting, for example, what do you seek to instill in your students? What's your central goal?

Dörrie. An interesting question because I was just offered a job at the HFF. When I gave my first lecture, I realized German students need something completely different from American students. German students have to be encouraged to write. The German school system never encourages creative writing. Writing is not considered a craft in Germany. It's a talent you're born with. Otherwise you can never become a writer. That's still the general idea of writers here, I think: You cannot learn how to write. In America there's a long tradition of creative writing, of seeing writing as a craft. I pretty much try never to teach German students any rules, tricks, formulas, or formats because they are so eager to stick to formulas. I think German students have to be encouraged to talk about emotions. That seems to be something that's really lacking in German theaters and, in general, in the German art world. Emotion. We have difficulty talking about emotion, but as a storyteller, I think, it's your main job to talk about emotion. So I'll try to get my German students to talk about emotions. With American students I find it much easier to gain access to their creative

fountain from which they're writing. They're not as eager to hide what their motivation might be to become a writer. German students, I think, are very timid,
very shy, and would rather conceal why they would want to become writers.

Phillips. How has reunification impacted your films? Do you see greater
opportunities now?

Dörrie. There are many more great actors available now as a result. For my
last movie, *Nobody Loves Me*, it was a great coincidence because I was looking
for a black actor, and there aren't too many black actors around in Germany. We
started casting shortly after reunification and I found this magnificent black actor from Eastern Germany, Pierre Sanoussi-Bliss, whom I could not have cast
before reunification.

Phillips. Multiculturalism is becoming an increasingly significant element in
your films, as demonstrated by *Happy Birthday* and *Nobody Loves Me*. You seem
to be underscoring the particular German problem with multiculturalism. In
Nobody Loves Me, Orfeo professes to be from "Uagnosch," which is "Schongau"
spelled backward.

Dörrie. You're probably the only one who realized that!

Phillips. And even in the casting, as you already indicated; in *Happy Birthday*, Kemal Kayankaya, a Turk, is played by Hansa Czyprionka, who is a German of Polish origin; in the same film, a Turk masquerades as an Italian waiter
because it's socially more acceptable to be Italian at this point. That's hardly farfetched, since my favorite Italian restaurant in Germany is run by two fellows
from Iraq who are trying to pass for Italian. Do you try to impart a lesson consistently and consciously to your audience? Are your films didactic?

Dörrie. I don't very much like didactic movies myself, so I try not to be didactic. At the same time, clearly, I do want to get something across. Concerning multiculturalism, I more or less was trying to depict the way Germany is
right now, which *is* multicultural, but nobody seems to want to acknowledge it.
We have been multicultural for the past twenty years or so, and still nobody really wants to see this and accept it and work with it. That is something I wanted
to get across in *Happy Birthday* as well as in *Nobody Loves Me*, which is a very
naturalistic movie; when you walk through the streets of Cologne, it is a very
multicultural city, more so than Munich, for instance. That's not something I
made up or invented in order to be didactic about German angst of foreigners.
It's there.

Phillips. I raise the point principally because your two most recent films
have a dead-serious core yet are immensely funny. Good comedy has that serious core as well as a didactic function. Do German audiences have difficulties
with comedy that's critical of the way they perceive themselves and the world
around them?

Dörrie. We all were very afraid that *Nobody Loves Me*, which is a very dark
comedy indeed, would not be accepted for precisely those reasons; but the op-

posite happened; the film didn't just cross all age barriers and really was seen by quite different crowds of all ages, but it also made a lot of money; it was very successful, which is really great, not merely for us, but for all my filmmaking colleagues; to see that it is really possible, that you don't have to go mainstream entirely in order to make it work. In general, the tendency in Germany still is to be very mainstream, especially as far as comedies go, mainstream comedies that don't dare touch anything that's a little ambivalent or dangerous or difficult. We seem to have proven the contrary, which I hope will continue with other movies, not just with mine, but with others as well. That's something we have to keep watering, to take good care of that acceptance, and not to let it dry up again.

Phillips. Nobody Loves Me, the first German feature film distributed by Walt Disney's Buena Vista in Germany, was released theatrically in the United States by Cinepix Film Properties. Critical reaction, overall, has been quite positive, but I wonder how the expectations and sensibilities of American audiences and critics differ from the Germans' and translate into a different reception for the film.

Dörrie. There were enthusiastic screenings, especially in Chicago and San Francisco—those were the cities that I went to—also the festival in Toronto, where we had a premiere before twenty-five hundred spectators, and that was pretty overwhelming, the level of enthusiasm. I think the reception really was pretty much the same as in Germany. People seemed to react in a very emotional way to the movie. A lot of people were weeping and laughing at the end. In Asia, the reception is completely different, though. I just went to Vietnam, and it's going to open in Japan soon. I attended a screening in Japan, and there, of course, the viewers immediately pick up on the movie's Buddhist background. I did use Buddhist themes consciously, of course. If you don't know anything about Buddhism, it's really not that important; you can understand it without it; but in Asia, that seems to be the central metaphor for the movie. I had interesting talks and discussions about the Buddhist themes in the movie. It really struck a chord because they are so familiar with them, and that was interesting to see. A Western audience may react the same way, but cannot see that because we are not trained to see that.

Phillips. Do your films address a particular audience? Do you make them specifically for a German audience, or do you think in terms of a more global viewership?

Dörrie. I don't think anybody knows who *the* audience is. When you think who the audience might be, you automatically think of your friends and family. Those are the people I think of when I make a movie. You and I are just as much *the* audience as anybody else. *Audience* is an anonymous term. When you look at your audience a little more closely, you realize it consists of very different kinds of people.

Phillips. Do you make your films for yourself?

Dörrie. I start working on the screenplay for myself. I find the center of the story, until I know what the story is about, really. Then I try to tell the story to somebody else. Just for myself would be incredibly boring.

Phillips. Does writing a novel or short story give you a thrill that's different from the thrill your movies give you? A different sensation, a different sense of accomplishment?

Dörrie. Oh yes, because it's much freer. I can move around in time and space and not worry about money. I can move bodies around much more easily, whereas in the movies gravity always holds you back. You have to get this actor, this "body," from one place to the other, into a car, out of a car, into a room, out of a room. Filming is much more gravity-stricken, which makes it much harder work, and to attain a certain light touch is much harder.

Phillips. Will you continue to do both?

Dörrie. Yes. A new book of mine is coming out this fall, *Samsara*, which again is a Buddhist term, meaning the wheel of suffering. It's also a perfume by Guerlain; I'm not so sure the perfume people understood what it means. Hmm, Let's spray a little suffering on my body today! And I will make the movie that we had to interrupt in the spring, *Am I Beautiful?* which is about a bunch of Germans who dream of going to Spain because they think that's where the real life is happening. I will do that movie next fall.

Phillips. What happens after *Am I Beautiful?*

Dörrie. I'll be doing a documentary this fall on working women. It's going to start out with me trying to get my daughter ready for school so that I can go off and shoot a documentary. Getting Carla ready for school is a major accomplishment.

Phillips. When you say "working women," do you have a cross-section of professions in mind?

Dörrie. No, it's basically my girlfriends, who are all working mothers and who are all quite privileged, like myself. They all work in the arts; one is a lawyer and it's mainly about that, that in order to be able to work, you really have to like your job and do something that you can be proud of. Otherwise it doesn't make any sense in Germany to be working because of our insane school and preschool schedules. From eight to noon, that's it. Nobody in the States would understand how that could be. It's good for the economy because it keeps the unemployment rate down.

Phillips. Which film are you most proud of?

Dörrie. *Nobody Loves Me.* I think I got very close to the ambivalence of life, happiness, and suffering at the same time. The fact that this movie made people react in such a strong, emotional manner is something I'm quite proud of.

Phillips. After the film opened in New York, one review [Barbara and Scott Siegel, Siegel Entertainment Syndicate] [4] promised, "You will not only leave the theater laughing; you'll leave the theater singing." Viewers have a tendency to leave your other films singing as well. They remember "No Woman, No Cry" at the end of *Me and Him*, and they remember "I Want to Take You on My Banana Boat" from *Men*. How do you select music for your films?

Dörrie. I find it very difficult to use music in the right way. In dramatic scenes music should not be noticed. It should reinforce what is happening, not overpower it. If you notice the music, you lose the emotion. Once in a while there's a scene when you can't really lose it because the scene's so well established already. Then I like to use music that really gets you out of your seat, makes you want to dance, jump up, and be part of what's going on on-screen. It's difficult to find that balance. If you insist too much on music that gets you up and dancing, then it's difficult to get the audience back into the story, so the end is always a good place to put that kind of music. In the middle it can be dangerous. And it's very difficult to find a composer who is humble enough to see and understand that music should never overpower a scene but just serve the scene. I did find a very talented guy, Niki Reiser, who did the music for *Nobody Loves Me*, who completely understood this. I think he's so talented because he's got a band and he's got his dance music and then his solo music on the side, which makes him much more understanding of film music. He doesn't need to have his own thing, his own act, in the movies.

Phillips. Some German reviewers[5] [Cf. Katja Nicodemus, "Thanatussi," *Die Tageszeitung*, 12 January 1995] felt that hearing Edith Piaf sing "No, je ne regrette rien" four times during *Nobody Loves Me* is a bit much. How would you respond to that?

Dörrie. I've never come across that criticism, but I think if it becomes too much for people, they tend to distance themselves from the emotion of the song and from the scenes in which the song is used. If you stand back and don't want to become completely wrapped up in what's happening in the story, I guess it can become too much. But if you really submit yourself to the emotions of those scenes, which deal with death and dying—the song, after all, deals with death and dying as well; "je ne regrette rien" means at the end of your life, if you can say, "I don't regret anything," that's what we all hope for—then I don't think it can become too much. I think it depends on how much you distance yourself emotionally from the themes of the song and the film, which are heavy sometimes.

Phillips. You've had astonishing successes, both professionally and personally, and you've also endured tragedy when your husband Helge Weindler passed away after a three-year battle with cancer. How do you deal with it? How do you see life?

Dörrie. During the last three years, something you might call tragedy was also something that was extremely lucky and a great gift to Helge, Carla, and me. Something I've always tried to portray in my stories and in my movies has really happened to me in real life, where, of course, it's more difficult to take and to digest than in the stories and in the movies. Everything is really very ambivalent. In the midst of tragedy things can become extremely light, very happy, because of the tragedy. But also the other way around: Sometimes you really can't enjoy your happiness; you become too impatient and you cannot really be in it and enjoy the special moment at which it's happening because you're too busy looking for something else already. The great ambivalence of things, which I've always tried to discover in all these stories that I've been telling for so long now, has really happened now in my own life.

Phillips. Orfeo's advice to Fanny in *Nobody Loves Me* about not wearing a watch because it's always the same time: now; does that reflect your own feelings?

Dörrie. It's something I had to learn when Helge became ill. It was really the hard way. I don't know whether I learned it for good. Something really strange happened to me when Helge was dying: I was standing in his hospital room and looked out the window; all of a sudden Orfeo's words came out of my mouth. I was looking at the clouds and I found myself whispering to my-self, "Wenn ich einmal weg bin, dann schau Dir die Wolken an. Alles verändert sich. Nichts bleibt so wie es ist, auch die ganze Scheiße" (When I'm gone, then look at the clouds. Everything changes. Nothing remains as it is, not even the bad stuff). And that was really strange. I was quite shocked that all of a sudden I was quoting one of my invented character's lines; but it made perfect sense. Nichts bleibt so wie es ist.

Notes

1. "So unterschiedliche schauspielerische Potenzen wie Elisabeth Trissenaar und Peggy Parnass vereinigen sich, dank Frau [!] Dörries festem Drang zum cinemato-graphischen Nullpunkt, in ausgeprägter Nichtigkeit" (Rainer Finne, "Dichter Boden-nebel: Doris Dörrie's Film *Keiner liebt mich* weckt viele Erwartungen und erfüllt keine," *Sonntagsblatt*, 13 [January 1995]).

2. "Nein, schreiben kann sie wirklich nicht. Denn zur Sprache und zu deren Mitte ln hat sie nur eine sehr flüchtige Beziehung" (Franz Josef Görtz, "Beiläufige Tragödien: Geschichten von der Filmemacherin Doris Dörrie," *Frankfurter Allgemeine Zeitung*, 14 March 1989)

3. "Die Dörrie duzt jeden. Cool und gnadenlos. Man darf sich aber nichts drauf ein-bilden, ihre Nähe hat nichts Wärmendes, weckt den Wunsch nach mehr Distanz. Denn sie trägt—nicht nur beim Parfüm—zu dick auf" (Sabine Pichlau, "'Ich bin ein netter Mensch' Erfolgsregisseurin Doris Dörrie: Wie "Männer ihr Leben veränderte. Warum sie die Filme ihrer Kollegen haßt. Und was sie über die 'häßlichen Deutschen' denkt." *Rtv* 43 [26 October–1 November 1991]).

4. Barbara and Scott Siegel, Entertainment Syndicate, *New York Times*, 29 October 1995.

5. For example, Katja Nicodemus, "Thanatussi," *Die Tageszeitung*, 12 January 1995.

IV

Images of Women as Social Ciphers

14

Commodified Body: Helga Reidemeister's
Mit starrem Blick aufs Geld (Blank Stares and Hard Cash)

Magda Mueller

While the construction of femininity has been discussed from a variety of angles, feminist theory has tended to focus on "imagined femininity," that is, the ideological production of femininity. Such an approach elucidates the constructedness of "imagined femininity" in theories on femininity in psychology, psychoanalysis, sociology, philosophy, and so on, or in representations of "imagined femininity" in film, literature, and cultural studies, but neglects what I will call the material production of femininity in the female body itself.

This essay will develop the significance of materiality as it manifests itself on the body of a fashion model who has to live with the imprint of time displayed on her aging body, and eroding the marketability of her body. On the one hand, Reidemeister's 1983 documentary on a particular fashion model is a multifaceted cut through several German feminist discourses that were *en vogue* in the early 1980s: the construction of sisterhood and its relation to real sister relationships, the feminist discourse on the female body, the Left critique of consumerism and its impact on society, and the discourses on women's film and its relation to documentary. On the other hand, this film anticipated a feminist discussion that did not materialize within German feminist discourses until the early nineties, and that reached its high point in discussions following the German translation of Judith Butler's *Gender Trouble* in 1991 and in discussions on postfeminism in 1994.[1] By anticipating the interconnectedness of these discourses, Reidemeister's documentary ultimately interrogates several ideologies held by the political Left, and also shows the limitations of any ideological framework. In this German context, the term *postfeminism* does not imply that feminist theories and discourses have come to an end but it signals that the subjects of feminist investigation have been expanded in reaction to various developments in feminist theories and praxis. This incorporates, for example, fashion, fashion models, and historical concepts of beauty. When applying the term *post-feminism* in this analysis, I use it in that contextualized meaning.

My conceptualization of materiality involves an intensification of women's recognition of themselves as lacking an image of themselves. The discrepancy between the female viewer's self-image and the physical form of the fashion model leads her to imagine a perfected image of herself patterned after the commercially produced pictures of fashion models and thus to seek to produce this image through the transformation of her own body and/or the purchase of the paraphernalia of femininity that create her image. While these ideas can be applied to the whole spectrum of the paraphernalia of femininity ("ideal" face and body, fashion, and its accessories), I concentrate only on the constructed body of the fashion model documented in Reidemeister's film. This materiality has a powerful effect on the production of the image of woman. Besides reading the film as text, I especially read the fashion model's body (a body that has to convey the impression of eternal youth) as a text within a text, and I also analyze the fashion model herself *as* producer of a production. My reading is therefore one expression of triangulated visions: the female body as consumer-producer/ produced-consumed/desired-desiring object.

Contextualization: The Female Body under Attack

The early eighties were characterized by a concerted resistance to the exploitation of the female body. In Germany, the most prominent voices were those of the journalist Alice Schwarzer and of the well-known popular actress, Inge Meisel. Their political campaign against the weekly *Stern* was initiated in order to protest against the objectification of the female body on the cover pages of magazines. Acting in the name of all oppressed women and representing all angry young women, Alice Schwarzer, journalist and editor in chief of the feminist weekly *Emma*, spearheaded the boycott. She had already shaped several feminist debates in Germany, including the famous statement "I confess, I had an abortion."[2] The 1981 campaign against the exploitative marketing of the female body was directed toward all agencies and toward all magazines that used the female body in order to sell products. Like several previous debates, this feminist debate had uncritically accepted the presumption that in a patriarchal society, the woman's role is automatically that of a victim.[3] Important too, in this context, is that in 1983 Barbara Sichtermann's collection of essays, reintroducing issues that had supposedly been resolved by feminists, was published by Klaus Wagenbach. By provocatively titling her critique of these issues in feminist discourse *Weiblichkeit. Zur Politik des Privaten* (Femininity: Concerning the Politics of the Private),[4] Sichtermann argued that femininity, depending on its context, could easily be reread as emancipation. Furthermore, she attacked the silent agreements existing between feminists who had stopped questioning certain presumptions such as the so-called object status of women, while, for example, the fight for houses for battered women reached an all-time high.[5] The publication of Christina Thürmer-Rohr's[6] critique of the women's perceptions of their own victimization, in conflict with the concepts of self-victimization of women, sparked a principled discussion within the German women's movement and was further theorized in the debate on female masochism.[7] At that time, discussions on whether or not pictures of naked women degrade women to objects of male scopophilia, were not included.[8] The feminist complainants had already made up their mind about *all* women's roles as sacrifices to patriarchal voyeurism and fetishism. This prepackaged viewpoint on women's status as victims blinded its proponents to the idea of asking women who actually work in the appearance business—models, actresses, and so on—about ways they perceive themselves.[9] Not so Reidemeister; creating an authentic social-historical context is central for her innovative filming technique of "staged" documentary. Her techniques radically question, as I will discuss later, widely accepted assumptions about victim status.

Blank Stares and Hard Cash captures fragments of the daily life in the everyday routine of the fashion model Hilde, a single parent, mother of two children, and the sister of the filmmaker. The documentary is exceptional in that it questions the fixed assumptions of the Left (and of the filmmaker herself before the making of the film) about capitalist consumer society and the exploitation of the human being within these societal constraints. By selecting an upper middle-class woman, the filmmaker juxtaposes the discourses already firmly in place concerning the German working class with those concerning the upper middle class. Simply by looking into the inner workings of the fashion world, Reidemeister already provokes the resentments of the leftist groups and what the feminists harbor against fashion *tout court*. Indeed, it is worth noting that from the sixties until the mideighties, German feminists and the Left shared one obsession: both ideologies opposed all expressions of fashion on principle.[10] Of course, notable exceptions notwithstanding (Georg Simmel, Theodor W. Adorno, and Walter Benjamin[11]), this contempt for fashion has a long tradition among German intellectuals. Despite several sociological studies[12] and despite Roland Barthes's[13] readings of the literature about fashion and his subsequent development of a semiotics of fashion and its German[14] reception, fashion as a serious field of investigation in the context of the recognition of cultural studies remains quite new within German intellectual discourse.

Sisters

While the ideology of sisterhood (understood as an idealized perception of close, essentially peace-loving, caring, and nurturing relations between *all*

women) remained a widely accepted model in feminist relationships throughout the 1970s, this notion was first problematized in *Schwesternstreit* (Dispute Between Sisters, 1983).[15] However, despite Margarethe von Trotta's films *Schwes-
tern, oder die Balance des Glücks* (Sisters, or the Balance of Happiness, 1979) and
Die bleierne Zeit (Marianne and Juliane, 1981), cinematic treatment of real sister
relationships has not often been a focus in German feminist film.[16] Here, too,
Reidemeister breaks new ground in that she and the fashion model she films are
connected in a very special way: they are real sisters. Reidemeister's younger sister, Hilde Kulbach, approached her older sister after having watched her second
staged documentary *Von wegen Schicksal* (Not at All "Fate," 1979), confessing to
her that she herself would be interested in helping make such a film. Reidemeister immediately agreed to this project. As they started to work on this staged
documentary dealing with the situation of Hilde Kulbach, a fashion and advertising model for most of her adult life, the sisters were trapped in competing
discourses. *Blank Stares and Hard Cash* was not intended as a portrait of an individual nor "a pure documentation of a profession." Reidemeister says that she
wanted "to show a woman who is by her circumstances caught in a spiral of
marketability, who functions in a certain manner and is sharply marked by her
age. I wanted to show the interconnection between professional and private life:
how the profession structures more everyday experiences than one can see from
the outside."[17] In the film, Reidemeister reevaluates her own relationship to her
sister, which had been under serious strain because of her own leftist identity
and by her own misunderstanding of her sister's glamorous life. Before her sister Hilde approached the filmmaker, a working-class woman portrayed in two
of Reidemeister's films had already suggested that she make a film about her
own class.

Reidemeister in the Context of Other German Women Filmmakers

As is a well-known secret, postwar Germany has produced numerous
women-filmmakers. The handbook for German women-filmmakers lists hun-
dreds, most of whom have been subsidized by the German government. In the
United States only a few of these many talented filmmakers have met with
the recognition they deserve. In the many books written in English about the
phenomenon of the New German Cinema, the omission of women is star-
tling.[18] When we look at alternative film journals (except for *Jump-cut*), women-
filmmakers fare little better. However, in journals such as *Discourse, New German
Critique, Diacritics*, and *camera obscura*, which are more concerned with questions of aesthetics and the avant-garde, the works of filmmakers such as Helga
Sanders-Brahms, Ulrike Ottinger, and Margarethe von Trotta are discussed.
What distinguishes Helga Reidemeister from her better-known sisters is her medium, the documentary, a form that is not considered a subject for discussions

of aesthetics. Furthermore, in contrast to Helke Sander, who started as a documentary filmmaker but who switched to feature filmmaking, Reidemeister belongs to the later generation of German women-filmmakers, who began producing films after the so-called New German Cinema was well underway.

Reidemeister's Development as a Filmmaker—Previous Works

Reidemeister had never planned to become a filmmaker. As a student, she enrolled in art courses and studied painting for several years. Her political awakening took place during the student movement in which she became an active participant during the late sixties, a time of social unrest in the Federal Republic of Germany (FRG) and in West Berlin. The students took to the streets to oppose a system that was involved in the war industry and imperialism but that did not talk about fascism. Not surprisingly then, Reidemeister's first film grew out of her political involvement with the student movement. Like many young people at that time, she wanted to change the world. She left her studies to become actively involved in the "march through the institutions," a political concept that implies belief in changing the system from within. As part of her political activism, she accepted a job as a social worker in a housing project in West Berlin, the Märkische Viertel, notorious for its concentration of persistent social problems. From 1968 on, she worked as a social worker with the inhabitants of this housing project and recorded her interviews with them to fuel with new material what has been called Protokolliteratur (i.e., literary documentation of current events).[19] These interviews were first published in the magazine *Kursbuch* and then reprinted as a book.[20] Working in this job helped her to realize that there was no alternative to the commercial movie theaters, which showed only violent action films or pornographic films. It did not take her long to understand that there were almost no films that dealt with the problems of the working class. National socialism had erased the popular memory of Berlin as the most politicized center of Western Europe, with the most visible and politically strong working-class movement, which had sustained several workers' theaters and workers' community colleges during the twenties. Berlin was also known for having a strong lesbian and gay culture and a large feminist community. All of this forgotten history had to be rediscovered by the generation influenced by the student movement. After these discourses and almost lost cultures had been excavated, they served as important material for leftist-oriented research on the Weimar Republic. Like the young, bourgeois generation of the twenties, these political activists of the sixties and seventies discovered their cause: the working class. Reidemeister identified completely with this free-floating ideology, which subsequently led her to combine two impulses in her life: political activism and the cultural tools of documentation.

Reidemeister noticed that mainstream filmmaking reflected only the problems of the privileged, and that the few existing working-class films never took into account the situation of working-class women. She knew that she did not want to produce films about women in the working class, since that again would mean objectifying these women. Reidemeister's solution to this dilemma was to make films *with* women and not *about* women. But, of course, before she could achieve her goal she had to study filmmaking first.

Before *Blank Stares and Hard Cash*, Reidemeister had selected subjects that were more in keeping with her leftist positions. She had made two staged documentaries about working-class families focusing on mothers. Her first film, *Der gekaufte Traum* (Buying the Dream, 1977), told the story of Irene, a woman with a part-time job, who submitted herself willingly not only to her uncertain working conditions but to her husband as well. In her second film, *Von wegen Schicksal* (Not at All "Fate," 1979), Reidemeister's main character is also named Irene, but this time, she is self-assured, has better working conditions as a cashier, and in the course of the film leaves her husband. From 1981 until 1983, Reidemeister worked on a two-part series about the left-wing intellectual activist and feminist, Karola Bloch.[21] Following her political agenda and desire to document the New Left's history in Germany, Reidemeister made a documentary about Berlin,[22] and about the children of the German student movement's idol and icon for the Left, Rudi Dutschke.[23]

With all of her films so far, Reidemeister has proven that personal experiences are profoundly influenced by politics. If we were to categorize her cinematic work it would be labeled a modified New Left feminist approach. She belongs to those New Left feminists who object to having the issue of emancipation polarized along sex lines or class lines. Rather, she prefers to work with two intersecting sets of social relations, capitalism and patriarchy, each with a material base, each with its own dynamics. As a consequence, it should not be a matter of privileging class over gender, or vice versa, for Reidemeister, but rather the much more difficult task of showing how and where such "intersections" occur.

The Staged Documentary

Work on this film took place between 1982 and 1983. It premiered at the International Forum of Young Film in Berlin on 26 February 1983, and won the Bundesfilmpreis (Federal Film Award) in 1983. Before *Blank Stares and Hard Cash*, Reidemeister's filmmaking and other artistic productions have always been inspired by a social movement. In her cinematic work on the staged documentary she developed the theory of self-representation of the main character. Actors did not exist for her. She wanted to work with real people "portraying" themselves. In order to achieve this, she talked for months with the person who would be the central figure of her documentary. The filmmaker and the woman who represents herself as the main character go on a retreat for several weeks, sometimes months, and just talk about the film they are planning to produce. This process is documented on tape and helps form the content of the documentary. In Reidemeister's understanding of a democratic relationship between the self-representing woman in the film and herself as the filmmaker, the most important category is that of self-determination. Reidemeister does not want to see the person in front of the camera as an object, but rather as a self-representing subject who is part of the decision-making process, and who codetermines that process. This approach is fundamentally different from creating a role for a woman, even about a woman, even one who is represented as relatively emancipated.[24] By selecting a fashion model as the subject for *Blank Stares and Hard Cash*, she cuts through thick layers of fixed sets of preconceptions: a fashion model is immediately stereotyped as an object for pleasure who must fulfill the spectator's voyeurism. Is she perceived as being emancipated or not? Feminism is at this point still in self-denial; it is in its early stages where contempt for fashion is a unifying sign; beauty is still something that is totally opposed to the high politics of feminism. In this regard, Reidemeister's documentary is clearly ahead of its time.

The carefully defined boundaries between feature film and documentary are not only blurred in *Blank Stares and Hard Cash*, but actually dissolved. Apart from its portrayal of exhausting and exploitative working conditions, the documentary is a close reading of the relationship of the sisters. For the filmmaker, the younger sister always meant competition. The younger sister was always more beautiful, more successful, had fewer problems, and seemed to enjoy life much more. Above all else, it was the younger sister's ability to enjoy life that was an ongoing provocation for the older sister. She resented her younger sister, calling her shallow, easy to seduce, and above all, pleasure-seeking. For years she did not communicate with her sister at all. She was interested neither in her professional goals nor in her achievements as a successful fashion model. She saw no point in her younger sister's daily hard work on her body in order to become more charming, alluring, and exciting. She interpreted all of this body work as merely superficial, with no value beyond the satisfaction of a consumer society.

The Price a Fashion Model Has to Pay

In the film, Reidemeister establishes her sister's professionality by emphasizing the daily hard work that every successful fashion model has to perform on her body. This maintenance requires, besides a rigid diet, extended exercise programs, the painful ritual of hair removal, and the erasure—by masks, emollients, and makeup—of all visible signs of aging; as a photographer bluntly says in the film "her body can still pass; the problem is her face." Beauty maintenance is captured in all of its brutality, anguish, and painfulness. Next to the excruciating removal of her facial hair, that of her legs seems almost relaxing. Reidemeister does not stress the artificiality of her sister's beauty; she rather documents her as the one who constantly and consciously maintains the brittle materiality of her still marketable, but aging body. Again and again, Hilde is shown to endure endless ordeals in beauty conservation and in beauty creation.

The fashion model is created like a piece of art, a process that is performed on her body. She contributes to this creative process by providing the raw material; her face and body serve as the surfaces on which the art is created. The boundaries of what is considered artificial and of what is defined as natural become blurred: the natural becomes artificial and the artificial becomes natural. In Reidemeister's film, however, the fashion model is actually *part of the production process*—even when she is being made up by makeup artists and when her hair is being coiffed by hairdressers—she has still brought a thoroughly exercised, dieted, worked over body and face to the studio or fashion show. The fashion model's active role is part of the triangular relationship that the feminists of the eighties missed: the fashion model is not a passive victim who gets used as a canvas but she actually becomes part of the active creator of the illusion. Furthermore, the military exactness with which the fashion model has to rehearse the choreography before each of her performances on the runway is as exhausting as a daily routine in a boot camp. (And soldiers are not required to be beautiful in spite of agonizing pain!) Models must always maintain their beautiful appearance, must always be alert and in full action, always ready and waiting to present themselves.

That the profession is stressful in a very particular way is clear; the irony lies, of course, in the fact that the stress must not be visible. As Paul Behrens points out, beauty is not associated with nervousness, depression, and despair.[25] Hilde does not define herself as fragile, though her fear and despair bring out the overly sensitive part of her personality. When she acts out the uncertain narcissist in herself, she dissolves into a sobbing, wailing face and her beauty disintegrates. In the film's next segment, Hilde is again the self-assured fashion model who knows how to carry her body self-confidently, turning it into a tool for advertising. She gets her self-affirmation from her job, since she is superior in it. Hilde characterizes herself with these words: "I am like a plant that assimilates itself—when I am asked to become red, I become red."[26] Yet Hilde's life is not free from fear of social downgrading. Reidemeister captures these emotions in scenes in which Hilde performs fashion shows in provincial cities, where the shows are less glamorous, staged in run-down and dirty places. Sometimes Hilde has to accept these engagements. She especially fears that with the coming of age these second-class places will become her only venue. Cut against segments that thematize these fears are segments where Hilde is at the pinnacle of her success and is surrounded by glamour, as in her performances for the Munich fashion king Dietl.[27]

Like Pandora's box, this film opens a variety of hotly debated questions that had been neglected for a long time in feminist discourse and that have just entered into the German debate on postfeminism. While the American university culture has often integrated areas such as women's, feminist, or gender studies, in German universities these fields of study are, if not completely absent, still marginalized. As a consequence, feminist studies originate in so-called Academies for Women (Frauenakademien) or in summer schools. These institutions are private associations though publicly funded. Added to their new catalog of discourses is one on fashion, the history of fashion, and the construction of the female body; a completely new one is the discourse on fashion models as creators of literature. The narratives the fashion models create are intended to enlighten the reading public and to correct "false perceptions" about the intellectual life of fashion models.[28] A similar contribution is developed by way of the narrative in Reidemeister's film. Since the impetus for the film came from the fashion model, that is to say, the filmmaker's sister, Hilde, the film can be seen as a precursor to this trend of models writing.

According to Roland Barthes, fashion does not serve women but it is fashion that constitutes the sign Woman.[29] While the image remains the center of fashion, Jane Gaines has emphasized the complex correlation between clothes, self-perception, and self-representation: "We are trained into clothes, and early become practiced in presentational postures, learning, in the age of mechanical reproduction, to carry the mirror's eye within the mind, as though one might at any moment be photographed."[30] Reidemeister's staged documentary questions these fixed assumptions in a time before the discourse on fashion and fashion models peaked internationally during the mideighties and within the German debate on postfeminism in the midnineties.

Camera: Reidemeister Interrupts the Voyeuristic Process

By changing the usual method of using her camera, Reidemeister examines problematic assumptions and contradictions concealed behind the masquerade that the model Hilde presents in public. She also problematizes the use of the camera as a voyeuristic tool or medium. In this way, she succeeds in capturing both the strain and the fear of her younger sister: the strain of the job, how the job determines her personal life, and her fear of getting older. This staged documentary is animated by filmed images that are cut in such a way that the fashion model's joys and fears are constantly present. Words are not supported by images; nor are images clarified by spoken discourse. Elements of a feature film, such as the frequent use of soft focus, reinforce the theme of glamour by creating a dreamlike texture for the constructed fashion world. In contrast, Reidemeister explores this masquerade and shows that Hilde's makeup is part of the context for her invisibility as a person. By concentrating solely on the model's face in one sequence of the film, the filmmaker succeeds in making visible the person hidden behind the image of the fashion industry. Sharply opposed to the glamorous image is Hilde's private face, without makeup. In this private performance, her emotions become visible on her face; they tell the story of loneliness and trace her constant exercise of pulling herself together. At the time of the shooting, Hilde had been working for twenty years as a fashion model and all this time she had been in high demand. Fashion models are themselves the commodity they are selling. While in other jobs, image became emphasized by modernism,[31] in Hilde's occupation, the commodity is her actual body, which must be kept beautiful and, at least in its staged appearance, young. No matter what her mood, when promised a couple of hundred dollars, Hilde is ready to transform herself and become the desired object, an artificially composed woman, a produced woman. When posing in front of the cameras, when doing her job, no pain can be seen on her face even though she may feel it intensely. At that moment, Hilde is the smiling face walking in a perfect body, ready to perform, ready to supply visual pleasure. At the same time, Hilde herself emphasizes the perspective of herself *as* producer of a production. Therefore, Hilde is not separate from the result (the image)—in this triangular situation; the image and its producer are coextensive. In her fashionable, contemporary look, she has to exude sexuality, which is her most marketable talent. The fashion and advertising industry works with real material products and with the flesh and blood of its models, but its ultimate appeal is to create desire and fantasy. That the filmmaker exposes the fashion and advertising industry to be ugly, degrading, and utterly unglamorous only serves to heighten the miracle of transformation that occurs in Hilde, a transformation away from reality into the realm of fantasy.

But are the working conditions for a photo and fashion model so different from those of other jobs? Reidemeister claims, and her film argues, that the only difference between this and other kinds of jobs is that in this particular profession the job controls the worker's personal life more thoroughly. Reidemeister wants us to understand her film neither as a portrait of an individual person nor as a pure documentary about a certain occupation. Her intention is to use Hilde and her particular profession as an example comparable to the situation of people in other careers. What is concealed in these professions appears more clearly, more glaringly, in Hilde's job: the fact that she sells herself bit by bit; that she is unable to extract herself from the entire process; that she does whatever is demanded of her.

Concepts of political correctness explode on two levels: on the emotional level between the sisters who had virtually no contact at all and on the level of leftist identity. Despite the inescapable fact that they are sisters, the women live in diametrically opposed worlds and each is shaped and molded by a different value system. Reidemeister's focus on the female body could only be interpreted within the leftist feminist movement as a critique of consumer fetishism. However, Reidemeister reveals a fashion model's work as time-consuming and back-breaking and painful on a number of levels, while at the same time she exposes the seamy side of the "glamorous" fashion world. By this very attentiveness to the process of creating the fashion model's identity, the filmmaker ultimately valorizes her sister's reality.

Most astonishing is that among all German women-filmmakers, it was this accredited Leftist intellectual who, focusing on the glamorous surface of commodity fetishism, saw beneath it. Reidemeister introduced a concept into German feminism that would take years to be further explored by other feminists. The debate on masquerade as a central feminist issue had already been introduced by American and English feminist film studies and had fueled international feminist debates. However, within German feminist discourse, Reidemeister's documentary inaugurated a debate that facilitated the entrance of postfeminist issues into feminist discourses. Known primarily for her documentaries on the legacy of the student movement, and on their prolific "leaders" such as Rudi Dutschke and the philosopher of concrete hope, Ernst Bloch, Reidemeister produced this documentary on the daily life of the fashion model who happened to be also her sister. While the filmmaker's critical consciousness might have been shaped by her choice of subjects, she has worked firmly in the center of major discourses. She entered the postfeminist discourse before it had emerged in Germany, and introduced it into the feminist debates on the exploitation of the female body, the production of beauty, and fashion.

Notes

1. Butler's book is translated in German as *Das Unbehagen der Geschlechter* and published by Suhrkamp. The German discussion on postfeminism is documented in *Postfeminismus*, Rundbrief 43 (December 1994) Frauen in der Literaturwissenschaft.

2. Alice Schwarzer, *So fing es an! Die neue Frauenbewegung* (Munich: Deutscher Taschenbuch Verlag, 1993).

3. *PorNo: Opfer & Täter, Gegenwehr & Backlash, Verantwortung & Gesetz*, ed. Alice Schwarzer (Cologne: Kiepenheuer and Witsch, 1994). This approach was contradicted by *Frauen und Pornografie*, ed. Claudia Gehrke (Tübingen, Germany: Konkursbuch Verlag, 1988).

4. Barbara Sichtermann, *Weiblichkeit. Zur Politik des Privaten* (Berlin: Klaus Wagenbach, 1983).

5. *Frauenhaus Köln. Nachrichten aus dem Ghetto Liebe. Gewalt gegen Frauen* (Frankfurt/Main, Germany: Verlag Jugend and Politik, 1980).

6. Christa Thürmer-Rohr, *Vagabundinnen. Feministische Essays* (Berlin: Orlanda Frauenverlag, 1987).

7. *Leideunlust. Der Mythos vom weiblichen Masochismus*, eds. Roswitha Burgard and Birgit Rommelspacher (Berlin: Orlanda Frauenverlag, 1989).

8. Silvia Bovenschen, "Auf falsche Fragen gibt es keine richtigen Antworten. Anmerkungen zur Pornographie-Kampagne," in *Autonome Frauen. Schlüsseltexte der Neuen Frauenbewegung seit 1968*, ed. Ann Anders (Frankfurt/Main, Germany: Athenäum Verlag, 1988), 266–79.

9. *Rheinische Post*, no. 106, 7 May 1983.

10. See *Die Listen der Mode*, ed. Silvia Bovenschen (Frankfurt/Main, Germany: Suhrkamp, 1986). See also *Reflexionen vor dem Spiegel*, ed. Farideh Akashe-Böhme (Frankfurt/Main, Germany: Suhrkamp, 1992).

11. Georg Simmel, "Die Mode," in *Listen der Moden*, 179–206. Theodor W. Adorno, *Ästhetische Theorie* (Frankfurt/Main, Germany: Suhrkamp, 1973). Walter Benjamin, *Das Passagen-Werk. Gesammelte Schriften* (Band V. Frankfurt/Main, Germany: Suhrkamp, 1982).

12. *Listen der Moden*, 28.

13. Roland Barthes, *Die Sprache der Mode*, Frankfurt/Main, Germany: Suhrkamp, 1985. Originally published in French in 1967.

14. Gerhard Goebel, "Einführung in die Literatur der Mode in den Anfängen des bürgerlichen Zeitalters," in *Ästhetik und Kommunikation* 21 (1975): 66–88. The journal has a Left readership.

15. *Schwesternstreit. Von den heimlichen und unheimlichen Auseinandersetzungen zwischen Frauen*, eds. Birgit Cramon-Daiber, Monika Jaeckel, Barbara Köster, Hildegard Menge, and Anke Wolf-Graaf (Reinbek, Germany: Rowohlt, 1983).

16. Janice Mouton, "Margarethe von Trotta's Sisters: 'Brides Under a Different Law,'" *Women in German Yearbook*, eds. Sara Friedrichsmeyer and Patricia Herminghouse (Lincoln and London: University of Nebraska Press, 1995), 11:35–47.

17. Stijepo Pavlina, "Aus dem Vollen schöpfen. ZITTY-Gespräch mit Helga Reidemeister und Klaus Volkenborn," *ZITTY* 9 (1983): 85.

18. An exeption is *Gender and German Cinema: Feminist Interventions*, ed. Sandra Frieden et al., 2 vols. (Providence: Berg, 1993).

19. Erika Runge, *Bottroper Protokolle*, ed. Keith Bullivant (Frankfurt/Main, Germany: Suhrkamp, 1968). Idem, *After the 'Death of Literature': West German Writing of the 1970s* (Oxford: Berg, 1989).

20. See *Kursbuch* 25, 27, and 37. "*Wohnste Sozial, haste die Qual*" (Living in a Housing Project Is Not Easy) (Reinbek, Germany: Rowohlt Publishers, 1975).

21. The film is entitled *Karola Bloch, Fragmente eines Portraits* (Fragments of a Portrait). Its first part "Dann nimmt die Frau die Geschicke in die Hand" (Then, the Woman Takes Life into Her Hands) was produced for two German television stations of two federal states, the WDR III (West German Radio) and the SW (South West Radio). The second part entitled "Ernst und Karola Bloch—die Tübinger Zeit" (Ernst and Karola Bloch During Their Years in Tübingen), emphasized the political side of the philosophers Ernst Bloch and Karola Bloch's involvement with the German Left and with Karola's feminist practical approach by working with the local group of autonomous feminists who were in the process of establishing a safe house for battered women.

22. *DrehOrt Berlin. Inszenierter Dokumentarfilm in beiden Teilen der Stadt Berlin (West) und Berlin, Hauptstadt der DDR* (Location Berlin: Staged Documentary in Both Parts of the City Berlin (West) and Berlin, Capital of the GDR).

23. *Rudi Dutschkes Kinder—Auf der Suche nach seinen Spuren* (Rudi Dutschke's Children—In Search of His Traces), 1987.

24. On the question of female subjectivity and autobiographical filmmaking see Jutta Brückner, "On Autobiographical Filmmaking," in *Women in German Yearbook*, no. 11 (1995): 1–12.

25. Paul Behrens, "Auftauchen oder untergehen?" *Rheinische Post* 106, 7 May 1983.

26. "Ich bin wie eine Pflanze, die sich assimiliert—soll ich rot werden, werde ich rot," *Basis Filmverleih* Press Release, 1983.

27. *Rheinische Post*, no. 106, 7 May 1983.

28. The fashion model Naomi Campbell's novel *Swan* is considered the first example of this new kind of literature. Using her status as a celebrity, she writes to revise popular preconceptions and prejudices. She intends to deconstruct stereotypes like "fashion models are beautiful but mindless." Campbell's intended goal is to establish herself as a beautiful *and* intelligent woman. Campbell, *Swan* (London: Heinemann, 1994). The German translation appeared in 1994. Gertrud Lehnert discussed this novel in detail in "Moden und Maskeraden," *Frauen in der Literaturwissenschaft*, no. 13 (December 1994): 26–30.

29. Roland Barthes, *Der entgegenkommende und der stumpfe Sinn, Kritische Eassays* (Frankfurt/Main, Germany: Suhrkamp, 1990), 3:120.

30. Jane Gaines, Introduction, in *Fabrications. Costume and the Female Body*, eds. Jane Gaines and Charlotte Herzog (New York: Routledge, 1990), 3–4.

31. Siegfried Kracauer, *Die Angestellten* (Frankfurt/Main, Germany: Suhrkamp, 1974), 25. In the context of the male and female white-collar worker, Kracauer ties the sophisticated work invested into appearance to the constant fear of unemployment.

15

Women, Film, and Writing in the GDR:
Helga Schubert and the DEFA
An Interview with Helga Schubert

Ute Lischke-McNab

When writing about the role of women in film and literature in the former German Democratic Republic (GDR), one cannot ignore either the work or persona of Helga Schubert. This dynamic, articulate, and humorous woman is both an accomplished writer and up-and-coming filmmaker who, in the prime of her life, still has much to offer. When I was in Berlin in February 1996 following some of the trends at the Berlinale (Berlin International Film Festival), I was beginning a new project dealing with women and film in the former GDR. Looking for women to contact, it quickly became clear that Schubert was one woman not to be missed. I began to telephone her at her apartment in the former East Berlin, but soon discovered that she had fled the metropolis for the quieter ambience of her seaside home. She had gone there not only to work, but also to recuperate from a broken leg. I also discovered quickly enough that nothing could slow her down. She readily consented to do this interview and was delighted to talk about her involvement in filmmaking. I am extremely grateful to her generous hospitality and to her willingness to share such exciting aspects of her life.

Schubert is a free-lance writer who now divides her time between Berlin and a small village in Mecklenburg, near the Baltic Sea. She studied psychology in Berlin and still works part-time as a clinical psychologist with adults. Her literary and film work have brought her several prizes, including the Heinrich-Greif-Preis in 1983 and the Heinrich-Mann-Preis in 1986. Her writings are autobiographical and emphasize the difficulties women face in everyday life, such as their attempts to combine work with family life, without having to sacrifice the need for individual fulfillment. Schubert's heroines do not symbolize the un-attainable heroic, but represent women with whom readers can identify. Her works include such diverse writings as *Lauter Leben* (Nothing but Life, 1975; in West Germany published as *Anna kann Deutsch* (Anna Knows German, 1985); a series of novels around *Bimmi*; a filmscript *Die Beunruhigung* (Apprehension, 1982), *Judasfrauen* (Women of Judas, 1990); and various radio plays and televi-sion scripts for the former GDR.

Film production in the GDR developed very differently from the system in the Federal Republic of Germany (FRG). Although women had been granted equal pay for equal work as well as equal rights and opportunity in theory, in practice it did not work out that way. Women carried the double burden of work outside and inside the home. When it came to assuming greater responsibilities at work, more often than not, women declined simply because of their respon-sibilities. It is for this reason that they remained, in the film industry, mostly oc-cupied as scriptwriters, cutters, editors, and set designers; very few became di-rectors and producers.

The films that were made at the Deutsche Film-AG (DEFA— German Film Corporation)[1] during the seventies and eighties, and that have women as their heroines, very much reflect the *public consciousness* of the former GDR. These films more often than not reflected the place of women in this society, and their search for self-fulfillment and meaning of life, in a society that had deemed them as equal.

Die Beunruhigung (Apprehension, 1982, director, Lothar Warneke) is one such film. Scripted by Helga Schubert, the heroine, Inge, a divorcée with a son, works as a psychologist. When she is diagnosed with breast cancer, she is filled with apprehension, questioning the usefulness of her life. Inge measures her life in terms of human relationships, which have been rather perfunctory. As she goes through the day, she waits for her married lover to come—until his pres-ence loses its significance. Concentrating on relationships, Schubert's autobio-graphical script was, for its time, certainly progressive in looking for new forms of male/female bonding in the GDR, with the emphasis being on partnership. This interview, conducted on 24 February 1996 in Berlin, gives us a closer in-sight into the values and ideas of this writer.

Lischke-McNab. You are a writer, dividing your time between Berlin and Mecklenburg. Can you tell us something about your life, growing up, living, and working in Berlin?

Schubert. I was born in Berlin in 1940. My father, a lawyer, died during the Second World War in 1941. My mother was an economist and later a research librarian. She didn't remarry and brought me up as an only child in East Berlin, part of the later GDR. It was because of her that I became interested in the fine arts and started to love books and music. In Berlin I graduated from high school

(Abitur) at a fairly young age—I was only seventeen. Actually, I then meant to move to the West as quickly as possible, since the borders within Berlin proper were still open. But because of my age and my mother, and then my first husband-to-be, who, for the time being, wanted to remain in the East, I still hesitated and applied for courses in psychology in East Berlin. For a year, I worked in a factory, a condition all had to satisfy before being admitted to the university, and then began my studies at the Faculty of Mathematics and Natural Science at Humboldt University in Berlin in 1958. I graduated in 1963. While studying, I married and had a son in October of 1960. Because of my baby, I intended to wait again for another few months before finally going to the West with him, where I wanted to continue my studies. At that time, I was already planning my divorce, when suddenly the wall was built in Berlin during August 1961.

Lischke-McNab. What were your reactions to the building of the wall and what were your options?

Schubert. It sealed the division of Germany. I consider this event to be a decisive turning point in my life—as it was for the other seventeen million citizens of the GDR. I had to adjust to a life under dictatorship and in confinement. This nightmare ended for me only when the GDR ceased to exist in 1989, when I was already forty-nine years old.

Lischke-McNab. What would you consider to be the beginning of your writing career?

Schubert. Shortly after the birth of my son, I started to write stories and poems, but I didn't start to publish these until fifteen years later, in 1975, when I was thirty-five years old. *Lauter Leben* (Nothing but Life) was the first book to be published.[2]

Lischke-McNab. You also wrote a filmscript around this time?

Schubert. I wrote my own script for a fifteen-minute film, which I submitted for my diploma. The film consisted of unconnected scenes and was used for the purpose of diagnosing neuroses. After I received my diploma, I worked full-time in the field of psychotherapy where I treated adults for twenty-four years until 1987. During the last ten years or so, actually since 1977, I worked only one day a week because I also wanted to pursue my work as a writer.

Lischke-McNab. Your literary production and style has been varied. Do you still experiment?

Schubert. I've tried my hand at different literary forms and found that the monologue suits me best. I wrote radio-dramas: *Eine unmögliche Geschichte* (An Impossible Story), *Anna, Ansprache einer Verstorbenen an die Trauergemeinde* (A Speech by the Deceased Addressing the Congregation in Mourning), short stories compiled into volumes: *Das verbotene Zimmer* (The Forbidden Room), *Judasfrauen* (Women of Judas), which consists of case histories of female denunciation during the times of the Nazis, *Die Andersdenkende* (A Woman Who Thinks

Differently), and finally in 1995 *Das gesprungene Herz—Leben im Gegensatz* (A Shattered Heart—A Life in Contrast), stories about political change and the consequences of dictatorship.

Lischke-McNab. You worked on a fascinating feature film for which you received a prize?

Schubert. I wrote scenarios for two feature films: *Die Beunruhigung*, in 1981, which was shown at the Biennale in Venice in 1982 and that was sold out at the Uraufführungskino (premiere theater) in East Berlin for five weeks. It deals with a day in the life of an East Berlin psychologist, who finds herself in the midst of preparing a class reunion, when she learns during this time of reflection that she will have to undergo surgery because of breast cancer. It's in black and white with a full-tone camera without postsynchronization by the documentary film cameraman, Thomas Plenert, and was awarded many prizes. The film showed the GDR without pathos and with laconic brevity.

Lischke-McNab. What were the opportunities for women in filmmaking in the GDR?

Schubert. There were three possibilities for filmmaking in the GDR, all of which were controlled by the State. First, you could be commissioned by the only television channel in the GDR. A couple of times I wrote hour-long portraits of prima ballerinas engaged at the Komische Oper (comic opera) in Berlin. One about Hannelore Bey *Und morgen wieder* (And Again Tomorrow) for which I also did the narration and the other of the prima ballerina Jutta Deutschland *Wir brauchen eine Blume* (We Need a Flower). This is a fictitious monologue of a prima ballerina. The monologue I had written was narrated by the actress Corinna Harfouch. On both films, I worked closely with the director, Petra Wirbatz. We used different camera crews for each film, which was absurd. But, we had to work with the crew on duty, so we had to explain everything again. We also used material from the film library for our work and had to do all the editing during the night, because whatever equipment and technology was available, was also needed for current affairs reporting during the day. The films had to be reviewed and approved by departmental managers. Their special job was to screen the films for their ideological content. While we worked on the script, one of the television station's full-time film editors was present at all times. It was impossible to film spontaneously, even though our topic was *uniquely* cultural. Everything had to be laid out meticulously in advance. I thought that this technique was very cumbersome. The second possibility for filmmaking was at DEFA, the only film studio in the GDR. The preparations were very time-consuming, as if time didn't matter at all. I thought that working on the scenario was too important since all ideological problems had to be eliminated beforehand. In addition to *Beunruhigung*, I also wrote *Ab heute erwachsen* (Grow Up Today, directed by Günther Scholz) and *Überprüfung des Kandidaten* (Examining the Candidate) as part of an episode in the movie *Verzeihung, sehen Sie Fußball?*

(Excuse Me, Are You Watching Soccer? directed by Günther Scholz). Several groups of producers working for DEFA were looking for authors. They dealt exclusively with the step-by-step development of the film material, which already required many hours of group discussions, before arriving at the exposé, followed by the discourse of the film, the treatment, and finally the script. Frequently no film resulted from all of this.

My short stories caught the attention of the producer Erika Richter, and so I wrote the scenarios for both DEFA films without the numerous preliminary steps, which meant that I didn't get paid for the intermediary steps. But, consequently, I wrote dialogues that were livelier and less influenced by a producer's interference. As an author, you could have spent your whole life in discussions, without ever seeing a director face-to-face. The directors were full-time employees. They were presented with the finished scenarios and could later decide whether to use them for a film script or not. There were always endless discussions, both before starting with the actual filmmaking and after the film was completed. But without a fully prepared script, there was no film. Everything was supposed to be under control. With this continuous interference by the producers, it took enormous efforts and strength to portray individuality, sarcastic humor, and a sense of the absurd in the scenario. The third possibility was presented by the Hochschule für Film und Fernsehen (Institute for Film and Television). In 1975, I wrote the scenario for Peter Wekwerth's thirty-minute-long thesis film, *Das Gastspiel* (The Guest Performance), a comedy. Later, I wrote a filmscript for another cinema student, Dietmar Hochmut. My narrative, *Heute abend* (This Evening) had been discussed with him beforehand.

Lischke-McNab. Has your situation changed very much since the Wende?[3]

Schubert. Because of the political events of the so-called Wende, a completely new situation has developed for me as an author. At first, I worked intensively in the political arena, for instance, from the beginning of December 1989 I worked as media spokesperson of the Zentralen Runden Tisch in Berlin (Central Round Table in Berlin), the institution, in which the unelected GDR government together with representatives of the opposition prepared and secured the first free elections to be held in the former GDR. After that, I returned to my desk, despite attempts to persuade me to become a politician, to make a documentary film with the director Frank Damrau. Damrau was a former classmate of mine, who had fled the former GDR across the Baltic in a dinghy. The documentary is about our first class reunion, which took place thirty-three years after our Abitur (graduation). I wrote the scenario after the rough cut and narrated the text myself. The film *Die geteilte Klasse* (The Divided Classroom) was aired by RIAS-TV during May 1990. I declined the offer made by a television station to write a serial because I'm mostly interested in the literary film essay and I prefer to express myself subjectively. So when commissioned by the film company Tellux, I wrote a one-half hour film about the prayer *Our Father in*

Heaven, directed by Jörg Foth, and right now I'm preparing a thirteen-minute lyrical film for Whitsunday, which, in all probability, will be aired by ZDF. Dagmar Brendicke will be the director.

Lischke-McNab. Where do you see your strength as a writer?

Schubert. I believe that I have found my writing style in prose as well as in film writing. It's close to the essay, a very precise, hushed, lyrical prose, that I would like to have control over, without doing the directing myself. The discipline that's required, which I don't want when I write prose, comes from directing. In all of this I can be much more creative. I can devote myself exclusively to writing and researching. When writing prose, I like to come up with my own topics, to rely only on myself, to have everything in my head, and to develop everything myself. For example, since the middle of 1994, I'm writing regular columns for a weekly journal in Hamburg; last year I wrote for the radio station Deutschlandradio Berlin, but also published in the newspaper *Weltwoche* in Zürich so I'm always moving within the borders of documentary and fiction. In film I am fascinated by the optical; I have a strong visual imagination, but it bothers me that you have to depend on so many other people while producing a film and that you have to make compromises with the director. So far I haven't had the courage to direct a documentary film myself, although this year I was encouraged to do so for the very first time.

Lischke-McNab. How would you define your life presently?

Schubert. Most of the time my second husband, Johannes Helm, and I, we've been married for over twenty years, live in a house that is very secluded, in Mecklenburg, near the Baltic Sea. Johannes is a professor emeritus in clinical psychology and he now loves to paint and write. We don't spend much time in our small high-rise apartment in the former border area facing West Berlin. Looking back at it now, especially since the GDR is a thing of the past, I enjoy living in a more democratic society. This is certainly something I have yearned for all my life—to live in a parliamentary democracy. But I also think that it was a good thing for my writing that I stayed in the GDR until reunification. Both, transfer and contrast, represent unique and happy experiences of my life.

Notes

I am very grateful to Heinz Blumensath, director, Berliner Institut für Lehrefort-und- weiterbildung und Schulentwicklung for introducing me to Helga Schubert. His kind and diligent efforts in seeking out relevant information and material that relate to women working in film in the former GDR have been an invaluable help to me. I would also like to thank the editors of this volume for their encouragement and suggestions.

1. DEFA or *Deutsche Film-AG* was founded on 17 May 1946 by the Soviet military and became the official film company that served the former German Democratic Re-

public as a state company with a monopoly of film production. The DEFA studio for feature films used, since 1947, the premises of the former Ufa (Universum-Film Aktiengesellschaft founded in 1917) Film Studio space in Neu Babelsberg. Until 1991, DEFA produced about eight hundred feature films, as well as television, documentary, and animation films. After reunification, DEFA came into the hands of Treuhand, the official German holding company, and was sold in August 1992 to a French consortium, the Compagnie Générale des Eaux, of which Volker Schlöndorff is a member.

2. *Lauter Leben* (Nothing but Life), 31 stories, Aufbau-Verlag, 1975, epilogue by Sarah Kirsch.

3. Wende refers to the period immediately after the collapse of the wall dividing East (GDR) and West Germany (FRG) in November 1989, a time of euphoria and hope for a reunited Germany.

16

Models or Misfits?
The Role of Screen Heroines in GDR Cinema

Andrea Rinke

Since 1945, West German mainstream cinema has been dominated by Hollywood and its main female stereotypes: the housewife, the glamorous sex symbol, and the demonized temptress. In contrast, a first overview of DEFA (German Film Corporation) films provides quite a variety of female protagonists from the Western screen images of women. Films in the ex-GDR tended to portray their heroines at their workplace, as ordinary average people, avoiding glamorous extremes. The majority of women on-screen are working mothers with one or two children, more often single than married. Throughout two decades of DEFA films, only three or four housewives are portrayed showing that this way of life was unacceptable on a social level and doomed to fail as part of a relationship. There was no explicit feminist approach to filmmaking in the GDR, the official view being that women's emancipation had been successfully accomplished by achieving women's economic independence.

However, a remarkable number of DEFA films feature female protagonists and address "women's concerns" in the 1970s and 1980s. According to Joshua Isaac Feinstein, it was the general turn toward everyday contemporary issues during those years, the focus on more concrete social domains conventionally associated with women, which favored cinematic representations of the female experience.[1]

Indeed, a large proportion of the films in the 1970s and 1980s deal with contemporary everyday life in GDR society—constituting a new film genre peculiar to the GDR, the so-called Gegenwartsfilm—and they did this remarkably often through the eyes of a female protagonist: of the roughly ninety Gegenwartsfilm produced from 1972 to 1988 more than half have a female character at the center of the story or a female-male relationship, as their main theme.

Does this mean that GDR audiences in the 1970s and 1980s were swamped with consciousness-raising films about women by female directors for female spectators, this is to say, with Frauenfilme (women's films) in the Western feminist sense? In fact, only a very small proportion of film directors were women: of all the directors of Gegenwartsfilms in the DEFA-Spielfilm feature film repertoire VEB from 1946 to 1992 (a group of twenty-seven to thirty on permanent contracts at any time) only three, eventually two, were women: Ingrid Reschke (1938–71), Iris Gusner (1941), and Evelyn Schmidt (1949).

But how then, did this strong interest by predominantly male directors in women's roles and gender relations arise in a state where the authorities assumed equality of the sexes to be an accomplished fact in all areas of society? What message did they aim to convey using female rather than male protagonists as vehicles? This essay will examine these questions, taking into account how the films under review related to their audiences and to the contemporary GDR society that they aimed to represent. Two of the lesser-known films of the early 1980s are chosen for closer inspection as representative for tendencies and strands of developments in the portrayal of DEFA film heroines. In *Unser kurzes Leben* (Our Short Life, 1981) by Lothar Warneke, the hero is an idealistic rebel who wants to instigate changes in society from within and could thus be seen as a model for renewal in a utopian sense. In contrast, *Das Fahrrad* (The Bicycle, 1982) by Evelyn Schmidt presents an antihero, a misfit who has dropped out of society.

Idealized and Real Heroines

In Gegenwartsfilme of the late 1960s and early 1970s, following the disastrous consequences of the eleventh plenary session of the central committee of the Sozialistische Einheitspartei Deutschland [SED] in 1965, filmmakers tended to portray women along the lines of the ideal "socialist personality." These model heroines participated in the process of social production and, being highly qualified, held down prestigious jobs, often in a formerly male domain, such as the university lecturer of mathematics in *Netzwerk* (Network, 1970) by Ralph Kirsten, the director of a research project in physics in *Liebeserklärung an G. T.* (Declaration of Love to G.T., 1971) by Horst Seemann, or the "Meisterin" (forewoman) in mechanical engineering in *Laut und leise ist die Liebe* (Love Is Loud and Soft, 1972) by Helmut Dziuba. This fact was criticized by Regine Sylvester, who pointed out that these idealized model heroines were not representative for the majority of women who were still at the lower end of the job scale doing menial jobs: "We shouldn't focus on the professionally advanced and successful woman in our films when the majority of women only experience interesting work vicariously at home in the evenings—as their husbands' work."[2]

In films of the later 1970s and 1980s the work women did on-screen tended to be a more "realistic" reflection of the position of female workers in GDR society. Although there were still female protagonists who pursued "exceptional" careers, an increasing number of DEFA heroines held down "ordinary" and traditionally female jobs, such as shop clerks and cashiers, cooks, cleaners, nurses, post office clerks, or teachers, as well as workers in textile or shoe factories or in other manufacturing enterprises. Following a famous statement by Marx about the relation of the sexes being an indicator of the achievements of society, the film critic Mihan concludes: "Heldinnen stehen stellvertretend für die Entwicklungsmöglichkeiten des Menschen im Sozialismus überhaupt"[3] (Heroines are representative of the possibilities of human development under socialism *tout court*). DEFA Frauenfilme were thus perceived as "seismographs of the condition of society."

After the promising albeit short-lived effects of Honecker's antitaboo speech in 1971, DEFA films started to challenge the rather simplistic view that had dominated in the late 1960s, that is, that once the work situation was sorted out, happiness at home would follow suit. In these films the protagonists aimed to achieve fulfilment and self-realization on an individual level, for instance, through a loving relationship, rather than through their role in society. They often critically addressed the discrepancies between the ideal and reality, between new opportunities the socialist state offered women, as well as outdated attitudes that prevented men and women from taking advantage of societal breakthroughs.

In Egon Günther's *Der Dritte* (The Third One, 1973), one of the most interesting and well-known DEFA-films, the gap between concepts of traditional gender role concepts still prevailing in GDR society and the progress women had made on a professional level, is addressed explicitly: the heroine Margit, a mathematician with a successful career, is divorced with two children from two different men, and is now looking for Mr. Right, the third one. In a famous scene she complains about the discrepancy she experiences between equality at work and the outdated role of the passive, submissive female she is expected to play in her private life:

> I am a mathematician. I work, think, and feel according to the technical, scientific, political level of the scientific, technical revolution under socialist conditions. But if I fancy a man, if I need him in my life, if I want him, I will most probably still make a fool of myself if I tell him.

Rebels and Individualists

So, on one level, DEFA films of the 1970s and 1980s presented women's changing roles to point out the social achievements as well as conflicts that con-

temporary GDR women experienced. On another level, filmmakers used female protagonists as vehicles to point out more general problems within society.
Women were perceived to be less conformist than men and were therefore seen
as able to signal the need for change more readily:

> Men adapt much more readily to conventions which originate from times
> when men exclusively had the say. Women, in their demand for change, signal
> much more clearly a general need for change in society.[4]

I would like to focus on two ways in which film protagonists express this general need for change within society: by rebelling against social conditions and
by promoting social change from a position within society, and by asserting
their independence as individuals in opposition to society's norms and expectations. An example of the first type of character would be Franziska from *Unser
kurzes Leben* (Our Short Life, 1981) by Lothar Warneke, based on motifs from
Franziska Linkerhand (1974) by Brigitte Reimann. The town planner and architect Franziska represents, on a professional level, the typical socialist hero, in that
she fulfills her role in society by actively creating the much needed living space
for her fellow men. As in many other DEFA films, the construction site is used
as a metaphor for the shaping of the new socialist country. However, Franziska
is also portrayed as a rebel against established rules, as a "Frau mit einer maxi-
malistischen Haltung"[5] (woman with a maximalist attitude). In her role as an
architect she raises a most delicate issue: she criticizes the official building plan
in the provincial town she chose to work. In the context of the acute housing
problems in the GDR in the 1960s and 1970s and the government's plan to
tackle this problem with a comprehensive building program, the slightest expression of doubts about this government program was regarded as an attack on
the working class and on its party leadership.

Franziska first provokes her boss Schafheutlin by insisting on her vision of
a more humane plan for the town center instead of the high-rise blocks of the
official building plan. However, in the end she has to accept defeat, as her project for redeveloping the old town center won a prize but cannot be realized.
Despite the controversial issues raised—which resulted in taking Warneke almost ten years to have the filmscript accepted by the DEFA authorities—*Unser
kurzes Leben* was a success with GDR audiences and with most critics in the
GDR. In my opinion, the eventual acceptance of *Unser kurzes Leben* was to some
extent due to the choice of a female protagonist. As I just outlined, it was mainly
women who were seen as representing a change and challenge in socialist society; they were expected to liberate themselves from traditional roles, allowed to
break new ground, and to make their mark in the work force. At the same time,
however, the authorities may have made allowances for female protagonists, if
women were still implicitly held to be the "weaker sex," thus representing a

rather more harmless form of criticism. The GDR film critic Bulgakowa argues that in many Gegenwartsfilme of the 1970s and 1980s female protagonists were chosen because they represented "das gemildert sozial Subversive"[6] (the subversive in a moderate form). The female could thus safely be used to address controversial issues in society and express feelings of dissatisfaction that were shared by the majority of viewers.

In the case of *Our Short Life*, the heroine is an attractive, very young woman, who poses no real threat to the prestigious government program and whose older and more experienced male colleagues keep telling her in a benevolent but patronizing tone that she will have to have her wings clipped. Indeed, the film ends with Franziska accepting compromise, seemingly conveying the message that it is part of the growing-up process to relinquish idealistic dreams, to come down to earth, and to face the limitations of the real world. Nevertheless, Franziska's remarkable openness, courage, and single-mindedness throughout the film can also be read as representing a serious attempt to reach beyond the immediately feasible and as the legitimate insistence on the right to have dreams of a better world and to fight for their realization. Warneke, when asked why he had chosen such a long and complex novel for his cinematic adaptation, replied that he had been fascinated by the novel's protagonist, admiring her rigorous idealism, and the uncompromising way in which she pursued her vision.

As he explained in an interview, Warneke himself saw women like Franziska as representatives of utopian visions of a better society:

> Everyone of us has to reconcile his decisions with the political requirements of the day, but also with the ideals of society, with the future. In this respect I regret that there are so few utopian films in socialist countries which express how we imagine the future to be.[7]

In *Our Short Life*, as in many other DEFA films, characteristics traditionally attributed to women, such as being led by strong emotions rather than by rational constraints, were used to express criticism of rigidity, conformism, and stagnation in society, usually represented by men.

The Private Sphere: Misfits and Dropouts

In some DEFA films of the 1980s, there was a notable shift of emphasis from portraying the heroines within their working context to an almost exclusive focus on their personal lives. Regine Sylvester suggests that the increased interest in the representation of gender-relationships in the home might have been a reaction to the fact that films of the late 1960s and early 1970s had primarily addressed practical issues resulting from women's new roles in full employment, portraying these from a social point of view, rather than looking at emotional problems on an individual level.[8] Oksana Bulgakowa goes a little further in her interpretation of the new focus on the private sphere in Gegenwartsfilms: she claims that this represented an intimate refuge from an otherwise strictly regimented collective life in the GDR: "Diese intime und erotische Landschaft wurde als Kochnische für versteckte soziale Probleme genutzt" (This intimate and erotic scenery was used as a niche to cook up hidden social problems). The frustrations, disappointments, and dissatisfactions these female figures expressed in the context of their personal lives on-screen could thus be read as representing feelings of a wider disillusionment with socialist reality experienced by the majority of people.[9] Moreover, as Marc Silberman points out, representation of private problems in interpersonal relationships very often experienced by female protagonists, helped filmmakers to account for negativity and failure as part of the human condition that socialist realism had tended to exclude.[10]

As a result of this development quite a different type of female protagonist appeared on the scene: the social misfit or Aussteiger (dropout). This is to be seen in the context of a general turn of the Gegenwartsfilme of the 1980s toward portraying individuals at the margins of society, addressing psychological and existential issues. The question of how individuals cope with illness, pain, depression, and death was raised, for instance, in Lothar Warneke's Frauenfilm *Die Beunruhigung* (The Apprehension, 1982).

Antiheroines and social misfits such as Nina in *Bürgschaft für ein Jahr* (Guardianship for a Year, 1981) by Hermann Zschoche; and Susanne in *Das Fahrrad* (The Bicycle, 1982) by Evelyn Schmidt and Christine in *Die Alleinseglerin* (The Lone Sailor, 1986) by Hermann Zschoche were met with a mixed, sometimes bewildered reception by GDR critics. Nina, Susanne, and Christine are portrayed as nonconformist individualists wrapped up in their own personal "little lives"; they seem to have no ambition to be recognized or to make their mark in society; they are quite content to pursue a modest degree of individual happiness in their private niche. As they are no good at expressing themselves nor able to represent their own interests in an appropriate way, they end up having to subversively avoid or violate society's rules; in the case of Nina and Susanne, they even resort to deceit, theft, and fraud. Similar to other female protagonists in DEFA films of the 1980s, they are single working mothers in unglamorous jobs that they don't enjoy. Their life-styles and behavior can be read as subversive because they refuse to go along with the socialist code of conduct: they do not seek approval, advice, and help from the collective at work; they are not team players and having successful careers is not one of their priorities. They rather look for personal fulfilment and social recognition in alternative subcultures such as pubs and discos or in total solitude.

A film almost always mentioned together and compared with *Bürgschaft für ein Jahr* is *Das Fahrrad* (The Bicycle, 1982), a Gegenwartsfilm by one of the few female DEFA directors, Evelyn Schmidt. Susanne, an unskilled factory worker and single mother is struggling to make ends meet. One day she can't take her monotonous and lonely job at a metal stamping machine (Stanze) any longer and walks out. It is harder than she expected to find another job, especially since the responsibility for her child rules out night shifts, work on weekends, and travel abroad. The child becomes ill and the child's father refuses to advance money to tie her over the crisis, all of which lead to her following her friend Marry's advice: to report her bicycle as stolen and to claim the insurance money. Meanwhile she has met Thomas, a successful engineer, in her local nightclub, they fall in love, he persuades her to move in with him, and gets her a job at his company. When her insurance fraud is discovered and she is faced with a court case she confesses all to Thomas. He is confused, irritated, and worried that her "shame" will reflect on him at work but gradually comes round and decides to help her somehow. His initial reaction hurts and alienates Susanne to an extent that she "freaks out" and eventually leaves him. The film ends on a positive note, however, as she is determined to continue the pursuit of happiness in her own carefree way, stubbornly rejecting caution, moderation, and sensibility. *Das Fahrrad* shows the problems that an allegedly emancipated working woman, with child care provided for by the state, still has coping with love relationships and day-to-day life. Again, the film portrays this ordinary everyday life with documentary realism and in graphic detail.

Evelyn Schmidt pointed out in an interview that she wanted to draw attention to those people who fall through the cracks, who are a marginalized, silent minority of nonheroines; that is to say, "The social portrait of a woman who is at the age of 30 still being dragged down by bad luck, doesn't know how to take advantage of opportunities, who on the whole: hasn't got much, isn't very good at most things and above all, doesn't know what she wants." [11] Unfortunately, Schmidt was swimming against the cultural political tide at the time: in 1981, the newspaper *Neues Deutschland* had published a (bogus) reader's letter entitled "Was ich mir mehr von unseren Filmemachern wünsche" (My Wish List to Our Filmmakers)—which some people suspected was written by Honecker himself. The author of this letter had looked at some contemporary DEFA Gegenwartsfilme and had found them wanting, asking pointedly, "where are the works of art which make us aware of the—let me call it—titanic way in which we have built a thriving, stable blossoming Workers' and Farmer's State?" [12] This public rebuke was to have far-reaching consequences for subsequent film releases. *Das Fahrrad* was not advertised in the GDR, released only briefly in a very few cinemas, and was thus noticed by the majority of the audience only by some venomous attacks in the papers, such as the one by the well-known film critic Renate Holland-Moritz for whom Susanne is "a screwed up dropout, suspicious towards everybody except her obscure drinking buddies in the disco cellar." She dismisses the film as "a lame expression of grumpy discomfort with society." [13]

As there was certainly nothing titanic about the hero's achievements in *Das*

Fahrrad, it is hardly surprising that Schmidt's promising career that she had started as Meisterschülerin of Konrad Wolf, was nipped in the bud; she fell from grace and was eventually banned from directing feature films for the DEFA. However, the film was sold abroad eleven times and was shown on West German television's ZDF (Channel 2) in July 1986 as part of the summer festival "Filme von Frauen" (Films by Women). The presenter introduced the film to West German audiences with praise for its well-observed details and for its honest portrayal of ordinary people in the GDR.

Thomas's role in this film generally seems to be to provide a contrasting character to Susanne. He is a young dynamic mechanical engineer who has managed to rise to head of department in his company through hard work and by obtaining a degree in evening studies. When Susanne and Thomas meet for the first time in the film, their contrasting worlds and backgrounds are represented by the upper and the lower level of one building, by light and darkness. While Thomas's promotion is celebrated by his collective on the bright ground level of the Kulturhaus in a rather stuffy way, Susanne has a free and easy night out with her friends in the dark disco cellar. He is attracted toward this "underworld" almost against his will and tries, in the course of the film's story, to pull Susanne up to his own level of propriety. Although portrayed as a likable, sincere young man who is genuinely fond of Susanne and her child, his role does seem to have touches of Herr Saubermann (Master Proper), the model working-class socialist hero who will always play by the book, or the "White Knight" who comes to his lady's rescue, and eventually of Pygmalion who wants his creature to behave the way he expects her to, out of gratitude for having saved her from the gutter. She, however, insists on doing things her own way, even if they do go wrong a lot of the time. This is exactly the point that irritated GDR critics about this antiheroine: why did she have no qualifications, why did she have unreasonable expectations of happiness despite her few achievements, and why didn't she at least try to follow the shining example of that young man and mend her ways? According to some reviewers, such unfortunate people did not exist in socialist reality or were a negligible minority who had only themselves to blame and were certainly not worth being portrayed in a film. Both Susanne and Thomas's inability to articulate their feelings and to connect with each other is reflected in a scene on an excursion boat: they are sitting inside opposite each other at an empty table. The scene is totally silent, filmed with soft focus, resulting in a blurred, dreamlike quality. As if in a bubble, the couple is shut off from the outside world and wrapped up in its own thoughts. They don't physically touch or even look at each other; Susanne is slightly turned away from him toward the camera while their off voices alternatingly express their thoughts in parallel, interrupted streams of consciousness. Only in their thoughts do they seem to be able to verbalize their need for each other.

Susanne's relationship with her child is portrayed as loving and caring throughout the film, and it is significant that this is where she does know what she wants: raising her daughter as best she can is *the* priority in her life. She declines the only immediate well-paid job she is offered because this would mean leaving her child in a kindergarten during night shifts. She cuddles up with Jenny in bed telling her fairy tales and, when Thomas in their final argument challenges her with the question: "Was haste denn getan bis jetzt, was denn!" (What have you accomplished up to now, tell me!), Susanne replies with calm confidence: "Ich hab Jenny erzogen" (I've raised Jenny). He snaps back: "Ja, die irgendwann mal stiehlt!" (Yeah, who'll start stealing one day!) Susanne is deeply hurt by his contempt, closes her eyes briefly, swallows, and says in a very low, controlled voice: "Jetzt reicht's" (That's enough).

In *Das Fahrrad*, the director E. Schmidt deals with three aspects of social reality that some young mothers in the GDR had to face. She points out the bleak aspects of women's lives by focusing on a single woman without any job qualifications who does not fit the official image of the assertive, confident heroine and who does not live in presentable conditions but who struggles with poverty and deprivation, but as one review put it whose "life consists of monotonous work, child care and occasional disco nights. This is a far cry from happiness. And there are enough women who live within these limitations who are so inactive." [14]

The film's presentation of Susanne's day-to-day routine reveals that she is not able to take advantage of the privileges that supposedly facilitated the reconciliation of employment and motherhood, so that the pressures of sole responsibility for her child are almost too much for her. In her household as well as at her job she faces conditions that officially didn't exist within socialist society: poverty and alienation at work. The one aspect that one could argue reveals a specifically female perspective on a woman's issue, is the presentation of male and female attitudes toward child-raising. Throughout the film Susanne is confronted with attitudes that belittle or don't recognize the hard work of child-raising as an achievement in itself. Thomas in particular reflects "traditionally male" values and norms of achievement, and an inability to empathize with other people's circumstances. This is contrasted with values represented by Susanne, such as her loving patience with the child and her unconventional, lively behavior with her friends and neighbors, as well as her feelings of solidarity with a female colleague at work, a single woman with three children who doesn't leave her partner although he beats her.

The social system in the GDR is indirectly criticized through Susanne and Thomas's relationship: Thomas wholeheartedly believes in state justice and in equal opportunities being offered to everyone and criticizes Susanne for not taking better advantage of them. His attitude toward Susanne mirrors that of the GDR state toward the individual, in that it is dominated by patriarchic structures: Susanne is helped back on her feet and looked after. This feels secure and comfortable for a while, but when Thomas starts patronizing and criticizing her for being ungrateful, declaring her as totally incapable of anything without his help, she realizes that this imbalance of power is in fact weakening and paralyzing her and it is only then that she is able to break away from his controlling care.

Evelyn Schmidt, when asked why she preferred to portray female protagonists, explained that it was a simple issue of identification, of being closer to women's experiences than to men's. And that she wanted to plead, especially on behalf of women, for the disadvantaged which, she claimed, existed even in this society of proclaimed equality, "the man was in the army, was able to study, always instinctively did the right thing at the right time. He just has better opportunities in our society. I believe that you can't deny the existence of different social positions, of different chances and abilities for self-development. . . . To develop self-confidence is an important issue for me, . . . especially in terms of women."[15]

The heroine in *Das Fahrrad* ultimately opts for a life as a cyclist rather than as a motorist: on the bicycle, moving under her own steam, she is closer to life; the bicycle represents autonomy and intensity of experience at a basic level. However, it also means a solitary journey through life and direct exposure to its adversities, such as the cold shower from a lorry on a rainy day. The bicycle is sometimes used as a metaphor for Susanne's spontaneous capacity for enjoying life's little moments, conveyed for instance in a scene in which Susanne takes her young daughter on an impulsive Spritztour ins Grüne (a spin in the country). After a picnic by the river, that is incidentally one of the few scenes of bright sunshine in the film, she teaches Jenny to ride the bike. This motif is taken up again in the final scene that ends the film on a hopeful note: she teaches the girl to ride around a fountain, trying to pass on to her daughter her own sense of spontaneous joy, of autonomy and risk taking. This time the daughter succeeds; the proud mother joyfully encouraging her daughter with little cries of delight.

Conclusion

The DEFA Gegenwartsfilms under review are Frauenfilme in the sense that they focus on a woman's experiences rather than on a male protagonist's. As I have tried to show, female protagonists in DEFA films are neither portrayed in the roles of the sex object or as wicked temptresses nor are they presented in the passive, dependent role of the housewife.

In all films, there is criticism of the state of gender-relations by presenting men and women's inability to communicate with each other. In many films, women are portrayed as emotionally stronger and morally superior or as having a more advanced social consciousness than their men—by whom they are generally let down. This could be interpreted as a reflection of what was seen as women's achievements in fulfilling the roles of workers and comrades, mothers, and lovers all at the same time, and the newly gained confidence that went with it. They were perceived to have more rigorous expectations of life and their partners, resulting in dramatic conflicts that made them more powerful protagonists than their male counterparts. In most films, there seems to be a binary opposition of male and female qualities, in which the male stands for external authority, the public sphere, stability and stagnation, entrapment and denial, whereas the female stands for a more valuable interior psychic reality and the private, spontaneity and openness, indulgence and emotional excess. Yet, within this representation based on traditional gender attributes, female protagonists manage to question and qualify manifestations of institutionalized power. On the surface, DEFA heroines seem to fight a losing battle and have to face defeat at some point in their lives. Nevertheless they come across as strong, resilient women, and were seen as "models for identification" by their viewers. They fight for their ideals and dreams against all odds, and they passionately voice their views.

After German Unification, at a film seminar in Berlin about DEFA Frauen-filme, female West German participants criticized the DEFA women as "heroines," that is to say, as socially romanticized *stehaufmännchen* (puppets that always manage to bounce back).[16] In my view, the female protagonists are portrayed as resilient, determined, and indestructible figures who make strong points about where things were wrong in their society and to show the way forward, possibly presenting utopian visions of a better future. Women's further advancement on the way to true equality and humane relationships is reflected in the films' themes of "Ausbruch und Aufbruch," of breaking out, starting fresh, and searching for a new role, for a meaningful life.

Notes

This article is a revised version of a chapter from a book published by Berghahn Books (New York: Oxford, 1996).

1. Joshua Isaac Feinstein, *The Triumph of the Ordinary: Depictions of Daily Life in the East German Cinema, 1956–1966* (Ph.D. diss., Stanford University 1995), 205.

2. Regine Sylvester, "Filmfrauen: Suche nach neuen Konturen," *Sonntag Nr. 25* (1975).

3. Mihan, Hans-Rainer, "Sabine, Sunny, Nina und der Zuschauer," *Film und Fernsehen* 8 (1982): 12.

4. Wolfgang Kohlhaase in Was heißt denn "happy end". . . Ein Gespräch über *Solo Sunny*, in *Film und Fernsehen*, 1980/81, p. 15.

5. "Eine junge Frau von heute zwischen Ideal und Wirklichkeit. Interview mit Lothar Warneke zu seinem neuen Film *Unser kurzes Leben*," *Die Union*, Dresden, 19 January 1981.

6. "Die Rebellion im Rock," in *Außerhalb von mittendrin: Literatur/Film*, ed. Annette C. Eckert (Berlin: Neue Gesellschaft für Bildende Künste): 98.

7. "Eine junge Frau von heute zwischen Ideal und Wirklichkeit. Interview mit Lothar Warneke zu seinem neuen Film *Unser kurzes Leben*," *Die Union. Dresden*, 19 January 1981.

8. Regine Sylvester, "Film und Wirklichkeit: Einige Gedanken zu Fauengestalten in neueren Filmen der DEFA und des Fernsehens der DDR," in *Theorie und Praxis des Films, Sonderheft 1975: Emanzipation der Frau—Wirklichkeit und Illusion* (Berlin: HFF, 1975), 97.

9. Oksana Bulgakowa, "Die Rebellion im Rock," 98.

10. Marc Silberman, "Narrating Gender in the GDR: Hermann Zschoche's *Bürgschaft für ein Jahr*" (1981), in *The Germanic Review. Special Issue: German Film*, ed. Richard J. Murphy, 66, no. 1 (winter 1991).

11. *Filmspiegel*, 5 April 1982/13, p. 20.

12. Alleged reader's letter by Hubert Vater in *Neues Deutschland*, 17 November 1981.

13. *Eulenspiegel, Kino-Eule*, 27, no. 8 (1982).

14. *Filmspiegel* 1982/13, p. 20.

15. Ibid.

16. Annette C. Eckert, ed., *Außerhalb von mittendrin*, transcript of a seminar discussion after film screenings (manuscript).

17

Wenders' Genders: From the End of the Wall to the End of the World

Scott Spector

> *Die Kunst schafft, die Wissenschaft zerstört die sinnliche Welt; darum ist der Künstler erotisch und sexuell, der Wissenschaftler asexuell. Die Optik zerstört das Licht.*
>
> Otto Weininger, *Über die letzten Dinge*

In the space between art and technology is poised Wim Wenders's *Until the End of the World*. If this is a negotiation that comes with the terrain of filmmaking, Wenders pushes the question to its limits in this particular film. But there is another pair of principles that is brought into focus in Wenders's film, just as forcefully and with the same discomforting ambivalence. As with Weininger's dichotomy, one is immediately conscious of the promise that gender will be mapped onto this binarism. Here I will be looking at *image* and *history*, and the way in which their contest, as in Weininger's contest, spills out into the realm of "vision"— the project of filmmaking.

First, though, one ought to rehearse the presumed feminine and feminist origins of this film. From the moment of its original conception and almost immediate advance promotion in the aftermath of *Paris, Texas*, Wenders staked out the film *Until the End of the World* as the terrain of the feminine narrative. It was to be Solveig Dommartin's story, the first Wenders road film with a woman at its center, one where Wenders could "look at a film with a female point of view," and the concept was supposed to have been suggested to Wenders by Dommartin almost ten years before the film was made.[1] It will not take much to dissolve these illusions of Wenders's. The story that Dommartin came to Wenders with had, as we see from various versions of the plot-line released since the mideighties, almost nothing in common with the film that was made. Dommartin had the idea for a love story, and Wenders decided to have the force that strung it along be essentially a travel agenda. His road movies always have this prime mover: shooting sites, landscapes that attract him *visually*. So the images associated with the authorial subject's favorite places, either familiar or exotic, come first, while the story linking them together is secondary, is determined by them. Indeed, since the format of the road movie is already a signature of the auteur-director par excellence Wenders, how is any such film to be figured as Dommartin's story? The opening credits acknowledge the film as derived from an original idea by Wim Wenders and Solveig Dommartin.

Of course the primary way in which Wenders's claim that this is "the first road film with a woman at the center" is fraudulent has to do with her "central" place itself. It becomes clear as the film develops that the narrative is the property of the writer Eugene (Sam Neill), Claire's patient lover and friend, who at a critical moment in the film reaches a crisis in his work and begins to write *Claire's Story*, the one the spectator has presently been reading. *Claire's Story* is Eugene's novel. Her central place, as the object of the author's unrequited sexual longing, is in this sense completely conventional in a way that I will come back to. Her construction as willful and capricious is also familiar in the filmic constructs of woman, and as we know from those many constructs, these qualities do not add up to any sort of autonomy from the male gaze. In fact the action of this particular film is not structured around Claire's independent caprices, but to the contrary, the impulsive decisions taking her from Paris to Berlin to Lisbon to Moscow to Beijing to Japan to Australia are nothing more than a chase after a man who repeatedly exploits her (Trevor MacPhee/Sam Farber, played by William Hurt). In this sense, if Claire is a feminist heroine it is rather along the lines of Billie Holiday. If she is bound to Eugene by way of the word, her relationship to Trevor turns on the eye, as she holds his open and subjects it to her gaze in the scene where they meet. So in these very obvious ways, it seems, woman is not at the "center" of this narrative as a subjectivity, but is sandwiched centrally between two male subjects in a—once again, conventional—love triangle.

While it is in this sense that Wenders meant this to be a feminist narrative, and therefore in this sense that it fails, there is much more at stake in this film, and more complex ways in which gender works within various conflicting structures of meaning. The primary conflict of the film is represented by the confrontation of two terms: *image*, in the first place, pictures that with the hypertextual technologies of Wenders's 1999 seem to spin out of control in the film; and on the other hand *narrative*, story, or, as its German equivalent foregrounds, the related trope of history. As with all such binarisms, this one, too, is gendered. But what is interesting about this film is that Wenders's own position toward the tension between image and history shifted during the development of this work, which as previously stated was conceived in the mideighties but filmed in the turn to the present decade, the Wende, which was ironically, for Wenders, a return to history. The problematics of this turn are played out over a prefigured complex of dynamics inherited from a powerful German literary tradition of figuring woman in specific and predetermined relations to the male authorial subject and to the (his) textual product. The confluence of this predetermined gendered scene with the historical shift taking place around the making of this film make a gendered reading of *Until the End of the World* particularly productive. The future, which is the site of the film, is an "historicist future" in a Jamesonian sense—the viewer is aware of the proximity of this future to the present; both present and future are inscribed in terms of their relation to history— the historicity of the moments recorded in the film (Claire takes a turn off the road that would change her life and "all our lives"); and, finally, this present/future is declared throughout to be the product of a particular illicit history.[2] Sam's family's dispersion is directly linked to Nazi persecution on one end and capitalist cold-war ruthlessness on the other, and the landscape through which the characters move is one marked by revolutions, wars, and droughts—all spilling out into a technological present/future that has neither come to terms with, nor disengaged itself from, its past.

If you were among the majority of viewers of *Until the End of the World* who appreciated some of its breathtaking moments and poignant sequences, who enjoyed perhaps the music and the landscape photography, the special effect experiments, for instance, but who came out of the theater thinking that the movie was "a mess," perhaps this interpretive opposition of image and history can help explain why. In his rush to put on display a mad proliferation of highly technologized pictures that he has begun to identify with the present/future, Wenders puts the spectator through a series of visual experiences that can only be described as exhausting.[3] But the rapid succession of sensory experiences presented under rubrics of "Paris," "Berlin," "Moscow," "Beijing," and "Tokyo"— distinguishable from one another through the use of some self-conscious signs, but otherwise homogeneous in their high-tech urbanity—this "world" of the present/future does, as the title suggests, have its limits.

In the first half of the film, the images overwhelm the filmic space in a frenzy only weakly rationalized by the gestures toward a story that come barely together—a stolen invention, a fugitive tracked by a lover, her lover, a private eye, and a bounty hunter, comically exaggerated film-noir intrigue, something about stolen opals. William Hurt's pained eyes need a rest no less than do the spectator's own as Claire catches up to rescue him in a futuristic video arcade in Tokyo: she lays a hand on him as he is pressing his thumbs against his eyeballs. "Do you know who I am?" "Weren't you the angel in Lisbon? . . . Would you take me out of here? Please? I can't see very well." As she leads him on an escape from the apparently ubiquitous technological present, Nick Cave sings

"Thank-you, girl. I'll love you 'till the end of the world. With your eyes black as coal and your long blond hair." This conflation of woman as image and the image of woman recurs at other moments in the film, and foregrounds the disingenuity of the association of the sighted woman, as in this scene, as a self-propelled subjectivity. In a "traditional inn" in a small mountain town they are both suddenly able to sleep, for eighteen full hours, and to begin a healing process. Here, where the relentless images of the future-present stop, the healing can begin—and not for nothing is it here that a "coherent narrative" emerges. As Claire nurtures Sam back to health according to the herbalist's prescription (in which Claire herself is as important an ingredient as the herbs), he explains: "That camera takes pictures that blind people can see." He has a family—a father who invented the camera, a blind mother for whom he is collecting the images—and a motivation that becomes clear only within this family narrative: "All I want is my mother to see and my father to know that I love him."

But this scene is just a brief hiatus in the busy traffic of images that continues in San Francisco and on to Australia. It is here that the film really breaks into two, as the visual experience of this first film ends abruptly with the explosion of the rogue Indian nuclear satellite. The blast effects a literal break in the narrative, a rest for the mind and for the eye. As the world's electromagnetic fields are interrupted by the nuclear event in space, Sam and Claire are in a propeller plane flying over a severe Australian landscape. They glide down to a new earth, the end of the world in geographic as well as temporal terms. As Peter Gabriel sings "The Blood of Eden" we see "the woman and the man" walking out on a stretch of earth abandoned after the droughts of the midnineties, not knowing whether they might be the last two people from the past world or the first of the next. The rest of the film plays in a corner of Australia outside of the ecumene—as it was untouched by the video-clip-paced metropolitan rhythm of the first half of the film, it continues to live after that world is dead. Even its technology (because it is digital, it is feebly explained) buzzes on in Sam's father's laboratory, organically hidden within a mountain, while every car is stopped short and every computer memory wiped clean. On the blank page of this purged world, on a manual typewriter in the desert, the writer Eugene begins to write *Claire's Story* and we are watching a different film.

Narrative emerges in this new film in more ways than this. The seemingly random succession of cities and faces making up the disjointed pieces of the first film becomes domesticated within the frame of a family narrative that only now comes to the surface. Sam Farber is the son of the scientist (Max von Sydow) and the blind anthropologist Edith Eisner (Jeanne Moreau). His quest has been to collect images of Edith's family on his father's invention, a camera that can mediate images to the blind. And so in this way the fragmented wandering of the first film takes on meaning first within Edith's personal and family history, a history "broken" by the displacements of a refugee from the Nazis, and the product of which is a family of a German father, a French mother, American children, and aunts and uncles in Moscow and Beijing. The vision imparted by Farber's machine, therefore, is a historical vision in the sense that it is the place in which these disparate images of the present/future become disciplined into a narrative. As Edith is hooked up to the machine, the family is not reunited as much as it is united for the first and only time. Certainly one ought here to be reminded of the clumsy invocation of the term reunification (Wiedervereinigung) as these scenes were being filmed. Indeed, while the question of a politically forced family dispersal and the promise of *reunification* of the family holds the film together in a sense, this family narrative was as we know absent from the 1984 prospect for the movie. The touristy travel agenda that was originally to drive the action was displaced by this family narrative as the decade approached its turn.

The conflict between narrative and image is explicitly problematized in *Until the End of the World*, and the dichotomy is just as explicitly gendered. Claire's place in the schema is posited in the introductory sequence. The narrator (Eugene, as we later discover) describes the world's anxiety in 1999 over the out-of-control Indian nuclear satellite, adding that "Claire couldn't care less" about this story, preoccupied as she is with her own nightmares. In this movie as with others, the viewer is presented with a relational structure that will acquire meanings later in the film: the identification of dream with image; the association of Claire with image and of Eugene with narrative; the competition of image (the dream) and narrative (the danger to the world) as objects of concern. The association of vision with the feminine is reinforced by the figure of Edith Eisner, Sam's mother, as a "blind seer" (again, a literary convention rather than an innovation or even a refiguration); her scientist-husband has learned to accept her powerful intuition (and here we move from convention to cliché). Claire's struggle with nightmares presages the unexpected "turn" within the film with regard to vision: from the utopian promise of bringing vision to the blind, Farber's machine leads to dystopia, with Edith dying from the sorrow of sight and Claire left to learn to record and replay her own dreams, a purely narcissistic practice with addictive and highly destructive effects.

Wenders has reported that the movie was meant to have ended with the utopian moment of Edith's vision, but "so much had happened since I first had the idea for the film, the realm of images had exploded. . . ."[4] What had "happened," what narrative had intervened in the artistic vision for a film inspired by Roland Barthes's note on the epistemological privilege of "image"?[5]

In January 1990, just after the fall of the Berlin wall and just before finally beginning to shoot *Until the End of the World*, Wenders discussed both events in an interview. He describes his position after 9 November, cut off in the outback in preparation for the film: "I was in the middle of the Australian desert far from any telephone, and got wind of the opening of the wall with a three-day delay.

My Berlin office had sent parts of newspapers via telefax. Then I kept trying to telephone, and finally my office faxed photographs, so that I could see the unbelievable."[6]

Here, as in Barthes's note on loving and image, "seeing is believing," and the weight of stacks of fax paper reproducing half-newspapers collapses before two hazy photograph images: one of people who appeared to be dancing on the wall near Wenders's apartment, in the other a young man sat on the wall chipping away with hammer and chisel. And yet at the same time as Wenders reinforces the primacy of the image over the narrative report, he first betrays a growing suspicion of image, declaring: "*Too many* images, that makes the head ache. Even worse: too many images of oneself."[7] The title of this published letter, taken from a favorite Bob Dylan song, was "For the City that Dreams," and it is in the wake of this deployment of the term *dream* and this particular setting for an ambivalence toward images that the long-developing plot of the film took its critical turn. The addendum to the film in which the characters become addictively obsessed with their own dreams (Claire: "Look at me! That's me!" And "she's so lonely. . . .") shares a border with the dreaming city of Berlin, with its million seductive images of itself, dreams of its past and its future. Was Wenders speaking of Claire or of Berlin when he identified watching one's own dreams as an ultimate act of narcissism, "and essentially a narcissist is someone who isolates himself from the world and would rather look at his own image than an image of the world?"

While Sam thanks Claire for repeatedly rescuing him by stealing from her, locking her up, and abandoning her several times, the supreme narcissist in the film is this figure of woman. Sam, after all, is on a quest, a profoundly masculine venture. This quest, by the way, defined as the search of a man to bring sight to a woman, can itself be seen as a sort of convention in literature. Structurally similar is, after all, the convention crediting a woman as inspiration of the masculine creation, and in creating the impossibility of a physical relation between Eugene and Claire, Wenders only produces the precise conditions created by a formidable line of male German-speaking poets.

But there is another "convention"—a particularly powerful gendered discourse from German cultural history—which is instructive to set alongside this film. A little chapter in Oswald Spengler's *Decline of the West* is called "The Soul of the City," in which Spengler's pessimistic historical project is articulated in condensed form, and in familiar terms.[8] He opens with the example of the contrast between the youthful and naive, clearly masculine Mycenaean culture ("darkly groping, big with hopes, drowsy with the intoxication of deeds and sufferings, ripening quietly towards its future"), to the decadent and feminine ("elegant, light") Minoan culture of Crete, with history behind her. The gendering of this pair is reproduced in a series of world cultures, with a healthy virile supplanting a declining and feminized term: the "refined, somewhat pale and tired Civilization" of the Byzantine court astonished at "that bearish morning vigour of the German lands. . . ." Familiar enough is the series of associations of a healthy culture, soulful and rooted, organic and original, earthy and bounded, as against the boundless civilization of the great cities: "only in the Civilization with its giant cities do we come again to despise and disengage ourselves from these roots."

One cannot doubt the ambivalence inscribed in Wenders's technologized future/present, the nostalgia for some kind of rootedness, and for the recuperation of a history. That ambivalence has appeared in his films since somewhat before the fall of the wall, in fact, but it is most openly problematized in the post-wall films. The Spenglerian moment is not invoked to provide an easy mapping of Wenders's history, I do not think Wenders's is a Spenglerian history. For Spengler, remember, the precultural epoch is feminine (the "not-yet-Spring" of the Germanic migrations as "virginal, yet already maternal"), making possible the emergence of the masculine era. All this protects us from the danger of assuming that the construction of Claire as visionary, sometimes angel, even salvation of the future, constitutes a break from a patriarchal discourse on culture and history. In Spengler, too, there are alternations of valency that nonetheless lead in a predetermined direction, which is toward a feminized degeneration.

Farber's machine is not just an instrument of vision; it is one that recovers narrative through the filmic image ("seeing") fused with the historical consciousness ("memory") of the medium. It is explained that the creation of this kind of vision to the blind requires two steps: the original recording is "the act of seeing," and then that pure image (abstracted from its original object) needs to be reviewed by the image-taker and rematched to the original moment via an act of remembering. All this seems of course to be a rather literal metaphor for a redemptive filmmaking that unites image and history. The undecipherable, diffuse particles of vision projected on the monitor and in Edith's inner eye begin to become legible as forms first upon the insertion of this memory into the image.

But there is a snag. While a meaningful context for the faces recorded in the first part of the film comes first with the reconstitution of the family narrative, the pathology of that story intercepts the successful merger of history with vision. The remarkably vulgar "exaggerated Oedipus" that Sam Farber is revealed to be recovers all of his familial anxiety as soon as he enters the laboratory, and, hooked up to his mother—pressured, anxious, under the eager eyes of laboratory staff and the father who is always disappointed in him—he cannot make the connection. Crushed, he is little consoled by the pitying encouragement that he can rest and try again tomorrow.

History may be necessary to give sensible form to the abstracted image, but history has its baggage, some histories more than others. Wenders is not the first to wish for recovery from the dysfunction keeping the present discrete from the past, or to wonder how much forgetfulness one can afford in order to recuperate memory. Standing outside of the network of familial guilt, the narcissistic and intensely sensitive Claire is hooked up to the machine, and gets it to work. We observe Edith, as she experiences sight after fifty years—first an impassive staccato of decontextualized colors, which receive emotive content first as they take shape within the familial narrative:

> Colors. Blue. Yellow. Red. A person. . . . Sitting. . . . I wonder. . . . Blue hairband. . . . Yellow dress. . . . She's sitting, hands folded. . . . Could she be . . . our . . . daughter . . . Henry. . . . What a lovely face! Henry, look at her face!

Edith's sight—this true sight, that is, as disembodied colors become her daughter and granddaughter—is signaled by the covering of her eyes with her hands. The image of Edith watching, her hands over her eyes, bleeds into the cloudy image of her daughter and granddaughter, also looking out, and finally to the eerie image of Claire, concentrating deeply, staring out, with her eyes superimposed onto the regions of Edith's hands where her eyes ought to be.[9] The sort of vision represented at this filmic moment seems to be a utopian instant of fusion of narrative and image, as it is also the "reunification" (Wiedervereinigung) of a family that had never been together, for Edith and Henry ran away before their granddaughter was born.

But like the euphoria of that other ("re"-)unification, this one immediately gives way to depression and anxiety. Edith keeps to herself the secret that "the world was darker and uglier than she could possibly have imagined," and lets her life go on the eve of the new millennium. Even this sad turn to a happy ending, however, can no longer be the terminus of the story of visions and histories. In the aftermath of the fall of the wall, in the midst of what Wenders identified as an uncontrollable proliferation of idealized and abstracted self-images, the aforementioned addendum was tacked onto the film, and it is introduced as such: Eugene confesses that he thought this was to be the last chapter of the novel, not knowing that Henry was working on a new invention.

If the first invention held the promise of uniting the family through the merging of masculine and feminine principles of story and picture, the machine that allows the characters to view their own dreams breaks it apart. The extended family of aborigines abandons this immoral extension of the original experiment, and the narrator explains that although they "arrived at the island of dreams together . . . in a short time they were oceans apart, drowning in their own nocturnal imagery." This unhealthy self-pollution is the extreme form of narcissism, and operates in neat contrast to the heterosexualist union of narrative and image leading up to it. Claire is glued to her viewer, which displays in undisciplined flashes of color and light a visuality abstracted from the ordering constraints of consciousness. It is, in other words, purely feminine.

And who can rescue her from this "disease of images" but the narrator Eugene, who knows "the magic of words and the healing power of stories." Claire has to literally be locked up with her own story to cure her from the addiction of images—it is the forced penetration of image by narrative. In the aftermath of this violent conquest, as she turns the last page of the story (in which she turns the last page of the story), she smiles radiantly and asks, "What happens now?" The narrative has finally overtaken the filmic image. Eugene answers, cynically reinscribing the blatant fiction of feminine subjectivity driving the narrative, "That's up to you to invent."

What happens next is a kind of joke: after reaching the ends of the earth, it was only left for Claire to leave it, and the film ends in space on Claire's mission with the planetary environmental monitoring agency Greenspace. But in this epilogue, Claire's identification with the purely visual is sealed. She has acquired this position, we are told, by obtaining the highest score ever on the visual recognition test. As the men in her life appear to sing her "Happy Birthday" on her four-screen videophone from various corners of the planet—Eugene, the bank robber Chico, the private eye Winter, and a blank screen for the elusive Sam—she smiles again. She switches off the screens and turns toward the image of the earth. As the camera zooms in slowly on her face, her eyes scan the globe, glistening.

Notes

1. See Walter Donohue, "Revelations: An Interview with Wim Wenders," *Sight and Sound* (April 1992): 8–9.

2. See Frederic Jameson, "Historicism in *The Shining*," in *Signatures of the Visible* (New York, 1990); and idem, "Nostalgia for the Present," *South Atlantic Quarterly* 88, no. 2 (spring 1989).

3. Lorenzo Pellizzari notes the "highly personal" tour of diverse filmic genres that add to the "fusion and confusion" of urban images in the film. *Abitare*, no. 307 (May 1992), 183–84. In the press release for the film, Wenders refers to the combination of genres and motives of the road film, the love story, and science fiction. Cf. *The Act of Seeing. Texte und Gespräche* (Frankfurt/Main, Germany, 1992): 28.

4. Donohue, "Revelations," 11.

5. Roland Barthes, *Fragments of a Language of Love*, in "Image: In the Field of Love the Worst Wounds Blossom More from What One Sees than from What One Knows." Wenders cites this passage as the epigram for the earliest (May 1984) prospect for the film as well as in the press release after its production. *Act of Seeing*, 11 and 29.

6. "Zeit-Reisen," interview with Wolfram Schütte, Frankfurter Rundschau, 27 January 1990, see *Act of Seeing*, 22.

7. Wim Wenders, "For the City that Dreams," faxed from Turkey Creek, West Australia, to the French journal *Libération* on 15 November 1989, in *Act of Seeing*, 177–78.

8. Oswald Spengler, trans. Charles Francis Atkinson, *The Decline of the West* (New York, 1932), 87–110.

9. I thank Geoff Waite for the astute observation that the daughter's image is a reproduction of a Vermeer portrait, layering images over histories over images.

V

Recovering (from) History:
Memory and Film

18

"The Robber Bridegroom" in Helma Sanders-Brahms's film
Deutschland, bleiche Mutter:
Erzähltes Märchen und erlebtes Greuelmärchen

Rosmarie Thee Morewedge

The central significance of the fairy tale "The Robber Bridegroom"[1] in the film *Deutschland, bleiche Mutter* (Germany, Pale Mother), was recognized by Helma Sanders-Brahms and has been corroborated since by the critical literature.[2] I shall analyze the meaning of the fairy tale for the film, focusing on the parallels and contrasts between them. My interpretation reveals a *narrated tale* leading to success, the reconstitution of the family, and social justice on the one hand and an *experienced horror tale* leading to a sense of failure, isolation, and the victimization of the heroine on the other.[3] For a definition of the fairy tale that is especially apt, I turn to Dietz-Ruediger Moser, who emphasizes the importance of problem-solving paradigms in fairy tales: "Grounded in strict views of morality," he states, "the fairy tale has the purpose of modeling how conflicts can be resolved. Actions related in the fairy tale can depart from the realm of experience; however, the conflict portrayed remains anchored in reality."[4]

Beginning with "Little Red Riding Hood" and "Sleeping Beauty," the film relies on fairy tales as framing devices to construct and explore the identity of German women, the central theme of the film. Early in the film, establishing shots show Lene walking resolutely through an idyllic forest next to a lake. The mood changes abruptly when some uniformed Nazi youths set a German shepherd dog on her. She manages to fend it off by herself without calling for help in a performance that prompts Hans and Ulrich, the admiring onlookers who observe the entire scene from a rowboat, to agree that she is a "real German woman." Lene's cultural identity is thus established as "a real German woman" through the idealizing heroic framing device of the fairy tale. The framing device appears particularly appropriate from the perspective of the daughter, whose consciousness determines the perspective of the film, since it permits a relational construction of identity: idealized, mythical constructions of the self and negative repressed perceptions of the Other, constructions that are subsequently corrected and modified through historical and biographical framing devices.[5]

Before turning to the tale, let us ask what it means for Lene, introduced as "the real German woman," to make use of the fairy-tale genre. Christa Kamenetzky and Jack Zipes have shown that during the Third Reich the fairy tale, and especially that of the Brothers Grimm, became the mouthpiece for the Nazis' political, racial, and cultural propaganda. National Socialism encouraged mothers to pass on norms of behavior recognized as "German" through the telling of heroic tales.[6] As an institutionalized genre, folktales had, of course, been popular before and were used by the Nazis precisely because of their popularity; nonetheless, by using the fairy tale to instruct her daughter, Lene is delivering an ambivalent and complex message. Part of that message is conformism to parenting norms approved by the Nazis;[7] part of it emerges through the camera's careful framing, which manages to suggest strong analogues between motifs of the tale and the racial policies of the Nazis as well as the horrific results of these policies. Still another part of the meaning emerges through the juxtaposition of social roles in the tale and in the construction of roles in the film that stand for the roles played by the protagonists during World War II and in the postwar period. Most importantly, however, the fairy tale introduces horizons of expectations to which the film speaks in a variety of ways. Offering a close reading of the tale before exploring its significance for the film will allow us to recognize that the film challenges us to focus as much on the development of the identity of the daughter and women of her generation as on the role of the mother and her position in history. Let us turn to the tale "The Robber Bridegroom."

The death of the biologic mother, even though central to the tale, is not mentioned. The father, interested only in the financial security and upward mobility of his daughter, marries her off for pragmatic reasons. The daughter demonstrates intuition and purposeful, rational thought—character traits more often associated with successful male heroes in fairy tales. In spite of her inner aversion to the suitor selected for her, she complies with his request to visit him, but demonstrates independent thinking by strewing lentils and peas, which will show her the way back, in case the ashes, with which her bridegroom promises to mark the way to his house, should disappear. If the ashes symbolically link the bridegroom with death, the lentils and peas she strews connect her to the organic, living order of nature. Death motifs in the fairy tale are connected to dismemberment and destruction caused by the Nazis,[8] a link emphasized cinematically: bunker and plane are engulfed in flames, followed by a severed head and a bloody hand. The polarization of images relating to men and women is as acute within the fairy tale as it is in "reality." Portrayed cinematically as being close to nature, Lene goes into the forest with Anna just as the young bride in the tale goes into the deep forest. Like many of the Grimms' heroes, she enters the forest full of uncertainties but emerges with certitude and a sense of moral purpose. It is important that her experience in the "house of death" leads to development and inner growth.

She finds the house deserted, except for a caged bird, who warns her of the mortal danger she is in. Birds in fairy tales often symbolize the development of higher consciousness or knowledge. She realizes that she is as trapped in this house as the bird is in its cage. Yet she bravely investigates every room and even descends into the cellar, the darker, deeper level often associated with a descent into the unconscious or death.[9] The motif of the curious woman references tales, such as "Bluebeard" and "Sleeping Beauty," where curiosity is punished; here it is rewarded. In the cellar she finds an old woman, who resembles the witch of many fairy tales. However, instead of running away from "the witch" she addresses her courteously and boldly. The appeal functions as a test of her character and legitimizes her to receive special help. In return, the old woman offers sympathy, the confirmation that the bridegroom is a wanton murderer, corroboration of the murderer's intent to kill and devour her, and an offer of joint escape. The old woman valorizes the young bride's cleverness and strength of character, replaces the girl's dead mother, and is thus symbolically linked to the archetypal Great Mother.[10] This bonding helps the young woman discover her own strength. Whereas the bird can still be seen as a magical object, it is important to note that magic is replaced in this tale by the heroine's intuition and rational intelligence. Aggressive masculinity is monsterized, whereas women collaborating against male aggression appear initially privileged. The loss of enchantment is made up by a greater reliance on the intelligence and wit of the heroine. In *Dialektik der Aufklärung: Philosophische Fragmente*, Max Horkheimer and Theodor W. Adorno relate the success of Odysseus, the exemplary "bourgeois entrepreneurial hero," to his reliance on intelligence, wit, and cunning rather than on magic. Like Odysseus, who hardens himself to the sacrifice of his shipmates to ensure his own survival, the hero of our fairy tale relies on reason (or perhaps, even on her ability to rationalize) and hardens herself to the slaughter of the Other bride.[11]

While silently observing the fate chosen for her perpetrated on the emotional Other bride, who is first intoxicated and heartbroken, then killed, mutilated, and eaten, the young bride learns to live by the reality principle. Cook suggests that the undressing of the Other bride and her placement on the table are a thinly disguised rape, linked to the rape that is shown taking place in the film.[12] It bears repeating, that it is her own fate that the young bride sees perpetrated on the Other bride, from whom she tries to differentiate herself. From the hermeneutical perspective, the content of the self and the Other is relative and can be defined only in relation to each other. In "The Other Within," Ernst van Alphen explains this idea:

> The other is not the description, not even an interpretation of a reality, but the formulation of an ideal, desired identity. . . . The preference for the other is not produced by an interest in and subsequently by knowledge of the other, but by a negative view of the observer's own identity or culture. An attempt at reading the other remains caught in evocations of utopian self-images or feared self-images. . . . Alterity is thus a screen for the imagination, while "identity" is the content of that imagination."[13]

Psychologically speaking, "Self and other are no longer counterparts; . . . the other is part of the self; we are our own others. The other is always the other within."[14] Like the uncanny, the Other is known and familiar, but invented and repressed, made strong, and thereby displaced onto an alien Other.

This hermeneutical and psychological framework, which depicts the young bride as beautiful, rational, connected, obedient, purposeful, self-controlled, silent, intuitive, and observant, and the Other bride as emotional (broken-hearted), helpless, disconnected from her family, lacking self-control, intoxicated, drugged, and victimized,[15] reveals the portrayal of the Other bride as based on a denial or of a negative cultural view of those qualities by the young bride. It is important to note that these qualities are projected onto the Other, her alter ego, although they are really part of the self. The young bride defines herself with culturally canonized values: self-control, courage, and rational action—marginalizing those, like the Other bride, who cannot control their passions. Her identity is formed through a repression of Otherness or Alterity; the self she has constructed appears to be valorized through the public exposure of the gang, which brings the outlaws to justice. The Other is perceived in many tales as a lower self that is killed or dies, allowing a higher self to emerge.[16] If one can speak of the voice of the bird as a symbol of higher consciousness and of the descent into the cellar as the intuitive, sympathetic bond with the Great Mother archetype, then one can speak of the emergence of the young bride's ego, which is governed by the reality principle, as she exercises the utmost self-control in the presence of the murderers and good judgment in holding on to the incriminating evidence, as she returns to her father's house accompanied by a mother figure that had been absent in the past. Her father does not attempt to dominate or to silence her, as is common practice in fairy tales, according to Ruth Bottigheimer.[17] Although the young bride's identity develops in the act of telling, and her narrative strategies foreground her uniquely, the tale does not provide closure to the young woman's future (she remains unmarried), leaving her role in society indeterminate. Will she follow the model of the mother, the old woman, who has become silent again? Will she be silenced and dominated by men in the future, or will she continue to be her own person with a voice, thinking divergently, bonding with women and men, occupying an acknowledged place in society? Will there be a place for such women? Or will the fate of the mutilated bride set the pattern for women in the future in Germany, having been inscribed psychologically on their spirit as the Other that has not been encountered? Both patterns are offered by the tale as alternative patterns for women in Germany, especially for those of Anna's generation.

It is one of the contradictions of the film, that while Lene narrates to her daughter a fictional model that exemplifies female resistance to male aggression, Lene embodies the passive woman victimized by male aggression in the second part of the film. While narrating the model of the problem-solving, proactive bride that Lene resembles before the return of men from the war, Lene models the fate of the coerced, mutilated Other bride first as American soldiers rape her.[18] Although not killed in the rape, she feels victimized and depersonalized ("That is the prerogative of the winner, little girl. One takes things and women"[19]). While the fiction of the tale posits a strong, exemplary woman, the reality captured by the camera in the second part of the film belies it. Lene's reality after the war demonstrates that women are strong only until normalcy is reintroduced when the men return from the war. The physical and psychological mutilation that did not take place during the rape by the American soldiers takes place when Lene's husband and dentist decide, against her will, to pull all her teeth. The mutilation is also understood symbolically through Lene's facial paralysis during the *Wirtschaftswunder* when "de-Nazified" men are again at the helm of society and women are rendered passive, victimized, silent, and domesticated bourgeois housewives who carry out prewar rituals with chagrin in their living rooms. Reduced to this dependent social status, Lene wishes to die. She becomes, in effect, the Other bride of the fairy tale: intoxicated, drugged, screaming, and incapable of asserting herself when oppressed by her husband and by patriarchal institutions. As the young bride watched the mutilation of the Other bride in the fairy tale, Anna observes the transformation of Lene.

The major task of the fairy tale, then, is to model the social and cognitive growth of the hero/ine in the process of solving nearly impossible tasks. In so doing she achieves self-mastery that enables her to escape victimization, to acquire a voice, and to restore social justice. As has been pointed out in significant parallels, motifs in the fairy tale describe Lene's family history and Germany's history.[20] The final part of this essay will address the function of the tale for Anna in the postwar period, depicted in the second part of the film.

As a blueprint for society, "The Robber Bridegroom" offers various scripts for women in Germany in addressing women's oppression; they can

1. act silently in complicity with men, waiting for the opportunity to escape;
2. endure oppression privately but confront it publicly, describing and denouncing it;
3. become a victim and be destroyed by it.

It is evident that Anna has learned from Lene to speak and to narrate, that is, to follow the model of her mother. During the opening scenes of the film, Sanders-Brahms's voice-over for the film states, "My mother, you say that you have learned to be silent. But you have taught me to speak. My Mother tongue."[21] From Lene's narrative and song about women, Anna has learned to speak and to use her voice to confront injustice.

Even though the film's primary focus is on the mother (Lene), whose fate parallels Germany's fate in many ways, the film is narrated by the voice-over of the daughter. The daughter's consciousness refracts Lene's story, the family story, her bonding with the mother, her relationship to her father, the painful separation from her mother, her decision not to get married, and the development of an identity that emerges through her understanding of her parents and her conscious differentiation from her mother. Cook, too, focuses on Anna's narration in interpreting the film as a double redemption: in the fairy tale he finds the redemption of the mother, who was both victim and silent partner of the robbers, that is, the allegorized figure of Germany; in the second part, in the story of the family history, "the melodrama," as he calls it, he finds the redemption of the mother by the daughter through the daughter's retelling of their tale. Tale telling, he suggests, becomes a way out of the silence imposed on women in patriarchal society. Cook regards Lene's redemption following her suicide attempt as an emancipation, even though there is nothing, in my opinion, to suggest that Lene is freed from the roles prescribed for mother and wife in the Wohnstuben culture of postwar Germany. By contrast, I see intentional indeterminacy in the ending.

By telling the tale of the "Robber Bridegroom," the mother teaches the daughter that community and speaking out in public are vital for women's survival. However, by living the antifairy tale or the horror tale in the battle zone of the living room, Lene provides a subversive subtext and a very different horizon of expectation for her daughter and for women of her daughter's generation.

What does the daughter learn from the tale? It teaches her the importance of content and form, of message and medium. She learns that cognitive development and survival are possible for women, even under patriarchal oppression. Her mother's tale speaks of survival, while she lets the daughter see the destruction around her. Fairy-tale discourse of fantasies of magic, enchantment, innocence, and success is deconstructed by the reality Anna begins to see.[22] But the point is, that precisely during the telling of the tale Anna awakens, stating: "I want to see," and Lene lets her see the rotting corpse in the spring wood. Telling leads to seeing. And instead of breaking off her story after the rape, Lene continues her tale in spite and perhaps because of the rape, affirming thereby the importance of telling for survival. In Lene's mind there is no rupture between the tale and historical reality. But from the mutilated bodies around her and from the rape of her mother during the narration of a tale that speaks of the heroism of women, the irony of the situation is driven home to Anna and to the daughters of her generation: though telling is necessary for survival, the heroic story rings hollow as they see evidence of the victimization of Germany by Nazis and of mothers, like Lene, by soldiers, by their husbands at home, and by society at large. The medium, that is, the narration of the fairy tale, appeals for a time, when the voice of women will be heard in Germany. The filmmaker, that is, the daughter, makes use of this medium, the narration, on the one hand to expose and challenge the patriarchy in Germany that continues to victimize women and on the other hand to claim a position for women in the cultural hegemony of postwar Germany. The subversive strategy of tale-telling reveals both the victimization of women and their exclusion from the public sphere as it denounces male oppression.[23]

In sum, Anna has learned from her mother to recognize victimization. Like the young bride in the tale, she has learned to stay single. She has also learned that women are strong only if and when they use their voice. Through her cinematic tale, she demonstrates that she has learned that tale-telling is a way out of the prison of silence imposed on women in patriarchal society and she has decided to continue the narration her mother started as she probes the allegorical question contained in Brecht's poem with which the film began: how Germany's sons have defiled their mother and how the mother's silent complicity in the sons' atrocities led to her shame among nations.

Notes

1. Jakob Grimm and Wilhelm Grimm, *Kinder und Hausmärchen* 1819; KHM, (Darmstadt: Wissenschaftliche Buchgesellschaft, 1969), 239–42.

2. Helma Sanders-Brahms, *Deutschland, bleiche Mutter: Film Erzählung* (Hamburg, Germany: Rowohlt, 1984), 116. Anton Kaes, *From Hitler to Heimat: The Return of History as Film* (Cambridge: Harvard University Press, 1989), 149–50. Barbara Hyams, "Is the Apolitical Woman at Peace?: A Reading of the Fairy Tale in *Germany, Pale Mother*," *Wide Angle* 10, no. 3 (1988): 40–51. Roger F. Cook, "Melodrama or Cinematic Folktale? Story and History in *Deutschland, bleiche Mutter*," *Germanic Review* 64 (1991): 113–20. Ellen E. Seiter, "Women's History, Women's Melodrama: *Deutschland, bleiche Mutter*," *German Quarterly* 59 (1986): 569–81. Angelika Bammer, "Through a Daughter's Eyes: Helma Sanders-Brahms' *Germany, Pale Mother*," *New German Critique* 36 (1985): 106–9. Irene Heidelberger-Leonard, "Brecht, Grimm, Sanders-Brahms—Drei Variationen zum selben Thema: *Deutschland, bleiche Mutter*," *Etudes Germaniques* 39 (1984): 51–55. E. Ann Kaplan, "The Search for the Mother/Land in Sanders-Brahms' *Germany, Pale Mother*," in *German Film & Literature: Adaptations and Transformations*, ed. Eric Rentschler (New York: Methuen, 1986), 299.

3. Roger C. Cook, "Melodrama," also recognizes the two sides of the tale. The other side, the "mirror image" focusing on the daughter's narration, transforms "the film

into a cinematic folktale," where the daughter "assumes the reverse role of narrating to her mother her own tale about women's subjection to the male aggressor instinct" (118).

4. Dietz-Ruediger Moser, "Theorie—und Methodenprobleme der Märchen-forschung: Zugleich der Versuch einer Definition des 'Märchens,'" *Jahrbuch für Volkskunde NF* 3 (1980): 61.

5. Seiter ("Women's History," 573 ff.) calls the visualized family history the "melodrama"; Bammer ("Through a Daughter's Eyes," 100–101) states that in the film history is seen obliquely and indirectly and personal relationships can be understood only within historical and sociocultural coordinates. She criticizes the partiality of the film that appears to place women outside history.

6. Karen Rowe, "To Spin a Yarn: The Female Voice in Folklore and Folk Tale," in *Fairy Tales and Society: Illusion, Allusion and Paradigm*, ed. Ruth B. Bottigheimer (Philadelphia: University of Pennsylvania Press, 1986), 53–74.

7. Bammer, "Through a Daughter's Eyes," 106–7 refers to the fairy tale as the most reactionary part of the film.

8. In contrast to Hyams, I do not link death and destruction with the patriarchal order in general, for the fairy tale splits the male image clearly into the negative, destructive figure of the hoodlum and the positive socially conscious father figure, who supports the restoration of social justice. Anna, too, recognizes the basic decency in her father before he goes off to the front.

9. Bruno Bettelheim, *The Uses of Enchantment: The Meaning and Importance of Fairy Tales* (New York: Vintage, 1989), 107.

10. In discussing the structure of the archetype of the Great Mother, Erich Neumann cites the representation of the image symbol in the psyche (i.e., the mother) to produce a compelling effect on consciousness, that is, to provoke flight. *The Great Mother An Analysis of the Archetype*, trans. Ralph Manheim. Bollingen Series 47 (Princeton: Princeton University Press, 1974), 5.

11. Max Horkheimer and Theodor W. Adorno, *Dialektik der Aufklärung: Philosophische Fragmente* (Frankfurt/Main, Germany: Suhrkamp, 1981), 61–99. For a contrary opinion, that the Grimm's fairy tales are opposed to enlightenment literature and to its emphasis on the primacy of reason, see Dietz-Ruediger Moser, "Keine unendliche Geschichte: Die Grimm'schen Märchen—eine Treppe in die Vergangenheit?" *Journal für Geschichte*, 3 (1984): 18.

12. Cook, "Melodrama," 115.

13. Ernst van Alphen, "The Other Within," in *Alterity, Identity, Image: Selves and Others in Society and Scholarship*, eds. Raymond Corbey and Joep Leerssen. Amsterdam Studies on Cultural Identity, no. 1, eds. Raymond Corbey, Joep Leerssen, and Arthur Mitzman (Amsterdam: Rodopi, 1991), 3.

14. Ibid., 11.

15. C. G. Jung would call the Other bride the "shadow heroine" for being "more instinctive than the heroine." Cf. Marie L. von Franz, *Fairy Tales* (New York, Springer: 1970) chap. vii, p. 1.

16. Bettelheim, *Uses of Enchantment*, 44 and elsewhere.

17. Grimm's *Bad Girls & Bold Boys: The Moral & Social Vision of the Tales* (New Haven: Yale University Press, 1987), 71–80.

18. Numerous critics, including Seiter, "Women's History" (580) and Kaes, "From Hitler to Heimat" (148) have objected to Sanders-Brahms's use of the American soldiers as perpetrators of the rape, since this rape obliterates the moral difference between Nazi criminals and American liberators.

19. Sanders-Brahms, *Deutschland*, 112.

20. For additional analogues, see especially Hyams, "Is the Apolitical Woman at Peace?" 45–48; also, Cook, "Melodrama or Cinematic Folktale," 115, 117–18; and Heidelberger-Leonard, "Brecht, Grimm, Sanders-Brahms," 52–54.

21. Sanders-Brahms, *Deutschland*, 112.

22. Kaplan, "Search," 299, would disagree; she sees the fairy tale as a means of isolating mother and daughter in a fantasy world.

23. Cook, "Melodrama," 119. Cf. also Jack Zipes, *Fairy Tales and the Art of Subversion* (New York: Wildman, 1983). Zipes calls it "an institutionalized discourse with manipulation as one of its components" (10). "Some [writers] even converted the fairy-tale discourse to subvert it" (11). Zipes demonstrates such subversion through symbolic innovation and involution especially for tales of the Weimar and Nazi periods in the last two chapters of his study.

19

Fairy Tales and Reflexivity in
Marianne Rosenbaum's *Peppermint Peace*

Susan E. Linville

The year 1983 marked the beginning of a three-year-long West German commemorative celebration of the birthdays of the Brothers Grimm. This bicentennial event produced an enormous outpouring of extremely popular psychoanalytic studies on the tales, studies which, in Jack Zipes's words, "preach the messages of the tales as though they could bring about salvation for one and all. The Grimms' tales are therapeutically messianic, as prescriptions for the good housekeeping of childhood development—unfortunately," he adds, "these general views of the Grimms' tales reign supreme in Germany today."[1] This year also witnessed a less celebrated but no less noteworthy event: the release of Marianne Rosenbaum's fictionalized, self-reflexive autobiographical film, *Peppermint Frieden* (Peppermint Peace).[2] This comic work recalls her childhood socialization into a wartime and postwar Germany ripe for social critique—and it focuses critical attention on the role of fairy tales and other lore in that socialization process.[3] While the celebratory psychoanalytic studies produced in the 1980s avoid certain questions—in particular, if "what appears to be a healthy resolution of psychological problems is merely a sexist [and majoritarian] resolution of power relationships"[4]—Rosenbaum's film tackles precisely these questions, and does it head-on. Unlike the dehistoricizing, ideologically mythicized studies described by Zipes, *Peppermint Peace* focuses critical scrutiny on *who* tells the tale and on the *context* of the telling.[5] Furthermore, it makes an imaginative contribution to the feminist project of resuscitating fairy-tale narration as a gendered social practice with resistant, historically conscious, liberatory ends.

A striking example of the film's attention to teller and context is its treatment of "*Der Hase und der Igel*" (The Rabbit and the Hedgehog). This beast fable is represented in the form of a Kinderfilm (children's film) screened under the aegis of the Nazis. Early in *Peppermint Peace*, Rosenbaum's autobiographical surrogate Marianne Worlicek (Saskia Tyroller-Hauptmann), a precocious child of about four, goes to the movies with her mother (Gesine Strempel) on an Easter Sunday. To the child's sorrow, her father (Hans Peter Korff) is absent fighting with the German army on the eastern front. And although her friend Dr. Klug (Gérard Samaan) had helped to fill the void left in her life by her father's absence, now he too is gone—"ist verreist" (has gone away on a trip) in her grandmother's words. The doctor's fate as a Jew is thus concealed from the child. Marianne, however, does not simply forget. Dr. Klug was imaginative, compassionate, and playful. He had healed her wounded hand and had charmed her by wearing a papier-mâché rabbit mask while making a house call. He gave her the mask as a gift, assuring her that rabbits "know how to double back"— his attempt, it would seem, to convince her that he would be able to elude the Nazis. The two films that Frau Worlicek and Marianne see are a Wochenschau (the weekly newsreel) and the Kinderfilm. The newsreel footage depicts groups of soldiers exuberantly saluting the Führer, while the children's film, as noted, dramatizes the tale of "The Rabbit and the Hedgehog," a fable in which the rabbit ultimately dies. The film screening is brought to a halt by an air-raid attack.

Not unlike the cinema, the Grimms' tales were seen by the Nazis as powerful tools for propaganda. Convinced of the utility of selection, German-centered tales for instilling their racist and peasant-centered Weltanschauung, the National Socialists systematically promoted the use of these Grimms' stories in public school curricula, in Hitler Youth functions, and in other venues. They believed the Märchen to be effective tools of ideological indoctrination for young and old alike. Moreover, as Christa Kamenetsky explains, "For teachers and youth leaders [the Nazis] organized conferences and workshops that were meant to help them to implement National Socialist guidelines for a new and uniform interpretation of the national folk heritage."[6] Not only did the Nazis insist on univocal readings of the tales, but they also banned "folk-alien" literature from the schools, libraries, and bookstores.[7] Select tales were considered a desirable and effective means to indoctrinate children even as young as four. In a 1940 essay "The Folktale Story Hour as a Preparation for History Lessons," Dietrich Klagges set forth the view that even very young children can be nationally socialized through fairy tales, and he cites as evidence a conversation between a father and his four-year-old daughter. Kamenetsky summarizes what Klagges reported as follows:

> "Father," she had asked him after listening to a folktale by the Brothers Grimm, "who is the most courageous person in the world?" "Well," the father had re-

plied, "I don't really know, but perhaps you know the answer." "It's you and Adolf Hitler!" the little girl had responded. According to Klagges, this answer proved that the Grimms' folktales were ideally suited even for the youngest children to teach the social virtues of the Third Reich.[8]

Read with the grain, the fairy-tale Kinderfilm within *Peppermint Peace* allows for an easy accommodation to Nazi ideology. Indeed, in many respects it seems cut to the measure of fascist desire. Set on a bright Sunday morning, the tale involves an earthy, lower-class, thoroughly "folkish" hedgehog, his wife, and their children; and a speedier, more aristocratic rabbit whom the hedgehog encounters while taking a stroll. The rabbit's condescending attitude toward the hedgehog annoys him, and so, seeking revenge, the hedgehog initiates a race and a wager: he bets that he can outrun the rabbit. First, however, he claims he must return home to eat a bit of breakfast. Once home, the hedgehog demands that his doubting wife follow him and help him win the wager. The hedgehog proceeds to deceive the rabbit into believing that two different but identical-looking animals—he and his wife—are one and the same creature: the hedgehog positions himself at one end of the race course and his wife at the other. Then, either one or the other pops up and is "already there" the moment before the rabbit arrives at either end of the course. Because the dumbfounded rabbit keeps wanting another go at it, and because the hedgehog never gives his duplicitous game away, the rabbit literally runs himself to death. Thus the hedgehog wins the race, the wager, and the wealthy rabbit's loot—a "happy" ending that is undermined in *Peppermint Peace* by the air raid that forces the evacuation of the theater.

It is not difficult to see why Rosenbaum selected this tale to represent the kind of narrative preferred by the Nazi party. The animal fable, recorded in Plattdeutsch (Low German—a colloquial dialect of northern Germany) by the Brothers Grimm, addresses and celebrates the common folk, and it affirms ideas and binarisms easily subsumed by national socialist values. In particular, the narrative concludes by drawing two morals, both folkish: one, a warning against condescension toward the lower classes, and the second, an assertion that if men want to be happy, they should marry others of the same social class (i.e., marry common folk) and of the exact same physical appearance as they—a conflation of classist and ethnocentric principles:

> De Lehre aver ut disser Geschicht is erstens, dat keener, un wenn he sick ook noch so vornehm dücht, sick sall bikommen laten, övern geringen Mann sick lustig to maken, un wöört ook man'n Swinegel. Un tweetens, dat et gerahden is, wenn eener freet, dat he sick 'ne Fro uut sienem Stande nimmt un de jüst so uutsüht. Wer also en Swinegel is, de mutt tosehn, dat siene Fro ook en Swinegel is, un so wieder.[9]

The moral, however, from this story is first, that no one, even if he thinks himself very aristocratic, should let himself be compelled to make fun of a lesser man, even if it were just a hedgehog. And second, that it is advised, if one is to be happy, he should take a wife from his own class, and who looks just like that (i.e., that she looks to be from his class). Therefore, whoever is a hedgehog, he should see to it that his wife too is a hedgehog, and so on.

The drama of the animal fable extends these principles, for it illustrates not only the idea that wives should mirror their husbands physically, but also that they should absolutely obey them, ape them, and unquestioningly endorse their behavior, just as the hedgehog's wife does when she goes along with her husband's ruse. (When she protests against the idea of the race, he responds, "Holt dat Muul, Wief, dat is mien Saak. Resonehr nich in Männergeschäfte. Marsch, treck die an, un denn kumm mit"[10]—roughly translated, Shut up and do as I say).

The didactic intent behind the screening of the fairy tale fails with young Marianne, however. In the comic tradition of the insightful naive, she reads against the grain, interpolating her own resistant meaning and point of view, simultaneously thwarting Nazi theory and defamiliarizing the tale for the spectator of *Peppermint Peace*. Specifically, the child sympathizes with the dead rabbit, a figure that becomes a representation in her imagination of her friend Dr. Klug. Seeing the dead rabbit, that is played by a man wearing a mask, she mournfully speaks the doctor's name out loud. Thus, despite the mechanisms of censorship and indoctrination that envelop her, and despite the lack of familial honesty, she comes to a realization of the probable truth of the situation. The girl aptly displaces the duplicitous mirror-image hedgehogs as the tale's heroes, implicitly positioning them as its murderous villains.[11]

Although *Peppermint Peace* shows us just a lap in the race and the race's end result rather than the Kinderfilm in its entirety, the tale's familiarity for German audiences presumably renders a presentation of the complete fable unnecessary. The clips and Marianne's spectatorial example are sufficient, in fact, to encourage the audience to mimic in a more self-conscious way the girl's subversive response to its assertion of "hedgehog" hegemony. Indeed, by reading still further against the grain and by broadening the interpretive implications that are suggested by the girl's empathic response to the rabbit as a stand-in for Dr. Klug, we are able to reflect on the Nazis' pedagogical apparatus and on our own status as film spectators. We can come to view the fairy tale as a narrative about a radically narcissistic and ethnocentric folk figure, a prickly patriarchal animal whose desire to exclude difference extends not just to his own wife but also to all those whose class, race, or genetic characteristics mark them as different from himself. This cultural meaning of this economy of the same is timely not just for the Germans of the Nazi era but also, in a different sense, for those of the

Communist-fearing, Red-baiting cold-war decades, an era that vilified "Der Ivan," the Russian Other, as the film later depicts.

Furthermore, we recognize that the tale and the folkish Papa desire more than just the exclusion of difference: the beast fable's ending registers a desire to kill difference off, to eradicate it altogether. The conclusion of the Grimms' tale smugly affirms that there were never any more races between rabbits and hedgehogs in Buxtehuder Heide, the race's setting—a development which, given the goals of the tale's appropriators, suggests a parallel to the Nazis' belief that there would be no more "Jewish threat," no more racial competition for resources, once the "final solution" was reached. The spectator also comes to realize that despite the aptness of Dr. Klug's name—he seems indeed to be intelligent, clever, and prudent—the doctor's survival strategy of protecting himself by, as he says, "doubling back" is too similar to the actions of the rabbit in the fable. Dr. Klug is doomed to fail because the trap is a complete circle, a fatally recursive loop, marked by repeated, indistinguishable, reproducible images that literally work him to death. (A later dream sequence emanating from Marianne's unconscious makes this idea more explicit.) Once again, a telling metacinematic, metafolkloric commentary can be readily inferred.[12]

Thus Marianne's spectatorship reflects on and directs our own cinematic spectation as adults. It also comments critically on childhood socialization and viewership as regulated by the Nazis. Yet Rosenbaum's evocations of fairy tale and fable are neither univocal nor monolithic and in this sense again contrast with both the Nazis and the 1980s psychoanalytic critics' approaches. Indeed, elsewhere in the film, progressively deployed motifs and topoi from fairy tales and religious lore are integrated into Rosenbaum's antirealist aesthetic, an aesthetic that further incorporates distorting lenses, extreme camera angles, slow motion cinematography, surrealistically coded uses of color, and dream sequences, to depict a child's logos of emotion. The film authorizes revisionist retellings and recontextualizations, and narratives and narrative strategies that historicize the motifs, bringing to life their liberatory, propeace, feminist potentials.

Motifs from Christian lore inform revised stories of the Virgin Mary, Marianne's namesake, during the cold-war segment of the film, which is set in Catholic Bavaria. During this time Marianne repeatedly imagines herself as a Madonna to the rescue. Revising the cult of the Mater Dolorosa, she refuses to tolerate the punishment God inflicts on "her Son" and will not abide his acquiescence to war—past, present, or future. Instead, she becomes Mary the activist performance artist. The "seven swords" that traditionally pierce her breast and betoken her "seven sorrows" become, instead, the knives that she throws toward a mounted radio, an apparatus for propaganda in the film. The girl thus imaginatively appropriates the role of author and hero of her own "divine" story, simultaneously inscribing Rosenbaum's interventionism in Mariology. Another example—contained in what is perhaps the film's most memorable postwar sequence—deploys secular fairy-tale motifs within a vignette that conjures up a utopic vision of world peace. The sequence also affirms the burgeoning Schaulust (scopophilia) and Wisstrieb (epistemophilia) of the girl, who is by this time about five.

This sequence begins with a medium shot of Marianne's look of outward regard. The girl smiles, lightly strokes her bare chest, then brings her fingertips to her mouth to moisten them, and strokes herself again. She steps closer to the sight that holds her gaze; the camera follows her, revealing in the distance the objects of her look: a swimsuit clad couple reclining and kissing on the shore. It is Nilla, an unmarried German woman, and her lover Mr. Frieden, an American GI (whose name and gifts of peppermint chewing gum give rise to the film's title). Marianne's parents emerge from the water. Her father sees his daughter's gaze, dons his glasses for a better look, registers his alarm, then to Marianne's annoyance, attempts to distract her by calling her attention to water flies and to the cry of the cormorant. When that fails, he tries to divert the small girl with bird calls, but succeeds only in prompting the human love birds to add some whistling to their billing and cooing. Frau Worlicek now pulls out her diversionary tools: she offers Marianne a sandwich, an apple, and a beach ball. Marianne finally accepts the ball and quickly creates a game of toss that includes Mr. Frieden and Nilla. At this point, to the accompaniment of the film's jazzy "Mr. Frieden" theme music, the sequence's marvelously rendered relay of gazes gives way to a relay of passes and pleased looks among the five. In faulty English, a jubilant Herr Worlicek exclaims to Mr. Frieden, "We are not more enemies!" The group's play breaks down barriers and hierarchies, momentarily uniting all—captured together in a single, joyful, utopic shot.

Certain elements here recall motifs familiar from the Nausicaa episode of *The Odyssey*—an episode played out on the fairy-tale island home of a matrifocal, pacifist society. They also evoke "The Frog King," though the film vignette differs considerably from the Grimm Brothers' sexually censored, patriarchally aligned version of this tale. Shared elements among the three stories include the topos of the shore or well, indicative of the unconscious; the ball, evocative of a globe, a world of utopic perfection, and of the girl's unrealized psychic potential; and the throwing of the object, suggestive of the girl's erotic awakening.[13] The utopic moment is brought to a halt by the appearance in the distance of the film's patriarchal alazon—the priest, Herr Expositus, whom the film associates with fascistic surveillance, sexual repression, and later, inflammatory anti-Soviet rhetoric.

The film's closing sequence depends on this utopic one for counterpoint. Ultimately feeling terrorized by the prospect of a third world war and betrayed by the Americans she had once associated with peace, freedom, and joy, Marianne asks her father where Korea is. "Very far away. Don't worry," he tries to reassure her, and he shows her Korea on an all too tiny globe. The film as a whole ends with a freeze-frame of Marianne's troubled, engaging look directly at the camera. She returns the viewers' gaze—and with this look, she passes directly to the implied audience the responsibility for reversing the insane race toward nuclear war that spanned both the cold-war time frame represented in the diegesis and the early 1980s, when the film was completed and released. That is, just as Marianne's gaze earlier creates a utopic interconnection among people through play, here her look conveys to us the obligation to recapture the kind of harmonious world symbolized by the ball as globe in the sequence by the shore.

Politically inflected, historically contextualized fairy-tale motifs such as these help to define the aesthetics not only of *Peppermint Peace* but also of much woman-centered German cinema from the past twenty years. Sanders-Brahms's *Germany, Pale Mother* offers the best-known examples, including the self-reflexive, historically charged telling of the complete "Robber Bridegroom" tale.[14] Among the somewhat less familiar instances are the fractured fairy-tale structure that subtends the entire narrative of Dörrie's *Straight Through the Heart*, and the motifs and topoi from "Hansel and Gretel" and from various doppelgänger stories—tales about doubles—that inform von Trotta's *Sisters, or the Balance of Happiness*.[15] These motifs span a number of von Trotta's films. Additionally, both *Peppermint Peace* and Verhoeven's *Nasty Girl* revise the topos of the "curious girl," whose negative prototypes include Red Riding Hood, Goldilocks, and, most notoriously, Eve.[16] Beyond these, Meerapfel's *Malou*, von Trotta's *Sisters*, Dörrie's *Straight Through the Heart*, and Sanders-Brahms's *Germany, Pale Mother* all allude to, critique, and refashion, "Sleeping Beauty"—that problematic paradigm of feminine acquiescence.

Insofar as these films authorize enunciative roles for females as tellers of the tales, they reclaim functions and practices that women possessed in the seventeenth and eighteenth centuries, the heyday of the genre as a literary form. During this time, especially in France, women-authors' fairy-tale narratives outnumbered and in some cases preceded the better-known work of Charles Perrault, himself a predecessor of the Brothers Grimm.[17] Although these women's narratives were not uniformly liberatory, as Zipes notes, at times they opposed patriarchal standards of female conduct: "The fairy tale was used in refined discourse as a means through which women imagined their lives might be improved." Zipes adds, however, that "gradually the tales were changed to introduce morals to children that emphasized *civilité* to the detriment of women, even though women were originally the major writers of the tales."[18] What is most memorable about the cinematic recastings, including and especially in *Peppermint Peace*, is that they emphasize sociohistorical dynamics over patriarchally identified, dehistoricized "universals." Where the fairy tale's retrograde applications are concerned, these films often demonstrate that distanciation or *disenchant-ment*—breaking the spell—is a necessary prelude to change. And where recla-mation is at issue, the films reveal that the "uses of enchantment," to borrow Bettelheim's phrase, include subversion, resistance, and social transformation.

Notes

1. Jack Zipes, *The Brothers Grimm: From Enchanted Forests to the Modern World* (New York: Routledge, 1988), 116.

2. Marianne Rosenbaum, director and screenwriter, *Peppermint Peace*, cinematogra-phy by Alfred Tichawsky, edited by Gérard Samaan, music by Konstantin Wecker; with Peter Fonda, Saskia Tyroller-Hauptmann, and Gesine Strempel (Nourfilm, Munich, 1983).

3. Although the film has received relatively little attention from scholars, it won five prestigious awards. Furthermore, Rosenbaum testifies that by 1984 she had traveled a great deal with the film and had spoken with more than ten thousand people about it. She reports that women-viewers' responses were especially positive (Bion Steinborn and Carola Hilmes, "'Frieden' hat für uns Deutsche einen amerikanischen Geschmack. Ein Gespräch mit Marianne S. W. Rosenbaum," *Filmfaust* 39 [May-June 1984]: 31). Up to the present, the film has continued to be shown on German television.

4. Zipes, *Brothers Grimm*, 126.

5. Cf. Marina Warner, *From the Beast to the Blonde: On Fairy Tales and Their Tellers* (New York: Farrar, 1994). Like Rosenbaum, Warner resists a universalizing emphasis and focuses instead on shifting social, political, and material conditions.

6. Christa Kamenetsky, *The Brothers Grimm and Their Critics: Folktales and the Quest for Meaning* (Athens: Ohio University Press, 1992), 242.

7. Mickey Mouse was also unacceptable. A Pomeranian newspaper article from the mid-1930s claimed, "Mickey Mouse is the most miserable ideal ever revealed. . . . Healthy emotions tell every independent young man and every honorable youth that the dirty and filth-covered vermin, the greatest bacteria carrier in the animal kingdom, can-not be the ideal type of animal. . . . Away with Jewish brutalization of the people! Down with Mickey Mouse! Wear the Swastika Cross!" (as quoted in Art Spiegelman, *Maus: A Survivor's Tale* [New York: Pantheon, 1991], 2:3).

8. Kamenetsky, *Brothers Grimm*, 245.

9. Wilhelm Grimm and Jacob Grimm, *Kinder- und Hausmärchen*, (Zurich: Manesse Verlag, n.d.), 2:496.

10. Ibid., 2:494.

11. Whether or not the *Wochenschau* footage recalls Marianne's father to her mind is left unclear.

12. Cf. Zipes's discussion of duplication in *Fairy Tale as Myth/Myth as Fairy Tale* (Lexington: University Press of Kentucky, 1994), 8–10.

13. For a discussion of these elements in "The Frog King," see Bruno Bettelheim, *The Uses of Enchantment: The Meaning and Importance of Fairy Tales* (1976; reprint, New York: Vintage, Random House, 1989), 286–91.

14. On Sanders-Brahms's use of this tale, see in particular chapter 18 of the volume. See also Roger F. Cook, "Melodrama or Cinematic Folktale? Story and History in *Deutschland, bleiche Mutter,*" *The Germanic Review* 66, no. 3 (summer 1991): 113–29; and Richard W. McCormick, *Politics of the Self: Feminism and the Postmodern in West German Literature and Film* (Princeton: Princeton University Press, 1991), 201–4.

15. See Lucy Fischer, *Shot/Countershot: Film Tradition and Women's Cinema* (Princeton: Princeton University Press, 1989), 123–24, 206–7, 213–15.

16. Warner, *From the Beast to the Blonde*, 396.

17. Ibid., xvi.

18. Zipes, *Fairy Tale*, 21, 24.

20

Interview with Helke Sander:
Reception of *Liberators Take Liberties*:
I would have hoped for a different discussion. . . .

Sabine Smith

I had the opportunity to interview Helke Sander in December 1995. Her most recent film, *BeFreier und Befreite: Krieg, Vergewaltigungen, Kinder*, was a few months shy of its fourth birthday, but the controversy surrounding its subject matter lingered on. The film, a three-and-a-half-hour-long documentary on the mass rapings of German women by Allied Forces at the end of World War II, had triggered an intense debate among historians, Germanists, feminists, and film scholars both in Germany and the United States. In the United States, the debate had played itself out at professional conventions,[1] dividing its participants into two camps that were opposed in an increasingly fierce intellectual battle over the merits of Sander's project.

In my conversation with Sander, I wanted to provide her with the opportunity to speak about the controversy. In the past she had responded repeatedly to specific accusations.[2] I was interested, however, in hearing Sander's views on the power dynamics surrounding the debate itself. In particular, it seemed that her film had given rise to research projects similar to hers.[3] Those, however, like the *Spiegel* report on children born to raped mothers at the end of World War II, had raised no public outrage. Nor did they rush to acknowledge the importance of Sander's preliminary work .

I also wanted to redirect the focus on the participants in Sander's project. Early on, Gertrud Koch had called Sander's interview style uncaring and disinterested.[4] The increasingly esoteric debate on *BeFreier und Befreite* seemed to have neglected the "human" aspect of the film. I was interested in Sander's views on what the film had accomplished for the participants involved, namely the

Helke Sander (l) and Hildegard Knef (r) in BeFreier und Befreite. *Perhaps you follow a different convention for designating left & right?*

men and women who had been victims, witnesses, and survivors. As ubiquitous images and "protagonists," the women were accorded a central role in the film. As a feminist, Sander had wanted to avoid portraying these women both as spectacles and as eternal victims.[5] Thus, I asked Sander about her views on an "alternative" documentary and interview style, having her identify some possibilities and limitations of feminist film art.

    Smith. Let's return once more to the controversy surrounding *BeFreier und Befreite.*

    Sander. Yes, I'd like to say something in general about this controversy. Well, it became a controversy at some point, but I was rather irritated by the sort of artificial way in which it was rendered into one. The film's first screening was in February 1992, and in November 1992, Gertrud Koch's article was published.[6] Immediately after the first screenings in Berlin, an abundance of national and international reviews appeared, and there was actually nothing of this controversy in them. In general, the film was reviewed favorably. Yet this article by Koch . . . is referred to in virtually all essays, and was quoted at times word for word at the New York conference. And whenever there were difficulties, or when there was resistance to the film, the critics referred again and again to this article, or to discussions with Koch. So she was always the source from which this controversy originated. And that's why it's a bit difficult to speak of a genuine controversy. . . . In Germany, it hasn't really been a controversy at all. There was Koch's article in the *Frankfurter Rundschau*—and I was able to respond to it right away and at equal length. That took care of it at the time. And the articles in *Frauen und Film* only appeared in April 1994.[7] *Frauen und Film*, like *October* are rather scholarly journals and don't have a very wide distribution. So, I'd say that it's a controversy within these journals rather than in the public eye.

Smith. Would you say that there was a difference between the critics and the audience's reception of the film?

Sander. No, I wouldn't, because I have at least three thick binders with critical reviews, and very few critics reviewed the film negatively.

Smith. How, then, did this second, negative wave of critical reviews come about?

Sander. Well, I don't have the faintest idea. I don't know what they actually wanted to prove with their accusations—labeling me as a revisionist strikes me as silly, to tell you the truth. I was very upset about it. I can't say that it harmed me terribly. But I thought the accusations were unjustified, and I don't think that they emerge as readings from the film. But life goes on, and the film was screened in at least twenty international film festivals; I received three awards for it, and it ran rather well in the theaters; and it has already been shown a few times on TV. My greatest fear had always been that the political Right would try to drag me into their camp. I really wouldn't have thought that the political Left would attack me this way. And I don't find it especially productive—I would have hoped for a different discussion. My approach in the film had been rather philosophical. I wanted to know what happens when a subject is repressed. I found out only in the course of my research that the rapes occurred on a massive scale, and I wanted to understand what this meant—when a subject that affects a lot of people isn't addressed in some kind of public forum. When it just disappears—without the possibility of rectifying the issues, such as problems of revenge. What actually happens to the people involved? I would have hoped for a discussion of these issues as a follow-up to the film. . . . My goal had been . . . to attain a basis on which one can conduct serious work. I consider my job done, and I think that historians should do the rest. And in part, I feel, and I'm not sure that I am right, I feel that I got caught in the machinery of experts. Up to this point, this had not been a topic with which historians had concerned themselves in a scholarly way—and when this filmmaker claimed that her data were sound, too, these scholars responded with irrational outrage.

Smith. Do you hold them responsible for sustaining the controversy?

Sander. Possibly. . . . Historians could of course make a point of addressing these issues—like patriarchal aspects in political debates. This issue had been relatively underexposed, and the film has surely contributed to its exposure. When the war in Bosnia began, . . . the film also helped people to understand what went on in Bosnia—although I don't want to compare the two, since the circumstances in Bosnia are different. . . .

Smith. Let's talk a little more about the issue of repressing a subject. Do you think that such a repression is going on right now, since you were criticized for talking about this subject?

Sander. Yes, but when a German talks about the injustices inflicted upon Germans—it is very difficult to do—if you don't want anybody to think that you're setting off one thing against another. That is, of course, the fundamental difficulty. I certainly had thought of the issues before I made the film. That contributed, among other things, to why it took me so long to even tackle the subject. Subconsciously, I had been thinking about the subject for a long time. It's almost inevitable, since the discussion of rape has been a part of the women's movement since the early seventies. Of course I thought about what had happened during the war, because I had witnessed some things myself. It bothered me that the Germans in particular, who had to learn the hard way not to repress memory and to confront the past, created at the same time, due to entirely different reasons, a subject about which nobody was supposed to talk. That's schizophrenic. I don't really understand it. Initially, I was even willing to assume that most rape stories were based on propaganda. That it turned out differently— well, those were the findings of my research. And these journals and documents to which Atina Grossmann refers now—those existed, except that most of them were published during the late sixties and early seventies, and even up to the late eighties—if they were published at all. And many of those who read from their manuscripts today took them out of their desks. There is indeed some material here and there, but there was no scholarly research on the subject.

Smith. Isn't it interesting that in the wake of your film, a number of publications appeared that address the subject of rape during wartime?[8]

Sander. Yes, I would say that the project gave rise to many others. Because since then, there are films and essays about the women abducted to Siberia, and so forth. There is quite a bit available now, like the stories on the children.

Smith. I assume you refer to the *Spiegel* article by Bruno Schrep?[9]

Sander. Yes.

Smith. To what extent did you think that your preliminary work had not been acknowledged?

Sander. Well, Mr. Schrep and I sat together numerous times, and I told him a lot, and he received a lot of material from us. In that regard I was a little taken back that our project wasn't even mentioned—I probably just have to accept it. I would have imagined it a little differently, I must say.

Smith. And to what extent did his article elicit a response similar to the controversy surrounding your film?

Sander. I don't know anything about that. I asked him about that, too, when he called me a few weeks ago to thank me. Apparently, he had received a number of letters, but nobody analyzes them once the article is written—they probably disappeared somewhere. By contrast, we still collected all those responses, and Barbara Johr will possibly write a research paper on them. We have kept in touch with some of the participants. One can't just suddenly break things off, since these people opened themselves up to us considerably.

Smith. I wanted to ask you about that, especially in light of Wiltrud Rosenzweig's article in the *October* issue.[10] It appears as if she was the only participant who came forward to defend your project. . . .

Sander. No, she wasn't. And it was even rather difficult to get her contribution accepted. She really wanted to say something about this controversy since she had been very aware of it. Her article was substantially shortened in the editing process. She was rather upset about it.

Smith. Is Rosenzweig's reaction to the controversy representative?

Sander. I wouldn't say that—because she is in fact an intellectual, and most of the other women who participated aren't necessarily. Moreover, she's much younger; that makes a big difference.

Smith. Would you say that the *October* issue did justice to your project, and that the contributions were balanced, differentiated, and fair?

Sander. Well, those articles were essentially the papers presented at the New York conference.[11] I did find them extremely aggressive and hostile—and partly inaccurate, too. The essay by Atina Grossmann, for example, rejects my claim of having violated a taboo.[12] My goodness, I don't insist on the fact that I violated a taboo, but I think it was a taboo. And in contrast to Grossmann I don't think one can consider it a public debate when women at the time talked about having been raped—about the fact that it happened. They would say "You, too?" or "How often?" but it hardly ever went beyond that. The debate was repressed because nobody was interested in it.

Smith. I'd like to ask you about specific details in the film. We said that the film's participants are very important. In *Gewaltakte*,[13] you mention conventional reports on rape victims and how they tend to revictimize women. To what extent did your project contribute to the women's revictimization, or their healing?

Sander. Well, I believe it had rather a healing effect on the women. A woman says so, by the way, in the beginning of part two. She is in this group of people in front of the TV screens. She says she felt something like relief and that for the first time it seemed permissible to talk about the rapes. It had always been inappropriate in the past—she refers to the entire postwar era. When interviewing the women I went to them with paper and pencil only. I told them about my interest in making the film—namely to find out whether the rapes had indeed occurred on a massive scale. And since this wasn't an intrusion, a barrier was removed, and that's why they were able to talk. Initially, I didn't want to know so much about them personally—how they had experienced the rapes. I asked, for example, in which streets it had happened so that I would get an overall idea—in which houses, which street numbers, who else had been there, how many people had lived in the house, and so forth. And all these facts allowed them to push the trauma to the side. And after having talked for one to two hours, then I would ask them if they were willing to speak about individual aspects of their experience in the film as well. I then talked to some of those who were willing. Frequently, I was the first or second person with whom they talked about it at all; that was something I hadn't expected. Many of them said that it felt good to finally unburden themselves. I thought that they might feel some incredible hatred toward the Russians—or the French—or whoever the rapists were. I virtually never encountered that. Instead, they often linked it with the question "What might German soldiers have done?" or "What do men do today?" Also, many women had been severely discriminated against by the men in their lives—because of the rapes. To many of them, this disappointment was more painful than the rape itself.

Smith. In the courtyard scene, the participants actually talk among themselves. That is, the film creates a forum in which women talk to men, exchanging their views on the rapes. Did your project possibly contribute to a dialogue between the sexes?

Sander. Well I wouldn't say it like that—but for the first time, they had a chance to talk about it in some kind of public forum. And that felt good. They told me that afterward. But I wouldn't want to draw any further conclusions.

Smith. The men said it, too?

Sander. Yes.

Smith. I'd like to focus on the last scene, Hildegard Knef's reading of Kleist's *Penthesilea*. To me, this scene stands in contrast to other parts of the film. It also brings up some of the issues for which you were criticized: on the one hand, you present the rapes as something specific and historical; on the other hand, you suggest they are universal. Furthermore, you address the need to change the situation, . . . but then you end on an almost pessimistic note when Hildegard Knef presents a "solution" to the problem in women's separation from men.

Sander. Well, I didn't mean that quite so seriously. The film is exceptionally long, and I wanted to come to an end, and I wanted to announce the ending with something that would make everybody aware that the film is over now. And I wanted to conclude with something that altogether departs from the level of the documentary. I kept wondering what that could be—I wanted something literary, too, and there isn't that much available. This story of the Amazons is not exactly a recipe. It's simply a literary quote that offers yet a different perspective. It's not a summary of what I envision as a solution. At least I didn't want it to be understood as such.

Smith. At the end of the film it does, however, occupy a prominent position—

Sander. Well, yes, but it is not, however, a one-to-one relation. This film is not a scholarly work. The film addresses so many different emotions, and this is just one more—and we don't know whether this took place or not—and I wanted to leave it in this in-between state so that it would convey yet another idea. But I really didn't want it viewed as a recipe.

Smith. You mentioned that you deliberately chose to end the film with something that goes beyond the documentary. Why?

Sander. On the one hand, one has to present the subject—of what happened in Berlin—very accurately. On the other hand, rape happens over and over again, though always in entirely different ways. And apparently, women draw different conclusions from the experience. By leaving the realm of the documentary, the film refers, in a figurative sense, to other ways of coping with the problem of rape and with other events that took place—and that have to be reassessed. Atina Grossmann reproaches me for saying that rape is ubiquitous and that all wars are alike, but that's not what I'm saying. I don't think that women are raped in every war, but in very many wars, rapes do occur.

Smith. It seems that the audience of *BeFreier und Befreite* consists mostly of women. To what extent do you see a disadvantage in this, or a missed opportunity? Is there is a gender specific reception of the film—and perhaps of the subject?

Sander. That's almost always the case—when you go to a reading, or the theater, or the opera—there are mostly women in the audience. . . . So yes, there are more women than men. I'd say 70 percent of my audience are women of all ages, but there were always men, too. Interestingly enough mostly older men . . . who seemed to be there mostly for personal reasons.

Smith. Would you say that the predominantly female audience is due to the subject of rape?

Sander. No, I think, generally speaking, it is women who read, who watch movies, who listen to presentations on whatever subject.

Smith. What is the place of *BeFreier und Befreite* within the context of your work and your personal history?

Sander. Well, every new film, every new project is closest to my heart at the time of its production. I focus fully on it and try to do it as well as possible. This film was different, though: never before did I have to discuss the subject so much afterward. With other films, you have a film discussion following its release, and then the film sort of makes it on its own. With this film . . . I had to talk so much—incessantly—about the film. It was indeed burdensome—all the interviews, the research, and what I found out in the course of it—that's why at this point, I actually have a hard time speaking about rape.

Smith. Except that I understood you to say that the topic of rape wasn't usually the focus of the discussions after the film's release?

Sander. No, but nonetheless you were continuously faced with these per-

sonal histories—with the most horrible stories. And when you hear them hun-
dreds of times—virtually every day, over years—it really brings you down.

Smith. What about *BeFreier und Befreite* within the context of the documentary film as such—to what extent is *BeFreier und Befreite* a different
documentary?

Sander. Actually, *BeFreier und Befreite* was supposed to be a short film between two feature films. It is of course difficult to make a documentary about a
subject this far in the past. You also asked me why I'm always on-screen. I simply wanted to place the different participants in settings specific to them. And
because the women told their stories to me—and not to the camera somehow—I couldn't let them be on-screen all by themselves. I didn't intend to be
in the frame so often, but I couldn't avoid it. I was some kind of catalyst.

Smith. Both in the voice-over and in your visual presence, you come across
as a partisan observer, as an active listener—who takes a stand by asking poignant
follow-up questions, and by noticeably steering the conversation in certain
directions.

Sander. Well, most of the time, I had the goal of finding out something
specific in these conversations. When I ask follow-up questions, I'm going after something that I consider significant. And I wanted to have it as accurate as
possible. I usually ask more specifically about the "how" and "where"—I usually ask for the facts.

Smith. Well, yes, but you edit and cluster the interviews; you arrange the
scenes; you use montage—it seems that not only the documentation is important, but also the process of filmmaking itself, since it discloses your partisan
interests.

Sander. Well, I am the director, after all. I was concerned with representing
the problem in a multifaceted way, and hence I tried to do it in the way that
seemed most appropriate to me.

Smith. In the past, you rejected the label of feminist filmmaker. To what
extent is *BeFreier und Befreite* a feminist documentary?

Sander. Yes, well Brecht and later Godard said, "I don't produce political
films, but I make films in a political way." So I could say the same about this
film: "I made this film in a feminist way." Let's put it this way: initially, my interest is not to make a feminist film, but as a person, as a citizen, I have an opinion. That opinion comes through, and it may be feminist. However, I am re-
luctant to use the term *feminist* at this point, because so many different things are
understood by it. I don't find it very fruitful right now.

Smith. Would you say that there is a feminist documentary style?

Sander. No, I actually wouldn't. Because we are part of so many different
traditions—as filmmakers, as political subjects, and as women so many different
things converge, and I believe that these categorizations aren't very helpful. I

think that one can always identify a film made by a woman, or locate certain feminist positions in it—if we can even agree today what feminism actually is, especially since nowadays even women of the radical Right count as feminists. That's why I tend to have scruples. I identify as a feminist, but not as a feminist filmmaker. Rather as a filmmaker who takes feminist positions in her films. I find that the term *feminist film* doesn't mean much, because there are horrible films—films that are horrible in terms of formal elements—which may, however, articulate certain feminist viewpoints.

Smith. One could, of course, make the argument that in a feminist film, there is a certain semiotics—a certain approach to directing, which is different from that in male-authored or conventional films.

Sander. Well, I don't think we'll reach a consensus on this. If I consider, for example, many avant-garde films: they may represent a patriarchal concept of women, or a very patriarchal viewpoint. And nonetheless, they may be incredibly interesting as avant-garde films, and we can learn a lot from them. . . . That's why I tend to reject the term in this abridged form.

Smith. What are you working on right now?

Sander. Well, that's a difficult question. I want to make a feature film next, and I am looking for the money—which is exceedingly difficult, but I don't want to talk about it at this point. . . . When you're stuck in these murderous financing negotiations, and so much goes wrong—I don't want to be asked again and again about projects that then don't go anywhere within the next ten years. I'm working, though.

Notes

1. The annual German Studies Association convention in Dallas in October 1994, the Goethe Haus/German Cultural Center colloquium in New York in October 1993, and the annual Women in German conferences of 1992 and 1993.

2. Helke Sander, "Erwiderung: 'Du machst es Dir viel zu einfach.' Helke Sander zu Gertrud Kochs Rezension ihres Film[s] *BeFreier und Befreite,*" *Frankfurter Rundschau,* 26.11.92. Helke Sander and Roger Willemsen, *Gewaltakte, Männerphantasien und Krieg* (Hamburg: Ingrid Klein Verlag, 1992). Helke Sander, "A Response to My Critics." *October* 72 (1995): 81–88. Stuart Liebman, "There Should Be No Scissors in Your Mind: An Interview with Helke Sander," *Cineaste* 21, nos. 1–2 (1995): 40–42.

3. Alexandra Stiglmayer, ed. *Massenvergewaltigung: Krieg gegen die Frauen* (Freiburg, Germany: Kore, 1993). Claudia Opitz, "Von Frauen im Krieg zum Krieg gegen Frauen: Krieg, Gewalt, und Geschlechterbeziehungen aus historischer Sicht," in *Sexuelle Gewalt gegen Frauen—kein Thema?* ed. Gisela Gräning (Münster, Germany: Waxmann, 1993), 11–28. Bruno Schrep, "Kinder der Schande," *Spiegel* 10.7.95. pp. 56–65. Since then,

Stiglmayer's volume appeared in a revised English edition: Alexandra Stiglmayer, ed. *Mass Rape: The War Against Women in Bosnia-Herzegovina*, trans. Marion Faber (Lincoln: University of Nebraska Press, 1994). See also Sander's comments in footnote 6.

4. Gertrud Koch, "Kurzschluß der Perspektiven: Helke Sanders Dokumentarfilm *BeFreier und Befreite: Krieg, Vergewaltigung, Kinder.*" Frankfurter Rundschau, 17.11.92.

5. Sander, "Erwiderung." See footnote 2.

6. Sander refers to Koch's review in *Frankfurter Rundschau*. See footnote 4.

7. Sander refers to the following articles by Koch and Atina Grossmann: Gertrud Koch, "Blut, Sperma, Tränen: BeFreier und Befreite—ein Dokumentarfilm von Helke Sander," *Frauen und Film* 54–55, nos. 1–4 (1994): 3–14. Grossmann, "Eine Frage des Schweigens: Die Vergewaltigung deutscher Frauen durch Besatzungssoldaten: Zum historischen Hintergrund von Helke Sanders Film *BeFreier und Befreite,*" *Frauen und Film* 54–55, nos. 1–4 (1994): 15–28.

8. See footnote 3.

9. Ibid.

10. Wiltrud Rosenzweig, "Some Very Personal Thoughts about the Accusations of Revisionism Made Against Helke Sander's Film *Liberators Take Liberties,*" *October* 72 (1995): 79–80.

11. See footnote 1.

12. Grossmann, "A Question of Silence: The Rape of German Women by Occupation Soldiers," *October* 72 (1995): 43–63.

13. See footnote 2.

21

Helke Sander's *Liberators Take Liberties* and the Politics of History

Marie-Luise Gättens

Helke Sander reconstructs in her documentary film *Liberators Take Liberties* and the book accompanying it the history of the rape of German women by soldiers of the Allied forces during the final weeks of World War II and the first months of the armistice.[1] Her reconstruction focuses on the rapes that occurred in Berlin that she and her coauthor Barbara Johr estimate numbered one hundred ten thousand.[2] Most of the rapes were committed by soldiers of the Red Army during the ten-day period between 24 April and 3 May 1945. For the documentary film and book, Sander explicitly states her aim as establishing these rapes as significant historical events. In the introductory essay "Remembering/Forgetting" to the volume *BeFreier Befreite*, she sums up her findings: "The results of our research made it clear that we were dealing with a singular event, comparable, perhaps, to the entry of the Japanese into the Chinese city of Nanking in 1937."[3] Thus she claims in an interview with the *Tageszeitung* in 1992: "I think that on the basis of the facts uncovered, the history of the postwar period must be rewritten."[4]

Like many feminist historians before her, Sander remarks that she was motivated by the silence that surrounded these rapes to uncover their history: "When I began to read literature about the postwar period, I was amazed. To be sure, there were always a few sentences about the rapes, but only as asides. . . . The void surrounding the word 'rape' began to irritate me."[5] And, at the opening of the film, Sander claims in the voice-over: "Everybody knew about it, but nobody spoke about it . . ." (*BeFreier* 108).[6] In both statements, Sander suggests rather than being surrounded by total silence—it was obviously spoken about if everybody knew—the rapes were talked about informally, "as asides." Sander wants to place these "asides" squarely into the dominant historical discourse that she is confident will have to be rewritten, if the rapes are to be fully incorporated into it. Sander clearly sees her work as an intervention into the politics of history, as an attack on a discourse that still systematically erases the traces of women's past experiences. *Liberators Take Liberties* brings us back to the questions asked by the speaker in Virginia Woolf's *A Room of One's Own* who is contemplating the empty space on her shelves, where the books on women's history should be, wonders whether a "supplement" of women's history can simply be added on to the existing history or whether this history itself will have to be rewritten.[7] Woolf's contemplation suggests that both dominant history and women's history are constructions, implying that adding a "supplement" to history always entails a critical reflection about the historical discourse—the mechanisms of inclusion and exclusion, the assignment of significance, and the assertions of (historical) truth.

Like many documentary films that explore a historical subject, *Liberators Take Liberties* tells about the past primarily through the use of archival film footage and the testimony of experts and witnesses. The film points in many ways to the constructed nature of the history it presents, through its montage of images, by clearly staging the interviews with the rape survivors and other witnesses of history and by incorporating the historian's search for the past, her efforts to make sense of it, which indeed underlines the very fact that history requires our active intervention. The film also shows that there are many competing discourses about rape, and while it clearly favors one, it does not simply unify all the various discourses but lets them stand in their contradictoriness. Through the layering of heterogeneous elements, the film, on the one hand, presents the complexity of the historical enterprise and, on the other hand, lays open the ways in which it was put together as a documentary film. All these elements denaturalize history and make it clear that the past is not simply an "it," an objective closed entity. Instead the film opens up questions about our knowledge of the past that Linda Hutcheon sees as central to postmodern preoccupations with history: "The past really did exist, but we can only know it today through its textual traces, its often complex and indirect representations in the present: documents, archives, but also photographs, paintings, architecture, films, and literature."[8]

Against the elements that present the historical enterprise as a fundamentally intertextual and interpretative one, runs a strong desire of the historian(s) for the archive as a place that stores objective, verifiable facts. This is primarily exemplified in Helke Sander and Barbara Johr's search for the number of rapes, but I think it is at work during the interviews, as well. For it seems to be their belief that it is primarily the *number* of rapes that embody significance and thus the challenge to the dominant historical discourse. Indeed, Sander asserts in "A Response to My Critics": "The film's contribution lies in its outlining of the ex-

tent of the rapes. The 'obsessiveness' with numbers of which I have been accused
. . . is correct."[9]

Like many women's histories, *Liberators Take Liberties* incorporates oral history testimonies. One reason for the interviews with women who were rape
victims is clearly the scarcity of archival documents and the limitation of their
content, which tell us nothing of the actual experiences of those who suffered
the rapes. Yet, the more important reason for these oral testimonies is to have
the film itself embody the many voices of those whose history it is. Thus, the
film also incorporates a trip to Minsk as an attempt to hear the memories of "the
other side." While the testimonies are also presented in a way that points to their
constructed nature, memory is not presented as an active process, in which past
events are worked and reworked. Instead memory is treated like a completed
process that represents the past that itself is stable and objective.[10]

In the following pages, I would like to leave the specific issues involved in
the use of oral testimonies aside and focus on the representation of the archive
in *Liberators Take Liberties*. While Sander presents the archive not as being outside of representation and interpretation, indeed the documentary film presents
the production of historical evidence as a profoundly intertextual process; the
archive, nevertheless, remains the repository of the facts that assure her project
historical significance.

The film begins with documentary images of Berlin in May 1945 and
Sander speaking in the voice-over:

> This is a film about rapes in times of war. Because I know the events in Berlin
> best, the film will deal with what happened here. Everyone knew but nobody
> spoke about them, just like today in Kuwait or Yugoslavia. (*BeFreier*, 108)

The opening lines as they present the project also provide an interpretative
framework: these are rapes during times of war. A common structure underlies
the rapes that occur during war time: thus the rapes that occurred at the end of
World War II can be compared to the rapes that occur today in Kuwait or Yu-
goslavia. The history of the past rapes is thus of significance for the present. The
opening remarks make it clear that Sander has no intention of examining these
rapes in their specific historical context, namely national socialism and its war
policies. This interpretative frame is confirmed by the images, which here, as
throughout most of the film, show the war from the end: The city of Berlin is
in ruins, the Red Army controls the city and its defeated population. The images emphasize the discrepancy in power between male military rulers and (female) civilian population. Nazism is largely absent in the images as well as in the
explanatory frame.

What we do not see here and will not see throughout the film is, of course,
the actual act of rape. The archival footage, while giving us some access to the

past, ultimately confirms the inaccessibility of the original event and thus documents the rift that is at the heart of any historical project, namely the non-identity between the past and the reconstructed past. The actual violence inflicted upon the bodies of women is paradoxically "embodied" in the non-diegetic music that we hear in this introductory sequence and that reappears throughout the film. The music reiterates a low F on the piano. The tonality drifts from F minor to A-flat (major/minor). The reiterated low F's are at eighty beats per minute, suggesting, perhaps, an accelerated heartbeat.[11]

In this opening sequence Sander also establishes herself as the historian. While the historian's knowledge is represented as situated and thus limited "because I know the events in Berlin best, the film will deal with what happened here," she nevertheless assumes the authority to interpret, conclude, and arrive at a generalizing argument. Throughout the documentary film it is Sander's physical presence, in which she assumes the persona of filmmaker as historian, that makes it clear that the past does not speak itself but requires active intervention and that guarantees the integrity of this historical enterprise. While the "embodied," fact-finding historian at first sight seems to limit the claim to historical truth, I think it indeed allows for the assertion of historical truth, albeit a more relative, contingent truth than the one claimed by traditional historiography. For it seems no longer possible to have the traditional disembodied, omniscient historian as the guarantor of historical truth. *Liberators* presents truth in a similar way as Linda Williams claims documentaries such as *The Thin Blue Line* and *Shoah* do, which simultaneously reveal a "clear sense that [documentary] truth is subject to manipulation and construction by docu-auteurs," but that nevertheless engage in "a serious quest to reveal some ultimate truths."[12] In addition to the persona of filmmaker as historian in the film, Sander has also spoken about the film and its historical project not only in the volume *BeFreier und Befreite* but also in the public arena of interviews, newspaper articles, responses to her critics, and so forth. While Sander as filmmaker—historian as she appears in the film and Helke Sander as the one who enters the public arena in order to speak about/for her documentary film are not identical, the public statements underscore her intention of intervention into the politics of German history.[13]

Right at the beginning of the film, after the introductory remarks and images that frame the project, we see Sander visit what is probably the most significant archive for her investigation—the archive of the hospital Kaiserin Auguste Victoria-Haus, which has an almost complete collection of all its files since its founding in 1909. From the birth records, which in most cases name the father, sometimes even explicitly record that the pregnancy was the result of rape, Sander and Johr calculate the number of children born with Russian fathers that at the end of 1945 and during 1946–47. Out of the numbers of children born with Russian fathers in this hospital, Sander and Johr calculate the number of children born with Russian fathers for the entire city of Berlin.

Sander introduces this sequence by giving us the name of the expert from the off: Professor Ballowitz. We see Ballowitz getting one of the hospital files. As it is impossible to use documentation in documentary films in the same way as history texts do—namely footnotes and bibliography—*Liberators* incorporates a sort of filmic documentation. In this sequence, as well as in several other ones, we see a close-up of the document. Sometimes the relevant passages in the document are highlighted, which the viewer is indeed able to read. Very often Sander reads these passages in the off. In these cases the camera almost assumes the status of scientific instrument, which in a version of vérité guarantees the scholarly nature of this historical project.

Professor Ballowitz's credentials as an expert are most obviously established through the meticulous naming of her titles. They are further reinforced through the visual elements of her white physician's smock and her position seated at a desk in the archive of the hospital. Sander remains invisible during this interview, foregrounding again the significance of Professor Ballowitz's status as expert. In the manner of the serious historical scholar, Professor Ballowitz explains the information contained in these hospital files and affirms that the number of children born in this hospital is probably representative for Berlin as a whole. This sequence establishes the rapes as verifiable historical facts, as the sort of scholarly basis for the memory work the film undertakes. The sequence is followed by an account of a rape survivor, which in turn establishes the rapes as the experience of actual women. The first sequence gives the calculation of the number of rapes its central, if necessarily problematic, status. At the same time, the visual and aural excess through which Professor Ballowitz's status as an expert is established also seem to ironize traditional history as scholarly enterprise.

In the second part of *Liberators*, Barbara Johr, introduced as "the calculator," literally "performs" the calculations through which she arrives at the rape number of one hundred thousand. In this sequence, we see Johr first punch numbers into a calculator. Then she writes numbers with a fountain pen into a math notebook, while simultaneously speaking about the numbers. While this sequence, too, has the function of authenticating the calculations and to make them transparent for the viewer, it also clearly points to the fact that the calculations are a performance and thus underlines the distance between the documentary film and the scholarly enterprise. The "properly" scholarly record of the calculations, however, is given in the volume *BeFreier und Befreite*, where Johr devotes an entire essay entitled "Die Ereignisse in Zahlen" (The Events in Numbers) to the detailed presentation of the numeric calculation of the rapes. It seems to me that the book overall has the function of supporting Sander and Johr's claim at having produced a serious and important work of history.

In a third "number" sequence, Sander interviews the statistical expert Dr. Gerhard Reichling, who has compiled statistics on German refugees from the East, about the significance of illegitimate births in Berlin during 1945, 1946,

1947, and 1948. Dr. Reichling interprets the numbers in a factual language that is ripe with (unintended?) irony: "Therefore, more illegitimate children were born. We know from the events, that the German soldiers were captured, taken into custody. Who was active there?" Sander: "Sexually active?" Reichling: "Who was active, who was the cause?" (186). He, nevertheless, agrees with Sander that many of the "causes" had to be soldiers of the Red Army. This sequence takes place in a seminar room. Reichling and Sander stand in front of a blackboard, which Sander lowers at the beginning in order to present her calculations to Dr. Reichling. This sequence again, in my opinion, points very self-consciously to its own constructed nature, to its performance of scholarship. All the number sequences undertake the calculations with rather outdated and old-fashioned tools, which give the scholarly enterprise a rather antiquarian aura. The irony of the sequence with Reichling, however, is checked again by Sander's commentary, which follows it. In it Sander stresses again the serious, if necessarily incomplete, status of her calculations.

In two other sequences, Sander discusses numbers with experts. The physician Renate Lutz-Lebsanft reports on her estimates of the rapes that occurred during the occupation of Freudenstadt by the French. Finally, Sander also questions the historians Clarissa Henry and Marc Hillel on their findings of the number of children produced by the German army during their various occupations. Both of these interviews have a distinctly different status from the other three I described. They serve as proof that other armies raped or engaged in sexual conquest. With respect to the German army, the interview is part of Sander's attempt to dismantle the myth that the German army behaved "honorably."[14] Both interviews take place outside the archive and thus make it clear that no fact-finding, as in the other three sequences, is involved.

Through the visits of the archives, Sander incorporates the historian's assimilation of data into her film, which foregrounds that we have no direct access to the past. We only know it through its particularly fragmentary, textual traces, which are thus open to interpretation: in the case of the Kaiserin Auguste Viktoria-Haus, a Russian father in the birth records is used for the calculation of the rapes committed by soldiers of the Red Army. This interpretation is based obviously not only on prior historical knowledge but also based on certain assumptions about the relationship between Russian men and German women. However, while presenting the problematic process of turning textual data into historical facts, the archive and the consultation of experts clearly also have the function of validating Sander's historical project. And while Johr's literal performance of her calculation of the rapes seems ironic, the numbers are nevertheless meant to be taken seriously. The production of the numbers seems so important for Sander and Johr because the numbers embody their scientific knowledge of the historical facts and as the historian Joan W. Scott writes: "(at least since the

Enlightenment) the power to control a particular field resides in claims to (scientific) knowledge."[15]

Sander and Johr's search for the number of rapes presents us with the political nature of the archive that is in no way an unambiguous and neutral storage place of verifiable facts. The meager and fragmentary nature of the data dramatically embodies, as Linda Hutcheon puts it, "the distinction between the brute *events* of the past and the historical *facts* we construct out of them. Facts are events to which we have given meaning."[16] Clearly when it comes to these rapes, there is a concerted effort not to give meaning. The men who commit the rapes are most unambiguously interested in leaving no historically readable traces, but also the women, out of shame or fear, are often not interested in reporting the rapes.

The records Sander finds exemplify the rape victims' radical loss of control over their own bodies, as the files are generated mostly through involuntary pregnancies or venereal disease. In light of this, it is perplexing that the film does not evaluate the requests for medical abortions on the grounds of rape, as Atina Grossmann found them, for example, in the Health Office of Neukölln.[17] In these records, the women appear less like completely passive victims, but rather determined to take some charge of their lives. Since Johr also claims that at least 90 percent of the raped women who got pregnant in Berlin had an abortion, this omission seems curious.

We must also consider the radically different access that victims and perpetrators have to the institutions that generate and administer the records out of which the historian traditionally forges her account. This difference occasions lopsided and meager data. After the chaos of the war, it is the victorious army that will reestablish in important ways the work of the institutions. The Red Army (like most armies) deliberately keeps no records about the rapes. Susan Brownmiller comments: "Documentation of rape warfare is something the other side totals up, analyzes, and propagandizes. . . . "[18] The historian Ingrid Schmidt-Harzbach discusses in *Liberators* the systematic erasure of any archival traces by the Communist party as they take over power in the GDR after the war. She thus points to the profoundly political nature of the archive itself. Particularly for the GDR, the history of these rapes was thus not given any status as "fact," but instead held to the level of (silenced) private memory. Frau Kleine, in a discussion among participants, refers to the prerogative of "Psst!" as a continuity of silence between national socialism and socialism. *Liberators* discusses the politics of the history of the rapes, however, only with respect to the GDR and fails to examine the representation of the rapes in the public memory of the old Federal Republic. This omission produces a rather one-sided view of the rapes as universally silenced.

The uniquely filmic form of documentation used in *Liberators,* as well as in many other historical documentaries, is that of archival film footage and photo-graphic images. As Bill Nichols observes, archival footage is usually accepted as "authentic signs of their times. We know the past by (re-)seeing it." The epistemological problems it poses, he argues, "are seldom confronted."[19] Archival footage is used in diverse ways in *Liberators*. At times it is used as evidence, exploiting the "scientific status" of the photographic and filmic image as pure record of the physical world. In the conversation with Werner Siebenhaar, for example, images are used to disprove his assertions. While Siebenhaar insists that German soldiers (in contrast to the soldiers of the Red Army) did not rape, we see images of German soldiers sexually harassing "enemy" women. This is, I believe, the only time in the film in which an oral testimony is refuted as false. Sander clearly aims at dismantling the myth of the German army as "honorable," when it comes to the treatment of the civilian populations in the occupied territories. She does this not only through the use of archival film footage but also through the presentation (in close-up again) of official documents that prove that the military leadership was not interested in prosecuting rape or violence inflicted on the civilian population in the East by members of the German army.

In other cases, Sander points to the fact that the archival footage was produced with clear ideological intent and can thus not be regarded as "neutral fact." In one sequence Sander shows pictures of dead and mutilated women who were raped. The pictures were made and published, Sander implies, purely for propaganda purposes, in order to document the other side's atrocities. Sander comments: "We see Russian women who were raped by Germans. German women raped by Russians. Russian women, German women, Russian women, German, Russian, etc." (131–132). Sander criticizes the use of rape for specific national propaganda purposes. Publicized are always only the rapes of "the other side." Photographic records thus ironically only exist because each side is eager to document the atrocities of "the other side." Sander's own use of these photographic documents is, of course, also not ideologically neutral. She constructs a transnational, common abuse of women. Thus, while dismantling the myth of the "honorable" German army and showing the German army's involvement in the sexual violence and murder, she "normalizes" the German army paradoxically. There are in my opinion two principal reasons for this "normalization" of the German army in *Liberators*. The film does not discuss the rapes committed by members of the German army in the context of national socialist war policies, and the film completely forecloses discussion of the Holocaust. In this respect, Sander's documentary film is not different from other German documentaries and fiction films. For as Thomas Elsaesser points out most German films about the Nazi past that were made in the seventies and eighties avoid the Holocaust and Auschwitz.[20] *Liberators'* almost complete avoidance of the Holocaust is the most significant difference to Brownmiller's discussion of rape during World War II in her classic study *Against Our Will: Men, Women and Rape*, which focuses on the systematic rape of primarily Jewish women within the context of the Holocaust.

Sander also employs archival film footage extensively in her exploration of military sexuality during World War II. She not only shows that all armies engaged in extensive sexual contact but also that the discrepancy between the (victorious) soldiers' power and the women is so great that rape exists within a broad context of exploitative sexuality. Despite its insistence on the universality of rape and sexual exploitation as vital ingredients of military pursuits, the employment of this archival film footage does indeed construct specific national identities, which fall back on the stereotypical notions of national character. Most of the archival film footage exploring sexuality is of American origin, as for example a U.S. army instructional film about the dangers of venereal disease and footage of the entertainment of the U.S. troops, in which sex is a vital ingredient. The use of this footage constructs curious national identities, with the Americans standing for an insidious form of sexual exploitation connected with the familiar American ingredients of puritanism and consumerism. The Red Army, on the other hand, appears in these images as clearly poorer and more backward, brutish counterpart of the American. Moreover, the Red Army is the only army that is identified by a piece of music: a piece of Russian folk music played on an accordion. This music, not only constructs the Red Army as a peasant army but indeed, subtly identifies the soldiers of the Red Army as the rapists. The Russian music is in the key of A-flat minor, acoustically reminiscent of the F minor/A-flat (major/minor) music of the opening.

During most of the oral testimonies of rape survivors, we see also archival film footage. We see houses burn and soldiers fight in the street. These images convey physical danger, particularly for women, as the streets are owned by soldiers. While the use of archival footage during the testimonies functions as evidence of the general conditions of the past, the footage also confirms the inaccessibility of the past, as the rapes remain unseen. Testimony and archival footage are also never synchronized into a sort of narrative, visual flow, thus emphasizing the disjuncture between narrative and images, and present and past. The ongoing process of (visual) textualization is suggested in a number of sequences in which we see participants in the documentary film watch other scenes of the film on video monitors.

Despite the employment of a great range of archival film footage and the many self-reflexive moments, I believe the film ultimately constructs a somewhat simplistic visual argument that constructs a binary opposition between the genders: (military) men appear as the eternal rapists and women as their eternal victims. This, I believe, is the result of Sander's avoidance of exploring German women's (nonmilitary) participation in the Nazis' war effort.

While Sander presents the archive as a place that is not only caught up in prior textualization and interpretation but also caught up in power relations, it nevertheless retains for her the status of the repository of historical truth. For as Linda Williams puts it: "(S)ome form of truth is the always receding goal of documentary film. But the truth figured by documentary cannot be a simple unmasking or reflection. It is a careful construction, an intervention in the politics and the semiotics of representation."[21] The production of this historical truth requires the intervention of a historian and as a result it obviously will have to be perspective. It is in her own status as a German feminist historian that I see a certain blindness in Sander's pursuit of her project. Thus, she never explores the inevitable relation of her estimated one hundred ten thousand rapes, which embodies historical significance so much for her, with the other gruesome numbers—particularly the number of dead in the Soviet Union and the number of victims of the Holocaust. It is precisely her strict avoidance of exploring these relations that raises the unfortunate issue of a "competition" in victim status. As we all know far too well, particularly with respect to the German past, not talking about certain issues does not make them go away.

Notes

1. Helke Sander and Barbara Johr, eds., *BeFreier und Befreite: Krieg, Vergewaltigungen, Kinder* (Liberators take Liberties: War, Rapes, Children) (Munich: Verlag Antje Kunstmann, 1992). The book contains, among other things, the dialogue from the film. Citations from the film's dialogue will be from this source and from my translation. They will appear in the text.

2. Johr, "Die Ereignisse in Zahlen" (The Events in Numbers), in ibid., 54.

3. Quoted from the translated version of the essay that appears in *October* 72, p. 17. Susan Brownmiller writes in *Against Our Will: Men, Women and Rape* (New York: Simon & Schuster, 1975) that the taking of Nanking "can only be described as an orgy of wholesale assault against the remaining civilian population" (57). At the Tokyo war tribunal in 1946, it was found that "approximately 20,000 cases of rape occurred within the city during the first month of the occupation" (60–61). Brownmiller compares the behavior of the Japanese to the German behavior during the occupation of the East. This is an interesting example of the politics of comparison.

4. *Die Tageszeitung*, (29 February 1992), quoted in Stuart Liebman and Annette Michelson, "After the Fall: Women in the House of the Hangmen," *October* 72 (spring 1995): 12.

5. Sander, "Remembering/Forgetting," in *BeFreier une Befreite*, 17.

6. Atina Grossmann criticizes Sander's unqualifying use of the term *silence* in "A Question of Silence: The Rape of German Women by Occupation Soldiers," in *October* 72.

7. Virginia Woolf, *A Room of One's Own* (New York: Harcourt, 1981); see also Joan Wallach Scott, "Women's History," in *Gender and the Politics of History* (New York: Columbia University Press, 1988), 17.

8. Linda Hutcheon, *The Politics of Postmodernism* (London and New York: Routledge, 1989), 78.

9. Sander, "A Response to My Critics," *October* 72, p. 84.

10. Gertrud Koch has criticized the way in which Sander conducts the interviews in her essay, "Blood, Sperm, and Tears," 34–37.

11. I would like to thank David Schwarz for his insights into music.

12. Linda Williams, "Mirrors Without Memories: Truth, History, and the New Documentary," *Film Quarterly* 3 (spring 1993): 12.

13. For a discussion of the various speaking positions inside and outside film with respect to German history see Thomas Elsaesser, "Subject Positions, Speaking Positions: From *Holocaust, Our Hitler*, and *Heimat* to *Shoah* and *Schindler's List*," in *The Persistence of History: Cinema, Television, and the Modern Event*, ed. Vivian Sobchack (New York and London: Routledge, 1996), especially 169 and 175.

14. In this interview Sander also follows the theme that the war led to a "gigantic mixing" of people that she seems strangely obsessed with. She also pursues the theme of female scapegoating by showing pictures of publicly humiliated French women who had sexual relations with German soldiers and who were branded as collaborators after the war by the French population.

15. Joan W. Scott, "Deconstructing Equality-Versus-Difference: Or, the Uses of Poststructuralist Theory for Feminism," in *Conflicts in Feminism*, eds. Marianne Hirsch and Evelyn Fox Keller (New York and London: Routledge, 1990), 136.

16. Hutcheon, *Politics of Postmodernism*, 57.

17. See Grossmann, "Question of Silence," 43 and 55–61.

18. Susan Brownmiller, *Against Our Will: Men, Women and Rape* (New York: Simon & Schuster, 1975), 37–38.

19. Bill Nichols, "*Getting to Know You*: . . . . Knowledge, Power, and the Body," in *Theorizing Documentary*, ed. Michael Renov (New York and London: Routledge, 1993), 177–78.

20. Elsaesser, "Subject Positions, Speaking Positions," 159.

21. Williams, "Mirrors Without Memories," 20.

Appendix

A New Home for the EIFF—
European Institute for Women and Film

Ute Lischke-McNab talks with Jutta Brückner

Since early 1995, the filmmaker Jutta Brückner has put much energy into establishing the Europäische Institut für Frauen und Film (European Institute for Women and Film) presently located in the Hochschule der Künste, Filminstitut/HdK Kunst und Medien (Film Institute in the School of Fine Arts) Berlin, where Brückner is also a professor. The institute, if Brückner has her way, will find a new and permanent home. There were several reasons for starting such an ambitious project.

Brückner came to the realization that most of the films made by women in the period between 1968 and the early 1980s are almost totally inaccessible. Women, who had actively participated under the rubric Frauenfilm (women's cinema) during that period, were not well-known abroad because their films were not screened in the cinemas. Having no access to research and film libraries that could lend out films, and in many instances having films with expired copyrights, many films were simply not available for audiences. Brückner came up with the idea that an institute had to be founded that could serve as a repository not only for films, but also for materials related in every way to the production of films. This institute must not only preserve films, but also make video copies available for the continued screening and analysis of film topics.

An institute for the dissemination of material related to the Frauenfilm is necessary since the Blütezeit (heyday) for these films had passed and in order not to completely lose track of this whole movement, an effort to preserve the materials related to these women's endeavours is important. The EIFF is conceived as being a research and film library that would house, preserve, catalog, and collect all materials that relate to *all* aspects of filmmaking at the same time concentrating on the work of women-filmmakers. Another role of the EIFF would be to assist young women-filmmakers in their profession, particularly by helping them to combine feminist film theory with practice, as well as to acquaint them with the latest in technological advances. The last important function of the EIFF is to provide funding and support for women-filmmakers with unusual projects, who, because their ventures are innovative and experimental, need help during the preproduction process.

Brückner, who has spent a lot of time organizing the founding of the EIFF, no longer has the time to continue this work. And although her Filminstitut/HdK (Film Institute) has offered to the EIFF the use of a studio for the first three years, Brückner is

273

looking for a permanent home for the institute. The following is intended to give the current status (February 1996) of the EIFF.

Lischke-McNab. Can you bring us up-to-date on the events surrounding the EIFF?

Brückner. There has not been any confirmation about financial support for the Institute. At the moment, the concept of founding the EIFF is enormous and its achievement can only be attained in stages.

Lischke-McNab. What is the relationship of the EIFF to the Filminstitut/HdK?

Brückner. The most important fact now is that it must be separated from me personally and be given institutional support by some other organization. At this moment, I don't have the time to spend on its organization, since I am involved in two very important film projects. Naturally, the Filminstitut/HdK has made space available for the EIFF, but as for myself, with my projects and my professorial duties, I really cannot see how I can continue to work on it. In the meantime, I have been looking for women who are able and willing to work on this project without remuneration. That, as you can imagine, was no easy task. Nevertheless, I have found these two women. It was important that they reside in Berlin, since the HdK is situated in Berlin. Their first role was to think about this enormous project, familiarize themselves with all its different aspects, and then set to work on writing the all-important funding proposals. Their proposal involves the preparatory steps that are necessary for the founding of the institute. The grant application is in response to a research program administered by the Berlin senator responsible for women's issues. The application form is in the process of being written and must be submitted within the next four days. Then it's a matter of waiting to see if there will be any monies forthcoming.

Lischke-McNab. How long will you have to wait before you find out whether or not you will receive funding?

Brückner. We really hope that we will know for sure in two to three months.

Lischke-McNab. If the funding comes through, what will be your next steps?

Brückner. We need to look for a building to house the research and film library. We will also need to plan the work that lies ahead, such as exchanges, networking, connections to the United States and Europe. I have already identified someone living in the United States who is ready to take on the work there, especially the German-U.S. liaison. Up until now, we have had women building up film programs, getting small bits of information here and there, having no access to films. This would be an opportunity for the EIFF to become very active in disseminating information and films. I really think that a strong working relationship between women in Germany and the United States is possible. Then, we must also look toward links with other European countries. This project will take time. But hopefully, with our first women in place, we will be able to build up a strong Research Institute.

EIFF Update April 1997

EIFF partners in the United States include FACETS, the Smithsonian Institute, and Women Make Movies, and in Germany Basis Videoverleih. All of these institutions will help with the collection and dissemination of multimedia materials for international distribution. They will help other cultural and educational institutions to establish research projects on an international basis. Julia Müller-Novak in Berlin is the contact person for EIFF. Dieta Sixt at the Goethe Institut in Washington has been generous in her support of EIFF.

Contributors

Nora M. Alter, assistant professor of German, is a member of the Graduate Faculty, Film and Media Studies Program, and the Women's Studies Program, at the University of Florida, Gainesville. She has written on German film and women, and is the author of *Vietnam Protest Theatre: Staging the Television War in the US and Abroad 1965–1979*.

Margrit Frölich teaches German studies at the University of Leipzig, Germany. She has written articles on German film, minorities in German culture, East German literature, and contemporary women dramatists, and is the author of *Between Affluence and Rebellion: The Work of Thomas Brasch in the Interface between East and West*.

Marie-Luise Gättens, associate professor of German at Southern Methodist University, Dallas, has written several articles on gender, fascism, and women reconstructing the past, as well as a book on this topic *Women and Fascism: Reconstructing History*.

Douglas Kellner, professor of philosophy at the University of Texas, Austin, is the author of many books on social theory, politics, history, and culture, including *Camera Politica: The Politics and Ideology of Contemporary Hollywood Film* (coauthored with Michael Ryan); and *Postmodern Theory: Critical Interrogations, Television and the Crisis of Democracy, The Persian Gulf TV War*, and *Media Culture*.

Marcia Klotz, assistant professor of German at the University of California, Irvine, has written extensively on German film. She is currently completing a book on German colonial discourse.

Barbara Kosta, associate professor at the University of Arizona, is currently researching the fashioning of the modern woman during the Weimar Republic. Her publications include *Recasting Autobiography: Women's Counterfictions in Contemporary German Literature and Film* and numerous articles on twentieth-century German literature by women.

Julia Knight, senior lecturer in the Media Arts Department at the University of Luton, United Kingdom, is the author of *Women and the New German Cinema*. She has recently edited *Diverse Practices: A Critical Reader on British Video Art* and is coeditor of *Convergences: The Journal of Research into New Media Technologies*.

David J. Levin is assistant professor of German at Columbia University. His works include essays in *October* and in *New German Critique*, an edited volume entitled *Opera Through Other Eyes*, and a book on aesthetics and aggression in the Nibelungen projects of Fritz Lang and Richard Wagner.

Susan E. Linville is assistant professor in English and head of Film Studies at the University of Colorado, Denver. Her research focuses on German autobiographical films directed by women. Linville's publications have appeared in *PMLA*, *New German Critique*, *Wide Angle*, and *Film Criticism*.

Henriette Löwisch received her master's degree in journalism and communication from the University of Munich; at the University of Washington, Seattle she researched her thesis on U.S. television coverage of the Gulf War. She is now at the news desk of the Agence France-Presse in Washington, D.C.

Barbara Mennel is a Ph.D candidate in German Studies at Cornell University, with a dissertation on masochism in German postwar literature and film. She wrote an article on R. W. Fassbinder, *Ali: Fear Eats Soul* and on the representation of Germany in Ama Ata Aidoo's *Our Sister Killjoy* and in Chantal Ackerman's *Meetings with Anna*.

Ute Lischke McNab, assistant professor of German at the University of Toronto, has published and lectured on gender, film, and the German Left in the Weimar Republic, and on women in Edgar Reitz's films. She was coorganizer of "Germany in Film: Post-Projections II" at the University of Toronto.

Rosmarie T. Morewedge, associate professor and chair of the Department of German, Russian, and East Asian Languages at SUNY, Binghamton, has written and taught courses on medieval German literature and on fairy-tale motifs in German literature and popular culture.

Magda Mueller, coordinator of German Studies at California State University, Chico, is the author of *Schein und Sein: Imageproduktionen der "Neuen Frau" in der Weimarer Republik*, and of *Karola Bloch als Herausforderung: Sozialismus und Feminismus*, coeditor of *Gender Politics and Post-Communism*, and an editor of *TELOS*.

I. Majer O'Sickey, assistant professor of German and women's studies at SUNY, Binghamton, has published articles on representations of gender, race, and class in German literature and film in journals and anthologies on cinema and culture.

Klaus Phillips, chair of the Department of Theatre Arts at Hollins College, Virginia, has instituted the annual Hollins Colloquium of German Cinema, and is editor of *New German Filmmakers: From Oberhausen Through 1970s* as well as author of numerous articles on the films of the New German Cinema.

Andrea Rinke lectures at Kingston University, United Kingdom. Her research interests are in the fields of contemporary German society, women's studies, and media studies. Her publications include *Wende-Bilder* and *Television Images of Women in Germany in Transition*. She is currently working on representations of gender relations in DEFA films.

Ulrike Sieglohr, senior lecturer in media studies at Staffordshire University, United Kingdom, received a Ph.D. for her work on the German film, theatre, and opera director Werner Schroeter. She has also written on various aspects of the New German Cinema.

Kaja Silverman, professor of rhetoric at the University of California, Berkeley, has published widely on cinema and on theories of film. She is the author of *The Acoustic Mirror*. Her most recent books are *Masculinity at the Margins* and *The Threshold of the Visible World*.

Sabine Smith received a Ph.D. in German Studies from the Department of German at the University of California, Davis, with a dissertation on the films of Helke Sander.

Scott Spector, assistant professor of Germanic languages and literatures and of history at the University of Michigan, Ann Arbor. His dissertation from Johns Hopkins now being revised for publication, is titled *Prague Territories: Nationality and Culture in German-Speaking Prague from Fin-de-siècle through World War I*.

Ingeborg von Zadow studied theater and German film in Germany and at SUNY, Binghamton. A playwright and independent scholar, her works include *Ich und Du* and *Pompinien*, both performed on German stages. Her current work is titled *Besuch bei Katt und Fredda*.

Subject Index

women, as actors, 13, 207; as fantasizing and desiring subjects, 160–161; danger of essentializing, 2; in GDR state, 215; as independent filmmmakers, 175; feminist filmmakers in the GDR, 202–203; in the FRG, 96, 97, 164, 176, 258–259; as filmmakers, 13, 20, 96, 97, 175, 195; Mongolian, 107, 108, 109–110, 112; nomadic, 107; self-constructed, 88; as spectacle, 144; as images, 1; as images deviating from traditional ones, 2; marginalized in studies on German cinema, 6, 188–189; representations of in Fassbinder's films, 33–40; represented in GDR films, 45–60; as sexually promiscuous, 73; as spectators, 13; Western, 108, 109, 110, 112

women-centered, filmmaking, anti-realist aesthetic in, 245; artistic and functional challenges to in the GDR, 43–46, 60; dimished chances for funding, 60; exception in canon of West German filmmaking, 20; in Germany, 180, 188; see also New German Cinema

women's, identity in and GDR cultural policies of, 45, 202; emancipation, 52, 97, image of self, 186; 190, 207; lack of agency, 87–88

women's history, as constructions, 262; oral history, 263

women's movement (West Germany), 89, 155, 187, 254; see also feminist discourses

Author Index